PRAISE FOR *NIGHT OF THE ASSASSINS*

"Here is a story largely unknown about a plot by Adolf Hitler to murder Franklin Roosevelt, Winston Churchill, and Joseph Stalin. . . . Paced like a novel, Mr. Blum will leave you waiting for the big Nazi reveal." —*Pittsburgh Post-Gazette*

"A truly thrilling exposé of the previously unknown Nazi assassination plot that could have changed history."
—Edward Jay Epstein, *New York Times* bestselling author of *The Assassination Chronicles*

"Blum tells the amazing tale of Operation Long Jump, the Nazi plot to assassinate the Big Three leaders at the Tehran conference in November 1943. Using Russian archival sources only made public in the last twenty years along with a huge collection of other primary and secondary sources, he weaves a fast-paced story of how Nazi intelligence services and special commando units tried to infiltrate an assassination team into Iran. . . . Ian Fleming himself could not have written such an improbable yet actual plot. The moves and countermoves in this tight and engaging story show that World War II was fought just as much in shadowy back alleys as on the battlefield." —*New York Journal of Books*

"Blum unravels the Tehran plot as a cat-and-mouse game between Mike Reilly, the U.S. Secret Service agent in charge of protecting Roosevelt, and Nazi foreign intelligence officer Walter Schellenberg. . . . Espionage fans will savor this wide-ranging, novelistic account." —*Publishers Weekly*

"An entertaining story of skullduggery. . . . A breathless drama in novelistic form with insight into the characters' conversations, thoughts, and emotions." —*Kirkus Reviews*

"Written like a thriller . . . this tale has enough twist, turns, and colorful personalities to make it a worthy and entertaining read." —*Bookreporter*

"*Night of the Assassins* is a suspenseful true-life tale about an impossible mission, a ticking clock, and the man who stepped up to the challenge and prevented a catastrophe." —Military Book Club

"Blum's book . . . looks at the plot which could have changed the world." —*Daily Express*

"More wartime derring-do and nail-biting with Howard Blum's *Night of the Assassins*." —Hamish Bowles, *Vogue*

"Riveting." —*Vancouver Sun*

NIGHT OF THE
ASSASSINS

NIGHT OF
THE ASSASSINS

The Untold Story of Hitler's Plot
to Kill FDR, Churchill, and Stalin

HOWARD BLUM

HARPER ● PERENNIAL

NEW YORK ● LONDON ● TORONTO ● SYDNEY ● NEW DELHI ● AUCKLAND

HARPER PERENNIAL

FIRST HARPER PERENNIAL PAPERBACK EDITION PUBLISHED 2021.

Library of Congress Cataloging-in-Publication Data has been applied for.

ISBN 978-0-06-287290-6

21 22 23 24 25 LSC 10 9 8 7 6 5 4 3 2 1

FOR SUSAN AND DAVID RICH,
my good friends

Who was the man who sowed the dragon's teeth,
That fabulous or fanciful patriarch
Who sowed so ill for his descent, beneath
King's Chapel in this underworld and dark?

—Robert Lowell, "At the Indian Killer's Grave"

The German leaders are aware that Germany is defeated but
others still hope that Hitler can work a miracle like an agreement
with Russia or some such stunt.

—OSS official dispatch, Bern, November 1943

Contents

Prologue:
"A Pretty Good Haul"

The New York Times

STALIN BARED PLOT AGAINST PRESIDENT

INDUCED HIM TO MOVE TO SOVIET EMBASSY, MAKING ANY TRIPS IN STREETS UNNECESSARY

Special to THE NEW YORK TIMES

WASHINGTON. Dec.17—President Roosevelt disclosed today what the Russians said was a plot endangering his life at Tehran, the knowledge of which caused him to move his residence from the American Legation to the Soviet Embassy.

Mr. Roosevelt, mentioning the matter during his press conference in discussing the need for security, did not say specifically whether the plot was aimed at all three leaders meeting there, although he implied as much.

While the President was at the American Legation on his first night at Tehran Premier Stalin sent word to him of a plot and urged him to move over to the Soviet

Embassy, which adjoined the British Embassy in the same compound.

Although he did not take much stock in the report, the President said, he moved the next day and everything went well from then on. All three leaders were in the same compound and did not have to pass through the streets. The American Legation was more than a mile from the Soviet compound.

The President observed that in a place like Tehran there probably were hundreds of German spies around and it would have been a pretty good haul for the Germans if they could have gotten all three of the conferees while they were going through the streets.

PART I

"THE INSCRUTABLE WORKINGS OF FATE"

1

AS THE CRISP, CLEAR MORNING dawned on the first day of June 1943, offering a hard blue sky and perfect weather for flying, the spy sat in the passenger terminal of Portela Airport outside Lisbon waiting to make a phone call. The call would be a death warrant.

His vantage point was a wooden bench shoved up against a rear wall, and his eyes surveyed the hectic scene playing out in front of him with a professional watcher's focus. It was just after six a.m., but the terminal was already crowded, a tempest of voices sweeping through the high-ceilinged room. It was a clamor fueled by desperation. Jammed into the boxlike space were men, women, and families determined to get a ticket on the 7:30 a.m. British Overseas Airway Corporation (BOAC) plane to Whitchurch, England—a seat on the lifeboat that would be their escape from a Europe that was a rapidly sinking ship.

Over the past three cataclysmic years, Nazi Germany had tightened its sharp coils around much of the continent, but a resolute Portugal had nevertheless managed to carry on as a neutral state. And as tens of thousands of refugees—Jews, artists, Communists, and other freethinking enemies of the Reich—gathered up whatever they could and hurried to flee from the advancing goose-stepping hordes, they poured into Portugal. It was an oasis—yet one that was both temporary and ominously precarious. The country's welcome, for one thing, was not open armed: refugees with the proper visas were granted a mere thirty-day residency. And while this statute was enforced by the Public Security Police more often than not with only a philosophical wink and a nod, the prospect of the country's continued neutrality created more genuine terrors.

Neutrality was a dangerous national strategy; it was a contract that was not even worth the paper that had not been signed. At any moment the winds of war might come blowing in over the Pyrenees from Falangist Spain or Vichy France—and the refugees would be trapped at the end of the continent, backed up against the roiling Atlantic as the Gestapo sighted them in the crosshair.

The twin-propellered DC-3 that made four commercial flights each week from Lisbon to Whitchurch Airport outside Bristol offered a way out, the opportunity to escape once and for all from the Nazis' murderous grasp. England would be a secure refuge; and from there, one could scramble to find a way to a new life in America, or Palestine. Dreams were fueled by such possibilities.

The obstacles to obtaining a ticket on a BOAC flight out of Lisbon, however, were formidable. One hurdle—albeit one that might be jumped by a nimble scheme or a king's ransom—was the requirement of a transit visa. The other, however, was more inflexible, determined by the laws of an inexorable mathematics: there were only thirteen passenger seats on a DC-3.

The terminal was very much a seller's marketplace. Day after frantic day, the bidding continued fast and furious.

Yet, like any fieldman on a mission, the spy would have found the discipline to pay only fleeting attention to the countless small and large dramas that fed the tumult storming about the terminal. He'd have concentrated on the faces. And, always conscientious, his glance would also have kept returning to the tarmac.

From his observation post on the bench, the view was perfect. Directly across the terminal, a row of three symmetrical windows, each as wide as a doorway and nearly as tall, gave an open view of the blacktopped runway. And there, with the early-morning sun simmering down on it as if a spotlight, the camouflage-painted plane, its name, *Ibis*, a tribute to the spindly ancient bird, painted in a cursive script under the cockpit window, the distinctive red, white, and blue BOAC stripes on its tail, stood, ready for boarding.

THE SPY WAITED, AND HE watched. He had been at the airport for days, ever since the order had been passed on from Berlin, and today was just like yesterday, and that had been the same as the day before. Yet his patience was undoubtedly fortified by the tenets any veteran professional would have learned the hard way: surveillance is a game played long; and more often than not, its diligence is without reward—the quarry never shows.

Worse, this assignment, he knew, was more improbable than most, its logic more a prayer than a certainty. Simply because the Distinguished Personage had returned to England the previous January from Bermuda on a commercial Boeing flying boat—the first transatlantic air trip in history by a world leader—that was no guarantee he'd repeat the experience. After all, even the Distinguished Personage, in soul-searching retrospect, had conceded that his last-minute decision to forgo the waiting battleship with its muscular escort of fast destroyers was "a rash thing." To think that he'd once again take the identical foolhardy risk, traveling on an unprotected BOAC flight in wartime, was like believing that lightning would indeed strike twice. Yet Berlin had its agents lurking about the souks and cafés in North Africa, and they were reporting a tantalizing rumor: at the conclusion of the military meetings in Algiers and Tunis, the Distinguished Personage would fly out of Gibraltar to Lisbon. From there, he'd catch one of the scheduled DC-3s home. It was a question of only what day, what flight.

So the spy dutifully maintained his vigil. He kept the image of the Distinguished Personage focused in his mind's eye, but he never expected to see it in the flesh. It was 7:25 and the propellers on the *Ibis* had started to twirl, quickly picking up speed. Soon the plane would be taxiing to the runway, and on its way back to England. He'd have passed another uneventful watch.

Then two events occurred, one more improbable than the other.

First, a couple exited the plane. Walking down the flight of steps that had been quickly wheeled up to the craft's passenger door were a young boy and an older woman. She, too, had the demeanor of a professional watcher, but her attention was more maternal than conspiratorial; the boy's mother, or perhaps the child's nanny, it clearly seemed. But why were they coming off the aircraft? No one gives up a seat on the plane to England. Unless—

And no sooner had a startling hypothesis begun taking shape, than it was confirmed. Climbing up the stairs was the stooped and portly figure of a man dressed in a voluminous pin-striped suit, a bow tie perched under the double chin, a seven-inch cigar wedged in the fleshy mouth, and a dark homburg resting on his head like a tea cozy. The outfit was as distinctive as any uniform. And for further confirmation, although none was really needed, there was the presence of the man trailing closely behind—tall, rail thin, and deferential, fitting to a T the description in all the intelligence reports of the Distinguished Personage's ever-present personal bodyguard.

Now it was immediately apparent why the boy and his keeper had left the plane. They had been bounced, their tickets revoked—to make room at the last minute for the two late-arriving VIPs.

In the electric moments that followed—and who could have blamed the spy if he felt as if war drums were pounding through his entire being?—he hurried to the nearest telephone to share his hard-won discovery: Winston Churchill, accompanied by the Scotland Yard inspector who habitually rode in his wake, would be on board the morning flight to England.

PERCHED HIGH ON A HILL in a stodgy, leafy neighborhood in the far reaches of Lisbon, the German embassy rose up behind a tall wrought iron fence like an impenetrable redbrick fortress. And on its very top floor, in a warren of dormer rooms that looked out toward the Atlantic and the unconquered world beyond the horizon, the Abwehr, the German military intelligence organization, had set up its headquarters. Albert von Karsthoff was the station chief, although few inside the embassy gates, and even fewer outside, knew it.

A major in the German army from a family of distinguished soldiers, he had, following the rules of his covert trade, reinvented himself with an assumed name (making sure, however, that his alias boasted a "von," same as the surname that had been his genuine aristocratic birthright). And, more pretense, he was listed on the embassy rolls under the deliberately vague diplomatic title of "adjunct." Even better, he lived his cover, as the professionals say with praise; and like the best disguises, it was rooted in his nature, only then some. Karsthoff tooled around Lisbon in a shiny Cadillac, often with his pet monkey sharing the front seat, and a vial of cocaine stashed in his diplomat's well-cut dark suit. Every evening was a fiesta. He cut such a flamboyant, fun-loving figure that it never occurred to the legions of Allied intelligence agents meeching through the shadows of neutral Lisbon that he was a fellow operative, let alone the Nazis' master spy in the city. It was Karsthoff's private line—five digits seared into every local Abwehr agent's memory—that the spy called from the airport.

As luck would have it, Karsthoff was at his desk—either just arrived or, no less likely, still in his evening clothes preparing to head home after a long night—when the early-morning call came in. He listened with attention; the details of the *Ibis*'s flight plan were essential. At once he knew he had to make a decision, one that could affect his career—and, more consequentially, the entire course of the war. He had only moments to make it.

The Wehrmacht, with typically tedious Germanic exactitude, was an armed forces fortified by its allegiance to rules and procedures. The method for contacting the Luftwaffe's air units in the North Atlantic had been set down in martial stone in "Luftwaffe

Regulation 16, The Conduct of the Aerial War," a work signed by no less an imperious authoritarian than Reichsmarschall Hermann Göring. The links in the chain of command, the manual decreed, must be rattled in a strict progression: first, contact the air fleet commander in Paris; if he concurred that something crucial hung in the balance, he'd pass the particulars along to the Flying Corps Regional Command based at the seaport town of Lorient, France; and from there an action order would at last be conveyed to the field commander at the Mérignac air base near Bordeaux, whose squadrons hunted in the skies above the pounding waves breaking across the Bay of Biscay. But with the tick of every second counting, as well as with a battlefield wisdom born out of sour experiences that had taught that intelligence was of value only if it were translated into timely action, Karsthoff made a decision. He defied the regulations. In an act that would become part of the legend surrounding the entire operation, he made flash priority contact directly with the flying leader of fighter wing KG 40 at Mérignac.

It was nearly ten a.m. at the Luftwaffe base when the klaxon finally roared, tearing the quiet morning apart. At once pilots and crew scrambled across the tarmac to their fighters. Eight Junkers Ju-88s, fast, well-armed attack planes, took off angled toward the sun. Their powerful Jumo engines rumbling, the fighters climbed above the clouds. They raced west in a tight V formation, the pilots in the glass-roofed cockpits scanning the horizon for their prey.

THE PILOT OF THE *IBIS* heard before he saw. Above him was the unmistakable sound of an aircraft. No, not one: two. Two planes hidden somewhere high in the clouds over his glass canopy, yet the whirl of their propellers and thrust of their engines and his sudden uneasy state made it seem as if they were close enough for someone to reach down and grab him by the scruff of his neck.

"I am being followed by strange aircraft," the *Ibis*'s pilot radioed. As he spoke, two Ju-88s came crashing through the clouds, homing in on their target. "Indians at eleven o'clock," the Luftwaffe flight leader announced.

The *Ibis*'s only hope was to outrace the attack planes. "Putting on best speed," the pilot, full of pluck, informed Portela air traffic control.

The lumbering DC-3 had no chance. The diving Ju-88s, with their supercharged engines at full throttle, emerged from the clouds at a dizzying speed, their guns trained like magnets on the slow plane. "A!A!" the Luftwaffe flight leader ordered. *Attack! Attack!*

At once a barrage of 20-millimeter cannon shells boomed across the sky and machine guns poured out bullets in a terrifying cascade of 1,200 rounds per minute.

"Cannon shells and tracers going through the fuselage," the *Ibis* radioed. "Wave hopping and doing my best."

Flames streamed wildly from the DC-3. Then the port engine gave out, and the plane fell from the sky.

Suddenly, three parachutists jumped from the plunging plane. But flames engulfed their chutes, and they fell from high into the sea as if weighed down by boulders. The plane hit the water, too. It seemed for a moment that it might float, but then it sunk quickly into the dark, frigid waters of the Bay of Biscay.

The eight Ju-88s flew around the crash site in slow, careful circles, their crews keeping a close watch on the ominously still sea. When they were convinced there were no survivors, the fighters returned to the base, their mission accomplished.

ONLY IT WAS THE WRONG mission. It did not matter that the operation was a tactical success. It was a complete and utter strategic mistake. The crucial error lay in the intelligence that had provoked the aerial attack.

There had been two last-minute arrivals boarding the flight to Whitchurch. And true, one was a rotund and rumpled man in a dark suit, a long cigar wedged between his ample lips and a homburg planted on his head; while the other, trailing behind, was long, lean, and sprightly. The problem was they were not the prime minister of England and his Scotland Yard bodyguard.

They were two doppelgängers. Leslie Howard, the fifty-year-old British actor who had won movie fame as the resourceful and in-destructible Scarlet Pimpernel had now been cast by the impulsive Abwehr agent as Detective Walter Thompson. The actor's business manager and traveling companion, Alfred Chenhalls—who, down to the telltale cigar, was dressed for the part—had been given the role of Winston Churchill.

By the time the enraged British papers reported the downing of the defenseless civilian Flight 777, the genuine prime minister's plane had safely landed in England. He had prudently taken off under the protective cover of darkness from Gibraltar in a military aircraft and had flown across the ocean surrounded by an attentive guard of RAF fighters.

In the rush of wartime days that followed, each measured out in countless unnecessary deaths and woeful tragedies, the Abwehr's misguided attempt to change the course of the war with one op-portunistic assassination was relegated to a small, sad footnote in the larger and still very much uncertain march of history. "The brutality of the Germans," observed the intended victim with an understandable anger, "was only matched by the stupidity of their agents." But even Churchill in the end took refuge in a weary, if not mystical, stoicism, consigning the needless murders of the fif-teen people unlucky enough to have been on board Flight 777 to "the inscrutable workings of fate."

YET THE ALLIES WERE A triumvirate, a three-headed monster. "A Hydra," was how the classically educated Abwehr head, Admiral Wilhelm Canaris, put it in a ruminative conversation in his office with his fellow spies not long after the wrong plane had been shot out of the sky. And in case they had not enjoyed the enriching benefits of an education similar to his, he thoughtfully went on to remind them how the Greek tale ended: Hercules succeeds in killing the beast, but only after lopping off *all* its heads.

In the strained and tense days that followed this discussion, it was decided by the Nazi high command that Churchill's escape had simply been bad luck, certainly no harbinger, no sign that all their subsequent efforts would be doomed. After all, Canaris had a point: the beast had many heads.

A decision was made to target the president of the United States and the Soviet marshal.

THE IDEA WAS TO COME at FDR from the sea. The daring scheme, hatched by Section 6 of the Reich Security Head Office (Reichssicherheitshauptamt or RSHA), would be a follow-up to Operation Pastorius (the name an ironic tribute to the founder of the first German settlement in America). In that June 1942 mission, U-boats had ferried rigorously trained Nazi agents to the beaches of Long Island and Florida. Their objective was to create terror—blow up bridges, factories, and railways, even poison the New York water system. And their bombs would have started exploding all across the country if one of the saboteurs, preferring to settle in America rather than blow it to smithereens, hadn't turned himself in to the FBI. With his alarming confession as their guide, the G-men swiftly rounded up the other conspirators.

But this failure—a logistical triumph doomed in the end by only a single shaky operative, the spymasters kept telling themselves—didn't mean a similarly designed mission to assassinate President Franklin D. Roosevelt would not succeed. Once again, they'd deliver agents to the beaches of Long Island. The assassins would make their way to Washington, and then a well-aimed bullet would bring the tyrant down. How could it fail? Even Hitler had endorsed its

underlying blunt practicality: a lone shooter can accomplish anything. "I understand why 90 percent of historical murders were
successful. . . . There can be no complete safety," the Führer conceded.

Yet while put down on paper, the plan was never set in motion. Why? Were the knotty tactical demands too daunting? Would
smuggling marksmen into America and then getting them close
enough to fix the well-guarded FDR in their sights present too
difficult a challenge? Or, as one of the men high up in the Nazi
foreign minister's office who'd read the operational memo flared,
was the very prospect of killing the American president "absolute
madness"? (His moral squeamishness, though, was voiced only after the war was over.) Whatever the reason, the spymasters' resolve
faltered.

WHICH LEFT STALIN. THE NAZIS' intention to assassinate the Soviet premier did—quite literally, in fact—take flight. A German
military transport took off from Riga with two turncoat Russians
aboard, as well as a bomb that was a masterwork of lethal ingenuity.
"Our experts produced a strange mechanism made exclusively for
this purpose—Stalin's assassination," the head of the foreign intelligence service of the Reich Security Office bragged with a proprietary pride. "The explosive was fist-sized and resembled a handful
of mud. It was to be affixed to Stalin's automobile. . . . The radio
transmitter, intended to activate the bomb, was no larger than a
cigarette box and could automatically explode the bomb from a distance of ten kilometers. The explosion was so powerful that almost
nothing remained of the car on which we tried it."

In the dead of a rain-swept Russian night, the two agents, the
valuable device carefully cushioned in a rucksack, parachuted from
the plane. Their objective was to make their clandestine way to the
military site the Abwehr had determined was the Russian marshal's
field headquarters. Once they'd identified Stalin's vehicle and stuck

the deadly glob of mud to the undercarriage, the rest would be easy: a matter of having the cold-blooded patience to wait until the precise moment to press the transmitter button.

They never even got close to the car. According to the German version of events, the two parachutists had the misfortune of touching down in the midst of a Soviet troop patrol. The smirking Russians, however, told a different, and more self-serving, story: the turncoats were not traitors, but double agents who all along had been in the employ of the Soviet intelligence service, the NKVD.

The result, however, was indisputable: once again the Nazis had failed.

MORE TROUBLING, THE TIMING COULD not have been worse.

And it wasn't just that the war was not going well for Germany. By the tail end of the icy European winter of 1943, after the demoralizing defeat of the Sixth Army at Stalingrad, after the Allies, invigorated by battalions of gung-ho American troops and newly built squadrons of US bombers, had begun openly discussing the inevitable invasion of Europe, most of the Nazi leadership had conceded that victory on the battlefield was a lost cause.

In its place, a resigned, coolly pragmatic endgame strategy had emerged: the Reich would snatch a stalemate from the jaws of defeat. The Wehrmacht would keep the world at arms, keep the life-and-death struggle going—until an acceptable peace could be negotiated. At the conclusion of the hostilities, Germany would emerge still strong and—or so went the wild hopes of the more optimistic true believers—maintain control over the eastern European territories it had conquered.

Preliminary back-channel talks—"officially unofficial," according to the deliberately obfuscating diplomatic jargon—for a negotiated settlement were already going on. In Bern, Allen Dulles, the chief American spy based in Europe, had met with civilian and military representatives of the German resistance. And in Stockholm,

Abram Stevens Hewitt, an American intelligence officer who was, he liked to boast, FDR's "personal representative," lay day after soothing day across a massage table as his aching back was expertly kneaded by the pudgy Finnish doctor who had been dispatched by SS Reichführer Heinrich Himmler. As the healing fingers of Dr. Felix Kersten—dismissed by some wags in the SS as "Himmler's Magic Buddha," but of course only when the Reichführer wasn't within hearing—prodded the spy's flesh, the masseuse and his patient entered into authorized discussions about what it would take to end the fighting.

In the meantime, until the last episodes of the war could grind to their slow conclusion on the battlefields, in the back rooms, and on the massage tables, it was Himmler who articulated the high command's new, quiescent marching orders. "Bravery is composed of faith," he preached to a gathering of SS generals and staff officers. "It's faith that wins battles, faith that achieves victories."

But then faith became impossible.

On January 24, 1943, the last day of the meetings in liberated Casablanca between the American president and the British prime minister, FDR took it upon himself to set the uncompromising terms that would end the war. "We shall fight until Germany's, Italy's, and Japan's unconditional surrender," he announced with stony determination at the conference's final press conference.

With those unyielding words—"unconditional surrender"—the Nazi high command's fantasies were ground into wistful sand. There would be no negotiated peace. Instead, the generals and their willing underlings abruptly understood they faced a rapidly approaching future in which they would have to answer to Allied military tribunals for their unforgivable crimes, for their methodical extermination of Jews and other civilians, for the horrors they'd so complacently let loose on the world. Retribution was inevitable. In the end, they would pay with their lives.

With this heavy knowledge, the string of unsuccessful assassinations was no longer one of merely poorly planned operations. Nor could these mishaps simply be dismissed with some forlorn words about "inscrutable fate." A grimmer realization took hold among the agonized men who controlled the Reich: These had been, it was now clear, do-or-die missions. Their significance had been historic. They had been the last chance to change the course of the conflict and the terms of the peace. Only they had failed, and the opportunity had passed forever.

PART II

SOWING THE DRAGON'S TEETH

2

SECRET SERVICE AGENT MIKE REILLY also had irretrievably failed, or so he sincerely believed at the time. He'd been expected to use his body as a shield for the president. It was the fundamental, inviolate rule of the job: *You take the hit.* Flesh stops knives and bullets. He was supposed to stay close, be ready to move in a split second to put himself in front of the president. But on that Indian summer afternoon in 1936, he'd blundered foolishly.

Over the course of a single horrible moment—an instant that stretched on for an eternity in his agonized mind—he watched as a dagger went hurling through the air straight at the president.

There was nothing either of them—not Mike, and certainly not FDR—could do to stop it. And while the incident would turn out to be nothing more than a close call, its malicious intent more theater than actual harm, it would nevertheless continue to haunt his thoughts. It became indelible, the scale by which he'd always measure all his fears.

UP UNTIL THEN, IT HAD been among the happiest of campaign trips in Mike's short professional life as a guardian of the president. It wasn't just that Franklin Roosevelt loved campaigning, the liberating opportunity to distance himself from Washington's petty, internecine battles by barnstorming across the country. Nor was it simply that he was good at it, and that his vain delight over the

tumultuous ovations from the crowds cheering his folksy, buoy-
antly optimistic speeches was infectious; Mike, despite the requisite
on-duty pose of detachment, couldn't help but be stirred. Similar
irrepressible joys had, after all, been part of the flavor of past outings
when the Boss (as Mike, with a breezy deference, always called the
president) took to the stump.

This swing around America, however, had its own unique animating quality. The 1936 presidential campaign—FDR dueling for
his second term against Alf Landon—had the feel of a victory march.
From Jim Farley, the president's canny, longtime campaign manager,
to John Mays, the dignified White House butler who had been ca-
tering to the whims of Great Men since the days of McKinley, there
was a solid confidence among those who basked in FDR's sun that
the election would be a mere formality. It was a sentiment that transformed the long, exhausting journey down the campaign trail into
an unusually agreeable adventure for the presidential entourage.

By the time FDR got to Erie, Pennsylvania, in the last days
of fall, Mike, along with the rest of the Secret Service detail, was
also feeling good about things; with the November election just
weeks away, they were in the home stretch. Not that any of them
could forget "the rough evening," as Mike would refer to it with a
professional's tact, that had nearly ruined the start of the reelection
campaign.

It'd been a night that had shouted out the seldom-spoken singular
challenge at the operational heart of protecting this president: FDR
was, as Mike bluntly put it, "a helpless cripple, incapable of walking
unaided a single foot." An autoimmune neuropathy (diagnosed at
the time as poliomyelitis) had left him, fifteen years earlier at the
age of thirty-nine, paralyzed from the waist down. It was a condition that those close to FDR conspired to keep, as best they could,
secret from the American public. The heavy steel braces on the
president's legs had been painted a deep black to blend in with his
trousers, and the press photographers were by and large sufficiently
complicit not to snap away when FDR was in his wheelchair. But

the men who guarded him knew that they were responsible for the safety of an immobile target.

This complication had been driven deeply home that night at Franklin Field. Twenty-four hours after the convention in Philadelphia had nominated FDR by acclamation, he had come to the cavernous college football stadium packed with well-wishers to give his acceptance speech. Holding tightly on to the arm of his son Jimmy for support, the nominee made his deliberate, stiff-legged way—each rigid step a small battle—through the narrow path behind the stage that Mike and the crew had cleared. Progress was slow; many people wanted to congratulate the beaming FDR. As he neared the stage, the president with his one free hand waved a salutary greeting toward an old acquaintance, Edwin Markham. The elderly poet, the white beard flowing down his chest giving him the countenance of a fiery biblical prophet, responded by extending his hand; FDR, with a veteran politician's reflex, reached through the sea of bodies to grasp it. And at that instant the crowd surged. Jimmy, overwhelmed, fell heavily against his father, and with the added weight, the president's right leg brace snapped. The president collapsed. His descent was hard and fast; he heaved forward like a tree felled by the final blow of an ax. But before he slammed into the ground, Mike, propelled by sheer instinct, managed to get his shoulder wedged under the president's right armpit. He also found the battle sense to scream at Markham, "Don't move!" He feared some trigger-happy agent, mistaking the wildly bearded man's good-spirited greeting as a deliberate assault, would shoot first and ask questions later. But Markham obeyed, or perhaps was too stunned to move. And then Mike, with a single mighty tug, lifted the president to his feet. He held FDR tight, doing his best to steady him. Both men were shaking.

Gus Gennerich, another member of the detail, refastened the screws that had popped on the brace. Yet the president, who even in the best of circumstance had little confidence in the efficacy of the heavy steel contraptions that bound his legs, was not ready to make his way to the stage. Supported by Mike and Gennerich, he stood inertly, his face a ghostly white. There was a long silence, and Mike supposed that what both the Boss and he were feeling was fear.

Finally, once more in control, FDR snapped, "Clean me up." And soon they were making their way to the stage.

The incident had been witnessed only by the people who'd been backstage, and, party loyalists, they rarely talked about it. The thousands of people jammed into the stadium's stands and field seats had no inkling of what had transpired. What they would remember about the evening was FDR's exhorting with a prescient author- ity, "This generation of Americans has a rendezvous with destiny." Nor would they ever forget a triumphant FDR circling the field in his open-topped car at the ceremony's end, and the collective full- throated cheer that rose up into the starry night sky above Phila- delphia, a sustained, gigantic noise loud enough, or so it seemed to Mike, to reverberate across the heavens.

But Mike never got over that "rough evening," and having made it to Erie without further incident and the end of a seemingly vic- torious campaign now in sight, he at last dared to allow himself a cheery confidence. Reinforcing his upbeat, end-of-term mood even further was the venue: the Boss would be talking from the narrow platform on the last car of the presidential train.

Vigilance, Mike would often moan, was the bodyguard's "un- ending headache." Still, in the course of his dutiful career, Mike had learned that some headaches were worse than others. Motor- cades, he felt, presented the greatest threats. "I guess the President is most vulnerable when passing slowly through a city," he'd decided from tense experience. "We watched the crowd along the route, the rooftops, the windows." Yet there was always the unsettling possi- bility that they might've missed something—the one window, the one rooftop, that hid an assassin poised to strike.

When the Boss was heading out on the presidential train, how- ever, the detail breathed easier. The train was as safe as a citadel, built by the Pullman Company with three-inch-thick bulletproof glass windows and a rock-solid body forged out of armored steel. A truck could hit broadside, sticks of dynamite could explode on the roadbed, machine guns could strafe—and the presidential car, as well as its occupants, would press on. There were even two intricate elevator systems in the rear compartment that allowed the wheelchair-bound president to be lowered to the ground, thereby avoiding the risk (as well as the indignity) of the Boss's being carried from the train like a child in the arms of a beefy Secret Service agent.

Another godsend: when the presidential train pulled into a town, there was no need for an automotive caravan to make a potentially dangerous trip to the waiting crowd. FDR would be propped up on the train's tiny back platform, his concealed braces keeping his legs as straight and rigid as telephone poles; the Secret Service agents would discreetly step back; and then the crowd would be ushered in, assembling on the tracks facing the president.

On that fateful afternoon in Erie, FDR, his usual genial smile animating his face, was standing upright on the rear platform in front of a waist-high rail while in his high, plumy voice he beseeched the crowd spread out below him to cast their vote for the Democrats and the New Deal. At the same time, Mike, experiencing no unusual concerns, had taken up a position among the onlookers.

Suddenly, a knife was hurled from the depths of the crowd. Its swift trajectory had the blade on a straight course toward the president's chest.

FDR saw it coming. But he was helpless. He could not move. His legs were locked stiffly in place.

There was absolutely nothing Mike could do. He stood in the crowd, watching impotently—his shudder giving way to the dreaded realization that the day of reckoning had come.

3

FOUR YEARS EARLIER, IT'D BEEN a matter of chance that Mike had signed on with the US Treasury Department, the government office that controlled the Secret Service. In fact, if he hadn't uncharacteristically splurged on the twenty-cent taxi ride that rainy day in 1932, then he wouldn't have had the conversation that set him on the path to become the president's bodyguard.

Mike had come to Washington as an unambitious twenty-two-year-old with the plan—more a casual choice than a decision rooted in either any genuine interest or conviction—to study law. He'd grown up in the wilderness copper mining town of Anaconda, Montana, at the foot of the lofty mountain range that had given the municipality its name. His father, Bernard, worked in the mine, and like most of the miners, had immigrated from Ireland; Saint Patrick's Day was, by the happy local custom, a weeklong, well-served celebration. And Mike had inherited his father's proud Irish, and devoutly Roman Catholic, soul, as well as dark, curly hair, brown, twinkling eyes, self-effacing wit, and, not least, fondness for drink. By many accounts (more bemused than judgmental), he was very much his father's son, spending long evenings belly up to the bar with a shot glass of whiskey grasped in his hand, and in the course of these marathons his moods would fly mercurially about, running the gamut from jokey to maudlin to sentimental in the course of draining a bottle. Mike, too, would sheepishly concede that he'd "known my share of hangovers."

But where the son differed from the father was in his sheer size.

Mike was a broad-shouldered mountain of a man with a fighter's thick brow, as imposing in his darkly handsome way as any of the peaks he could see from his childhood bedroom window. And while Mike could, when his dander was up or it suited his purpose, be an intimidating presence, he more often than not went about in a soft-spoken, unchallenging way, carrying his bulk with a born athlete's easy grace. It was this natural prowess, fortified by, once the game began, a suddenly competitive streak, that had made him a high-scoring basketball forward as well as a sure-handed right end on the football team at Regis, the Jesuit college he'd attended on scholarship in Denver.

When graduation came, he'd managed ("against all odds," he'd say with a typically self-deprecating honesty) to squeak gratefully by with Cs in most of the demanding Jesuit courses. Nevertheless, he'd made a name for himself on campus as an athlete as well as a jovial (at least when sober) and fun-loving frat boy, so when he asked the good fathers what he should do with the rest of his life, someone suggested law. The one thing Mike knew for certain was that he didn't want to go back to small-time Anaconda or the perpetual nighttime of working in the belly of a copper mine. With an amicable resolve, he agreed he might as well give law a shot. The old-boy Jesuit network found him a place across the country at George Washington University in DC. His first class was in September 1932.

After six months of struggling not only in the classroom but also making ends meet (law schools didn't bestow scholarships on former football players), Mike knew he needed a job. The university's placement office directed him to the newly created Farm Credit Administration (FCA). A division of the Treasury Department, the FCA was one of FDR's godsend creations to help struggling farmers get through hard times, and Mike hoped they could find room for another bureaucratic pencil pusher. He wasn't hunting for anything permanent, just part-time work, something that would pay enough so he could sit down to a decent meal for a change. He wasn't prepared to give up on all the imagined possibilities that a law degree would bring.

At the end of the FCA interview, however, the only offer made was for a full-time position. I'll think about it, Mike said without enthusiasm; and then, after glancing at his watch, he realized that if he hurried, he could still be on time for his next class at George Washington. With the rain pelting down and the clock ticking, Mike, despite his strapped straits, impulsively decided to hail a cab.

Mike instructed the driver to head to the campus, and the cabbie abruptly asked, "Do you go to George Washington?"

Mike confirmed that he did, and the garrulous driver continued his interrogation: "Studying law?"

An affirmative grunt, so the cabbie's monologue picked up speed. "I went there. Graduated head of the law class."

"Boy, that's pretty good," Mike said politely. Then he returned to his thoughts, mulling the unexpected choice the FCA interviewer had put before him. Only to burst out incredulously: "You finished at the head of the law class?"

"That's right."

Mike considered the cabbie's depressing career trajectory and swiftly came to the uneasy realization that his own legal prospects would be a lot dimmer. "Would you mind taking me back to the Farm Credit Administration building?" he asked. "Quick!"

By the day's end, Mike had become a full-time Treasury Department employee and a law school dropout. "American jurisprudence would have to carry on as best it could without Michael Francis Reilly," he decided equably.

It was a job with a steady paycheck, and he was quite happy except for the work: he spent his days making his dogged way through a small mountain of government forms. But Washington was a convivial city, and he made lots of friends. He could walk into downtown bars and someone would be sure to call out, "Hey,

Mike." And while former football players don't win law scholar-ships, they do win hearts. He was juggling several girlfriends, and it suited him to keep the relationships noncommittal.

Then, for reasons that were never explained to him, his FCA bosses plucked him from the rows of young men hunched over their desks to make him an investigator. The only qualification he had, as best Mike could figure, was that he possessed the intimidating look of a bruiser; "a large, strong character with normal brains and plenty of muscle," was how he sketched his own self-portrait. The powers that be had their eyes on a purportedly corrupt farm lending administrator in Tennessee and, he surmised, they'd reasoned that if it required a little pushing and shoving to get the goods, well, so much the better.

When Mike went down to Memphis, he made two discoveries, and each came as an unexpected surprise. First, the embezzler's sole crime was being a registered Republican, and while that, Mike would concede, "did come dangerously close to lawbreaking" in the South, it was not sufficient reason, he felt, for losing a job. A lifetime of going to mass had left him too much of a moralist to railroad an innocent man. And second, Mike learned that he gen-uinely enjoyed foraging in dark corners. He was, he'd say with modest pride in his newfound skills, "an Irish cop, more muscle than brain."

His evenhanded work on the case made him political enemies in Tennessee but won admirers in the department: the title of "inves-tigator" became, to his delight, permanent. Soon he was running across the country as he chased down one corruption suspect after another. A string of successes brought Mike to the attention of the Interior Department, and they recruited him to run to ground a cabal of energy profiteers. Here his tenacious work led, he'd cele-brate, "to indictments against some of our proudest oil and gasoline peddlers."

Then marriage put a sudden damper on his roving blood-hound's career. He had met a pretty red-haired secretary, Roby, who worked in the office of Senator Samuel Shortridge of California. Suddenly, all he could think about was commitment. After a whirlwind courtship, they married in 1935 and Mike realized he'd need a new job, one in which an investigator could stay in one place long enough to raise a family. Mike decided a transfer to the Secret Service (also part of the Treasury Department) would do the trick. "I would be assigned to a district somewhere in the United States, and the extent of my travel would be an occasional few days, not more than an overnight from home," according to the sensible future he'd plotted.

It all went as he'd planned, at first. In June 1935, his transfer to the Secret Service went through and he was quickly sent to his home state of Montana. He figured Roby and he would put down stakes close to his relatives and life would play itself out without any dramas. Which was just what happened—and it left him bored silly. After all the heady cases tracking down genuine big-time villains, he found it dispiriting to be shoved off to the hinterlands. His investigative challenges were mostly low-grade tax-avoidance cases. Worse, he knew many of the culprits from high school or college. In their former lives they had drunk a lot of beers, chased a lot of girls, played for the same teams. If Mike had his way, he'd simply give any of his old buddies, he'd suggested, "a clout in the mouth and let him go." That punishment would fit the crime. But having to put the cuffs on a man with whom he'd palled around— that didn't sit right with Mike. He didn't want to be the one who upended a friend's life. At the same time, he'd be violating his own sense of honor if he didn't do the job the Treasury Department was paying him to do. Rather than having to go on making uncomfortable choices, Mike put in for a transfer.

Before the year was out he was assigned to Secret Service District 16. That was the White House detail. His job: to protect the president.

AND THAT HAD BEEN, LARGELY, the professional career that had brought Mike to the unsettling moment in Erie, Pennsylvania: staring with wide-eyed rage as a dagger flew at the man he was to keep safe at all costs.

Mike was running on the balls of his feet, shoulders down, smashing his way through the crowd, when the dagger hit the president smack in the chest.

And then bounced to the platform.

Mike vaulted over the waist-high guardrail and held the weapon in his hand. Incredulous, he ran a finger along the blade. But even after that, it still required another moment before he could make full sense of what had happened. Before he finally came to terms with the fact that it was a rubber dagger. It had been hurled to frighten the president, not to kill him.

The president made light of the attack. Yet that was only a small consolation for Mike. Even after his anger subsided, he could not stop thinking about what might have been.

The next morning at mass, Mike gave thanks. And from the depths of his heart, he silently prayed that his luck would not run out.

4

THEN CAME THE WAR. And at once Mike knew his prayers had gone unanswered: his luck had run out. There was Before Pearl Harbor and After, and in the aftermath his job would never be the same.

Like the rest of the nation, Mike would always remember where he was when he learned about the Japanese surprise attack. Only he had the distinction of hearing the news before it reached even the president. Weekends in the White House were a slow time; a skeleton staff roamed through the corridors, and they went about in a relaxed walk, not the usual officious scurrying. On Sunday, December 7, 1941, Mike, on duty, found himself filling the empty afternoon sitting in the cubbyhole office of the mansion's chief usher talking fishing; a young naval aide, resplendent in his gold-braided uniform, sat slouched in an adjacent chair with his eyes closed as though trying to sleep while his boss, the naval secretary, ate lunch in the next room with the president. The phone rang, and Wilson Searles, the usher, interrupted his long-winded tale about some pesky trout that'd gotten away to answer it. He listened, and then offhandedly passed the receiver to the aide, explaining, "It's the Navy Department calling you."

The young man pulled himself from his chair and put the phone to his ear. At once all his previous lassitude vanished, and, immediately alert, he was bellowing into the receiver, "My God, you don't mean Pearl Harbor's been bombed?" Searles's story stopped in midsentence. Mike's head snapped back, as if a roundhouse sucker punch had landed, which it had. The reeling naval aide couldn't even manage to hang up the phone; it took him two tries before he succeeded in putting the receiver into the telephone cradle.

Then the initial shock passed, and they were on the move. The aide ran off to alert his boss and the president. At the same time Mike, careering down the carpeted mansion hallway like the right end he was a lifetime earlier, went straight to the White House switchboard. "Start calling in all the Secret Service men who are off duty," he instructed the operator. "All the White House police, too." Picking up a phone, he called Ed Kelly, Washington's chief of police, telling him to send sixteen uniformed men over to the White House right away, and "don't tell them why." Next he started reaching out to his superiors. Mike couldn't locate Colonel Ed Starling, the chief of the detail; Starling and his wife apparently were spending a sunny Sunday afternoon driving through the Virginia countryside. He did find Frank Wilson, the chief of the US Secret Service, who took the news with an icy calm, and then began tearing into Mike as if the war were somehow his fault. Finally, Mike spoke to Henry Morgenthau Jr., the imperious treasury secretary and the Secret Service's ultimate boss, and, the way Mike remembered it, for once Morgenthau's usual treacly reserve was overwhelmed. He let out a scream "as though stabbed." Recovering, he ordered that the guard be doubled immediately. But before Mike could act on that, Morgenthau was back on the phone, demanding that the guard be quadrupled and machine guns issued all around.

It was at that moment, the phone pressed against his ear, that Mike saw the president being pushed in his wheelchair to the Oval Office. "His chin stuck out about two feet in front of his knees and he was the maddest Dutchman I—or anybody—ever saw," he'd recall, the fierce countenance of the normally affable president locked in his memory. The Boss, he realized, was now a wartime commander in chief.

As the arriving agents and police officers were being deployed,

Morgenthau showed up. He wanted to hear all the protective measures the detail had taken. Mike ran through them, but it didn't seem the treasury secretary was paying much attention. Instead, his eyes kept darting to the White House's windows. Mike was perplexed until he realized Morgenthau was searching the sky for enemy aircraft. For the first time Mike fully comprehended that now anything was possible.

The next day, Mike was summoned to Frank Wilson's office. He didn't know what to expect. He feared the head of the service was going to reprimand him for not having done enough to protect the Boss in the first chaotic hours of this new war. He was blindsided, then, when Wilson announced that Morgenthau had just signed an order promoting Mike to supervising agent of the president's Secret Service detail.

At thirty-one, Mike found himself in charge of the safety of Franklin D. Roosevelt, the leader of a nation at war. The weight of his new responsibilities landed on his broad shoulders with a sudden, nearly crushing force. "It was something to give a man," he'd admit without embarrassment, "cold shivers in the daytime and nightmares in bed. It did both."

The Boss was no longer just "a high priority target" for the mentally unsound. At any moment the president could be, Mike imagined with a fresh shudder of dread, in the sights of "a regiment of Axis assassins." Mike understood it would be his job "to outwit them." And he knew they wouldn't come armed with rubber knives.

SHOULD THE WHITE HOUSE BE painted black?

But would that be sufficient? Perhaps engineers also needed to alter the course of the Potomac and Anacostia Rivers. Even if the mansion were camouflaged, an enemy pilot could still follow these waterways; the building was, any map made clear, a measured mile from their confluence. It would be an easy bit of navigation.

Maybe, then, the only secure alternative was to relocate the president's residence, find a home and office for him farther inland, away from the dangerous geography of the East Coast.

Such was the heightened anxiety in the uncertain days after America went to war that these precautions against aerial bombing attacks, as well as other similarly impulsive suggestions, were discussed with an earnestness that, only in retrospect, seems fantastic. Yet at the time the challenges were unprecedented. FDR was the first president who had to be protected against enemy nations that had aircraft that could fly across oceans to drop payloads of bombs or platoons of paratroopers from the sky above Washington. There were remote-controlled devices that, in the hands of spies or fifth columnists, could be detonated from a distance to blow up bridges, railroads, even buildings. And, if all the jittery rumors buzzing through the city were to be believed, the Nazis had high-powered rockets that could be shot off from faraway locations and strike with lethal accuracy. Mike's overactive imagination was grinding out one horror after another, and yet he knew however preposterous they might seem, he could not afford to be contemptuous of any of them: too much was at stake. Guided as much by his fears as any firm military expertise, he threw himself into the multifaceted task of making sure the White House was put on a wartime footing.

Before the war, Mike's persistent four-in-the-morning, staring-at-the-ceiling worry was fire. The White House, he judged with a professional's unsentimental objectivity, was "the biggest firetrap in America, bar none." Compounding his distress was the fact that the man he'd have to rescue from an inferno was unable to walk. FDR couldn't make his own escape. Mike, therefore, had fire chutes installed in the president's bedroom that (or so he tried to convince himself) would enable him to slide from a window to the White House lawn. And, a more realistic insurance against disaster, agents had also practiced, and practiced again, the procedure of grabbing the president from his bed and carrying him down a flaming staircase until they could do it blindfolded (which might as well have been the case if the flames and smoke were thick).

But that concern, Mike learned after his first wartime security conference with the building's engineers, was nearly insignificant when measured against another cause for alarm. A bomb wouldn't need to land directly on the White House; the tremors from even a near miss would cause the mansion, the engineers predicted with a dramatic certainty, to "crumble like a stack of cards." The building, they explained, was constructed with mere oyster shell mortar and limestone blocks. It wouldn't survive a bombing attack.

Spurred on by that unnerving appraisal, as well as by the horrifying mental image of Japanese planes unloading their bombs on the US Pacific fleet, Mike realized he needed to find a bomb shelter for the boss. *At once.* He swiftly located a suitable spot—only first he had to get the authorities to remove several tons of opium.

Across a narrow street from the White House stood the stately, stone-columned, neoclassical Treasury Department building. Years earlier in a more halcyon time, the department had built a huge vault constructed of heavy armor plates and reinforced with concrete beneath its marble halls. Its purpose, in part: to warehouse the nation's reserves of opium. Under Mike's direction (and after much more expert consultation with army, navy, and civilian engineers), the Federal Works Agency quickly began transforming this subterranean repository. Protective filters against chemical gases were installed. Escape hatches were carved out of the thick walls. And a zigzagging underground tunnel, with emergency exits scattered along the route, was hollowed out between the White House and the Treasury building. The president could be wheeled covertly from the mansion to the vault even in the midst of an aerial attack. (As for the tons of opium, Mike never knew where they wound up, yet he often wondered if the fumes still hung in the vault's air. But then again, he mischievously suggested, any lingering medicinal effects might be welcome in case the day came when the nation's capital was being blown sky-high.)

However, even as work began on this bomb shelter, Mike had no illusion that it was anything more than a stopgap measure. The president needed a safe place to hide without leaving the White House grounds. FDR grumbled that this was an unnecessary precaution, but then one morning as Mike, always persistent, made his case while the Boss was having his breakfast in bed, the president relented. Perhaps FDR realized that it would be easier to give in than to listen to Mike's constant badgering. Or perhaps, while comfortably propped up in his bed, the inconvenience of having to be wheeled through a twisting underground tunnel whenever there was an alert became apparent. Whatever the reason, the president instructed, "Tell Horatio Winslow to see me today." And before the day's end, FDR and Winslow, the White House architect, had sketched out a preliminary schedule to begin construction on the long-discussed East Wing—only now this much-needed addition would contain not just offices, but also a huge basement bomb shelter fortified by sufficient walls of lead and concrete to hold up against even a direct hit. In a further display of wartime prudence, the president insisted there should be a vault within the shelter to house state documents that were vital to the continuity of the republic.

Dive-bombing enemy planes, however, were just one of Mike's nightmares. He also worried about "Axis parachutists or an organized heavy fifth-column invasion" of the White House. And he had little confidence that even a beefed-up, machine gun–toting Secret Service detail could fend off a determined, well-organized attack. He shared this troubling scenario with the army, and the generals quickly got the point. After the initial discussion, though, the four-star chieftains' possessiveness took over; they'd be damned if they were going to formulate their plans to protect the commander in chief with a civilian. So Mike sat back and watched as the military went to work to transform the White House into an impregnable wartime citadel.

Overnight, or so it seemed, a combat-ready infantry battalion from nearby Fort Myer was bivouacked on the once pristine lawn. Artillery and heavy machine gun fortifications were excavated. An antiaircraft battery was set up on the mansion's roof, the long-barreled guns raised, Mike felt, as if already searching the sky for targets. And a crack unit of the Chemical Warfare Service took up residence in the building in case of a sudden gas or even biological weapons attack. When Mike asked if that was really necessary, he received a curt lecture: the Germans had cavalierly dispersed anthrax spores in the United States during the last war, and the Japanese are even more ruthless than the Huns. Of course it's necessary. By the time the industrious generals were done, the only thing the White House lacked, Mike liked to joke, was a moat.

Yet as the war dragged on, as the burden of his responsibilities pressed down on him, Mike found himself thinking that maybe the idea of a moat was not so outlandish. Not at all.

5

STILL, THE WAR HAD CAUGHT the Secret Service by surprise, and a sense of institutional shame was compounded by a feeling of helplessness: We should have seen this coming, we should have been more prepared. It didn't take long before this hand-wringing predicament was brought soundly home.

Just twelve hours after learning of the Japanese attack, the president informed the detail that he'd be riding from the White House to the Capitol to declare war against Japan. The entire journey was about a mile and a half, only a few minutes' drive. But Mike began to fear that FDR might not make it to his destination. In his open-topped car, the president would be a perfect target for enemy assassins.

Even before the war, Mike had argued that the Boss should travel in an armored car. Part of Mike's job was to read the belligerent and too often threatening letters that arrived at the White House each day, and that disquieting duty had left him with the acute realization that "there were literally tens of thousands of Americans who would love to shoot the president of the United States." It was a necessary, even commonsense precaution, he'd pleaded, for the presidential limousine to be bulletproof. His concern, however, was overruled by the Treasury Department. The problem, he was primly informed, was money. Government regulations explicitly stated that a maximum of $750 could be allotted for the president's vehicle. And while $750 would purchase a pretty nifty roadster, it

wouldn't begin to cover the sticker price of a car that was as indestructible as a tank.

On the momentous day of FDR's speech to Congress, then, the
best Mike could do was line the route deep with soldiers, the taller
the better. And he had Secret Service agents, the huskier the better, draped over the president's limousine. After taking those small
precautions, he could only, he recalled with a forlorn pang, "hope
for the best."

Wishful thinking, however, would not be sufficient to get the
president safely through the remainder of the hostilities. Mike decided he'd need to improvise. He quickly came up with a resourceful plan, one that would have to suffice until the money could
somehow be authorized to build the president a suitable wartime
car. And he soon got the opportunity to try it out.

Two days later, FDR announced that he wanted to go for a ride.
"I'm not going to spend the rest of the war in hiding," he barked,
glowering at Mike as if he expected him to object.

"Yes, sir. What time will you be ready?" Mike responded, a
model of obedience.

Within the hour Mike was wheeling the president to the White
House driveway as a car pulled up. It was a green Cadillac about
the size of an army truck, and at first glance, arguably twice as un-
wieldy.

"What's that thing, Mike?" FDR demanded.

"Mr. President, I've taken the liberty of getting a new car," Mike
began, relishing his straight man's role. "It's armored. I'm afraid it's
a little uncomfortable. And I know it has a dubious reputation."

"Dubious reputation?" the president repeated with impatience.

"Yes, sir. It belonged to Al Capone. The Treasury Department
had a little trouble with Al, you know, and they got it from him in
the subsequent legal complications. I got it from the Treasury."

The president stared quizzically at the mammoth vehicle, nine
thousand pounds of reinforced steel. Mike wondered if he wanted
to kick the tires, or, for that matter, possibly poke him. But in the

end, he simply accepted the situation. "I hope Mr. Capone doesn't mind," FDR said coyly. Then, fellow conspirators enjoying a shared joke, they went off for their ride in the new presidential limousine.

BUT THE PRESIDENT WAS NOT always so tractable. War or no war, FDR insisted that there'd be business as usual at the White House. And since the business was politics, that meant that streams of government officials would be forever marching through the mansion's halls. And on Christmas, just two weeks away, the gates would swing open and people would crowd the grounds for the tree-lighting festivities. The prospect of so many strangers, any of whom might be an Axis agent or a fifth columnist, in proximity to the Boss gave Mike the jitters. His impertinence reinforced by the terrors swirling around in his imagination, he tried to lay down the law to the president: the number of official visitors would need to be curtailed, and as for the Christmas ceremony, well, that would have to be abolished. It was an edict that nearly cost him his job.

It wasn't that the president said no; Mike was accustomed to FDR's turning him down. And it wasn't the terse, emphatic definitiveness of his response; Mike, too, had been lashed with that whip before. But what was unprecedented was the look of uncompromising resolve the president fixed on Mike. It was a tacit proclamation of presidential authority. Mike swiftly understood that if he dared to press the issue he would, he imagined, "very shortly be giving the bank teller at No People, South Dakota, a lecture on how to tell the counterfeit two-dollar bill from the true one."

In defeat, Mike once more had no choice but to turn resourceful. If he couldn't bar the doors to the White House, he decided he'd better fortify them. He resorted to what he came to dub with a sly relish his "gaudy collection" of "gadgets": "talking fences, seeing-eye doors, pocket-sized radio senders and receivers." The problem, however, was that some of these gadgets worked better than others.

The Alnor Door, for example, was one of his brainstorms. It was a freestanding passageway that let off a high-pitched alarm whenever someone concealing a gun or knife walked through the electrified, metal-sensitive portal. Mike ventured that this equipment, standard at prisons, would work just as well at the White House (which, if Mike were to have his jumpy way, he'd be only too happy to turn into a prison of sorts). On the eve of the tree-lighting ceremony, Mike had a couple of the intimidating Alnors, each one weighing several hundred pounds, plunked down at the White House's main gate, although in keeping with the Christmas season, he had each of them decked out with boughs of holly. Fifty thousand or so people walked through the makeshift passageways for the festivities, and there was a steady chorus of yelps from the machines. Yet at the end of the evening, all Mike had to show for his caution was a tall pile of confiscated metal flasks, which, to Mike's way of looking at things, was an unanticipated but nevertheless welcome fringe benefit. The detail would enjoy some extra holiday cheer.

Encouraged, he had a smaller version (although still by most residential standards an ugly, gargantuan piece of machinery) of the Alnor Door set up inside the mansion. But every time the solid interior doors swung open, their decorative brass and ornamental locks would set off a sustained series of angry electronic yelps. The Alnors were in place one day, and gone the next.

So Mike, tenacious, found an engineer who came up with another metal-detecting device—and this one weighed only eight ounces. It would be hidden away under an agent's suit jacket, with a connecting buzzer on his lapel. And it worked well—just too well. It emitted a nearly nonstop cacophony of noise as the buzzer-wearing agents roamed through the mansion, passing by the many guard posts manned by gun-toting members of the detail or the White House police.

That fiasco led an exasperated Mike to bring a fluoroscope machine to the building. A visitor would stand in front of the device, and in an adjacent room an agent would glance at a screen that revealed whether a weapon was concealed under a guest's coat. Or, the smirking agents quickly discovered, under a woman's dress. And that struck a red-faced Mike as "just a little indecent." The fluoroscope was quickly gone, too.

The "talking fence" also produced its share of indiscreet moments. A device originally deployed at ammunition depots and secret radar installations, it consisted of minute microphones attached by a nearly invisible cable to the tall iron fence surrounding the White House grounds. If an intruder attempted to climb the fence, the microphones would pick up the activity and a storm of lights would start flashing on a guardhouse control board monitored by the Secret Service. An ancillary benefit, however, was that the sensitive concealed microphones would also pick up even the hushed conversations of the movers and shakers walking in tandem by the fence. In the interests of wartime security, Mike decided the detail's overhearing a few bits of salacious gossip, or, on occasion, the stray official secret, was an intrusive price worth paying for keeping the president safe.

The entire detail, in fact, was on Mike's orders wired up for sound. Each agent carried a newly invented radio that was not much bigger than the package of Camels that Mike always had tucked in his suit jacket. This radio could receive messages from any transmitting station within one hundred and fifty miles or could send a message to any agent within three miles. That way, Mike very much wanted to believe, his men would be ready to respond in a flash to any emergency.

But while all his ingenious "gadgets" brought Mike a small measure of reassurance, he'd have only to look at the president to be reminded of what his detail was up against, and how the odds were overwhelmingly stacked in the determined assassin's favor. Attached to the president's wheelchair was an unobtrusive black box about the size and shape of one of the tort books Mike had briefly lugged around campus. Inside was FDR's gas mask, and he didn't travel anywhere—either inside the White House, or beyond its gates—without it.

6

YET EVEN AS MIKE THREW himself into the many unique challenges of protecting a wartime commander in chief, events continued to bring new, and often previously unimagined, dangers. Some were unintentional. Soldiers at the front lines, for example, thought it would be respectful to send FDR souvenirs from their hard-fought campaigns, and Mike had to be sure to intercept these ill-considered gifts as soon as they reached the White House postal drop. On several unsettling occasions, these mementos turned out to be still active German artillery shells or grenades. When Mike watched as they were detonated by the army ordnance team at its base just across the Potomac, he couldn't help but imagine what might have been if the well-intentioned package (What were these soldiers thinking? he wondered) had made its way to the Oval Office. He'd be unable to sleep soundly for nights on end in the aftermath, the boom of the explosions filling his nightmares.

There was also the unforeseen—and very demanding—problem of dealing with Winston Churchill. Keeping the British prime minister in good spirits when he came to stay at the White House just weeks after Pearl Harbor was, the president ordered, one of Mike's new responsibilities. It was a task that left Mike, as hard-drinking an Irishman as anyone he'd encountered, he'd proudly boast, "open mouthed in awe." "It was not just the amount" of brandy and scotch that the PM consumed with "grace and enthusiasm," Mike recounted with an almost reverential admiration, "but the complete sobriety that went hand in hand with his drinking.

Winston Churchill was the very best drinker that crossed the White House threshold in my memory, and I am including in that estimate the White House Correspondents, Inc. Collectively, that is."

Yet while the role of Churchill's occasional drinking companion was a gesture of American hospitality that Mike accepted with some relish, he was less enthusiastic about the added burden of having to protect another great man. Especially since, as wide-eyed experience had led him to complain, "the English do not take personal security very seriously." Too often, in his expert appraisal, the Brits let their prime minister wander about Washington more or less on his own. He cringed when he thought about all the opportunities there'd been for an assassin to get off a clean shot at the easily recognizable figure.

FDR was taken aback by this laxness, too. As Churchill was winding up his whirlwind June 1942 stay at the White House, the president summoned Mike to the Oval Office. With an uncommon brusqueness that at once put Mike on high alert, he gave the agent his new marching orders.

"Mike, Churchill is going home on the twenty-seventh. I am seriously worried about security. I want you to do everything possible to assure his safety." And that was how Mike came to save the prime minister's life.

Churchill was to fly off by plane, first stop Bermuda, and so Mike came up with a cautious plan. He'd have the PM bundled into a government car, which would then hightail it to the Anacostia Naval Air Station, just a three- or four-mile trip. The engines of a private plane would already be running, and the PM would be safely up and away twenty minutes after leaving the White House. Only, the powers that be at the British embassy in Washington refused to go along with such a circumspect departure.

"That sort of thing isn't necessary, Mr. Reilly," a snooty British diplomat pooh-poohed. "There is a British Overseas Airways base at Baltimore and if he flew from there it would be quite good for the workers' morale, you know."

Morale was the last thing on Mike's apprehensive mind. The British, however, would not budge. They refused to share his anxiety. "Absolutely nothing to worry about," was the often-repeated and always definitive official response to Mike's earnest warnings.

On the day of Churchill's departure, Mike did what he could to add precautions to what he was convinced was a fundamentally imprudent enterprise. He sneaked the PM, accompanied for this leg of his send-off by the president, out of the White House using the interconnecting tunnels that led to the Treasury Department building. ("I am going along with you, Winston, only to make sure that you don't steal any of Henry Morgenthau's gold," FDR joked, a remark that the man leading the bullion-depleted British Empire might not have found quite as droll as his host intended.) From there, an unmarked car, following a carefully chosen route through Washington's back streets and Maryland's country roads, drove Churchill to the BOAC terminal in Baltimore.

It was only as the car was approaching the hangar that Mike saw a baggage handler grappling with a uniformed BOAC guard at the door to the prime minister's plane. They were fighting for control of a pistol.

Mike leaped from the car and ran toward the two combatants. In the course of his mad dash he was trying to determine whether to shoot to kill, or if there was any preemptive blow he could inflict on the baggage handler—when he suddenly realized he had focused his attentions on the wrong man. The squat, burly fighter wearing overalls, he now recognized, was Agent Howard Chandler; Mike, as an extra touch of security, had instructed members of the Secret Service to disguise themselves as field employees. It was the wild-eyed BOAC guard who was the assassin.

"This jerk wants to shoot Churchill!" Chandler yelled to his chief as together they succeeded in wrestling the man to the ground. Applying the solid force of all his weight, Mike kept him pinned down while Chandler yanked the gun out of the guard's hands. A flock of agents, previously concealed about the field, hurried over to cuff the assassin and lead him off. "I noticed this guard—he's American by the way—standing near the entrance to the plane," Chandler, still trying to catch his breath after his exertions, reported to his boss. "I sort of eased up behind and beside him and he was saying, 'I'm going to kill that bastard Churchill. I'm going to kill him.'" Next thing Chandler knew they were grappling, but if Mike hadn't shown up, he conceded, it could have been anyone's contest.

Mike walked slowly across the tarmac to the prime minister's car, hoping to regain some calm, or at least enough discipline so as not to betray the commotion that continued to explode inside him. "Everything is fine, sir," he informed Churchill. But whether either of them was convinced by this small optimism was anyone's guess. All Mike could definitively remember was the prime minister's final, resigned words before he boarded the plane: "Mike, there are an awful lot of bastards in this world."

Which, Mike would come to agree, was an insight any presidential bodyguard should take to heart.

BUT OF ALL THE UNEXPECTED, as well as unprecedented, dangers the war wreaked on Mike's duties, there was one that left him with more shivery thoughts than any prior event. It was the president's decision to meet with Churchill in Casablanca at the tail end of January 1943.

Nearly three months earlier, just a day after the successful Allied invasion of North Africa, a heartening time when the gloomy war dispatches had abruptly turned more hopeful, Mike was summoned to an eight a.m. meeting with the president. FDR was sitting up in bed, sipping the coffee he made a point of brewing himself, and he was grinning widely. Mike assumed the Boss's good mood was further evidence that the invasion had gone as well, or perhaps even better, than planned. But he quickly learned that was only part, and at the moment a small part, of the president's buoyant mood. FDR was about to deliver a stunning bit of news, and, with an impish joy, he looked forward to his bodyguard's predictable reaction.

"Mike," he said, "I have to go to Africa."

"Africa, Mr. President?" Mike dumbly repeated—while at the same time he could not have been more surprised if the president had announced that they were going to the moon. And he was thinking: When FDR had wanted to go to a ball game across town at Griffith Stadium, it was a wartime excursion that had kept him fretting for days as he put in motion all the defenses against a large inventory of potential catastrophes. *Africa?*

"But there is grave risk," Mike blurted out. Then, remembering his place, he explained weakly, "Human beings and machines being what they are."

"Churchill and his Chiefs of Staff are going and our Chiefs of Staff will be there, too," the president went on with a generous patience. "Mike, there are many reasons why I must go."

And so it was settled. FDR would go, and Mike would lead the advance security team.

US naval surface patrols and rescue units fortified by seaplanes and blimps would monitor the route over which the Boss would fly—the first transatlantic presidential air trip—to Bathurst, South Africa, the initial leg of the journey. But this gave Mike little confidence as he looked down warily at the slate-gray sea from the narrow window of the converted B-24 ferrying him and the others who were paving the way for the president. German submarines remained active in the Atlantic, and their sharp-eyed antiaircraft gunners had time after time zeroed in on Allied bombers and transport planes. The ocean had swallowed up the remains.

When Mike landed at Casablanca, Lieutenant General Mark Clark promptly greeted him with more frightening news: "The bid and ask price on murder amongst the natives was so close to ten dollars, American money, that there was never much haggling when somebody wanted somebody else done in." And there was a good likelihood there'd be plenty of offers. Casablanca, according to the alarming army intelligence reports, "was crawling with Nazi agents." Hordes of potential contract killers and dedicated enemy assassins, however, were not the only threats. The skies above the suffocating, dust-swept city held danger, too. Two weeks before Mike's arrival the Luftwaffe had rained its bombs down on the native quarter. Hundreds of civilians were killed in a single merciless raid.

It was an agitated Mike, his nerves drawn taut by his frightful days spent reconnoitering the inhospitable town, who watched the president's shiny C-54 land as scheduled at 6:20 p.m. on January 12, at Medouina Airport, Casablanca. The aircraft taxied to a deserted part of the field, and Mike hightailed it up the ramp and into the plane.

"Mike, I had a wonderful trip," the president said in greeting.

The Secret Service agent could not be bothered with small talk. On edge, he abandoned all pretense of courtesy and, without prelude, swiftly jumped to the heart of the matter. "Please get your business over as fast as you possibly can," he found himself nearly begging the commander in chief. "Otherwise some of your finest generals will have to be retired with ulcers." "Even my cast-iron stomach has taken to quivering," he added plaintively.

FDR listened, and when at last he spoke it was with sympathy. "Mike, I'll get this over as soon as I can," he promised. In the next breath, though, his words carried the hard steel of a presidential reprimand: "Now stop worrying!"

But Mike couldn't stop. For the remainder of the three-week trip across fourteen thousand miles, much of the journey bringing the crippled president close to active foreign battle zones, the only small solace was Mike's growing realization that the fears pounding in his imagination would either be everything or they would be nothing. And if they were everything, it was probably too late for him to do anything.

When the president was finally back safely in the White House, Mike sternly told himself that he would never, never allow the president to put himself at such risk again. Not on his watch.

LATER THAT YEAR, IN MID-AUGUST, Mike had been enjoying a respite from the muggy Washington summer as he accompanied the president to balmy Quebec for a meeting with Churchill. Then he stumbled on some disconcerting news. Without trying, Mike had learned that the Boss and the PM had sent a joint message to Joseph Stalin: "At this crucial point in the war" they wanted the first joint meeting of all three of the Allied leaders.

With that the cooling summer breezes whistling in from Hudson Bay might as well have been transformed into a force 10 storm. Mike was rattled. He quickly began to conjure up all the far reaches of the globe where this hazardous wartime conference—the three commanders of the Allied armies in a single location!—might take place. Churchill and FDR had blithely ignored all the military warning, not to mention simple common sense, by meeting in Casablanca, a city teeming with Nazi spies, a city only a short bomber's flight from enemy bases. He shuddered to imagine where the three leaders would in their collective recklessness decide to convene. He wondered whether he could once again summon up the skill and attention that would be required to protect the Boss against all the large dangers such a foreign conference would create.

But no sooner had his raging concerns turned his world akilter than, benevolently, he heard further news that restored his equilibrium: FDR and Churchill had asked Stalin to meet them in Fairbanks, Alaska. On American territory. A city near American military bases. The Boss wouldn't need to travel over oceans, or through foreign lands. A conference in Alaska wouldn't involve outrageous risks, and certainly none for which Mike couldn't prepare.

1

Unlike Mike Reilly, who protected great men, Walter Schellenberg, the SS general who headed Section 6 of the RSHA, hunted them. But despite this defining difference in their duties—one the bodyguard, the other focused on cloak-and-dagger intrigues—the two professionals shared many similar qualities. They were both would-be lawyers and, at the identical age of thirty-three, young for their jobs. Each was guided by a strong sense of duty. And, not least, they both shared the experienced fieldman's adversity to risk. For Schellenberg, this restraining caution had taken permanent operational hold after his ill-conceived part in Operation Willi—the Nazi plot to kidnap the Duke and Duchess of Windsor.

The idea was Hitler's, but the summons on that July morning in 1940 came in an urgent telephone call from Joachim von Ribbentrop, the foreign minister. "Tell me, my dear fellow, could you come over to my office at once?" he asked in his typically florid way. Schellenberg, who keenly understood his underling's role, immediately agreed to the powerful Reichsminister's request, but when he tried to ascertain the agenda, if there were papers he might need to bring, Ribbentrop, full of authority and mystery, cut him off. "Come at once," he ordered. "It's not a matter I can discuss over the telephone."

Ribbentrop stood in front of his massive marble-topped desk, arms folded across his chest like a headmaster preparing to upbraid an errant student. The stern look on his face, the hard stare in his blue eyes, only added to Schellenberg's concern. The Reich was an adder's nest, strivers vying for power and Hitler's blessing, and the vain, old Ribbentrop, he had discovered, was among the most ruthless. A further concern: Schellenberg had long held the belief that the foreign minister, although lauded by Hitler as the greatest German statesman since Bismarck, was a profoundly stupid man, and that made his plodding machinations even more dangerous. His mind racing, Schellenberg feared some new contrived charge—he already had to defend himself against the accusations that he'd been having an affair with the attractive ash-blond wife of Reinhard Heydrich, his superior in the Reich Security Office—was about to be leveled.

Instead, the foreign minister began to hurl a series of questions at the intelligence officer about the Duke of Windsor. Had Schellenberg met the duke during his last visit to Germany? And—now affecting a deliberately conspiratorial tone—did he understand the *real* reasons behind the abdication?

Schellenberg had no idea where the interrogation was going, but he was immediately relieved: his head wasn't on the chopping block. Dutifully, he quickly started to share what he'd read in the newspapers: the duke had decided to abdicate his throne to marry Wallis Simpson, the American divorcee he loved.

Ribbentrop cut him short. "My dear Schellenberg," he said acidly, "you have a completely wrong view of these things—also of the real reason behind the Duke's abdication." The marriage issue had been a pretext to remove an "honest and faithful friend" of Germany from the British throne, he declared definitively.

Then Ribbentrop announced that he had a new mission for Schellenberg. It had come directly from the Führer. He was to offer the duke 50 million Swiss francs, the fortune (the equivalent of about $200 million in 1940) to be deposited in Switzerland, if the former king of England would make "some official gesture"

disassociating himself from the royal family and the British government. Hitler would prefer the couple to take up residence in Switzerland, but, in a spirit of accommodation, the Führer had agreed
that any neutral country would suffice as long as it was not beyond
the Reich's territorial reach. As for any attempts by the British Secret Intelligence Service to prevent the flight of the duke, it was up
to Schellenberg to deal with them—"Even at the risk of your own
life, and if need be, by the use of force."

The lawyer in Schellenberg could not help but point out the apparent contradiction in his orders. Was he simply to offer the duke
a bribe? Or was he, in fact, to kidnap him?

With a diplomat's skill, the foreign minister parried the question: "The Führer feels that force should be used primarily against
the British secret service. Against the Duke only insofar as his hesitation might be based on fear-psychosis, which forceful action on
our part would help him overcome."

It was a response that Schellenberg tried to unravel, and when
he did he came to only one conclusion: one way or another, he was
to get the duke under Germany's physical control. If an ex-king's
ransom wouldn't suffice, then the former monarch must be bundled up and carried off. Sensing Schellenberg's dismay, Ribbentrop
added knowingly, "Once he's a free man again, he'll be grateful
to us."

Ribbentrop explained the rest of the plan with a similar confidence, and a similar sparseness of detail. The duke, it had been
learned, would soon be hunting in Spain with some friends. Schellenberg should make contact with him then. The rest would be up
to Schellenberg; "All the necessary means will be at your disposal
and we have agreed to give you a completely free hand."

To seal the deal, Ribbentrop, with a showman's flourish, telephoned Hitler as Schellenberg rose to leave. He handed the young
general an earpiece so he could listen to the conversation. "Schellenberg will fly by special plane to Madrid as quickly as possible,"
the foreign minister reported. "Good," Hitler replied, in a voice

that struck the eavesdropper as strangely hollow. "Tell him from me that I am relying on him."

As for the actual mission, things initially proceeded with a reassuring operational swiftness. A meeting with the German ambassador in Madrid confirmed for Schellenberg that the duke and duchess would soon be coming to Spain for a hunting holiday, although the specific date had not yet been set. The country hacienda where they'd be staying was near the Spain-Portugal border; it would be easy enough to confront, and if necessary abduct, the duke as he meandered through the forest. And the top Spanish police and customs officials made it clear to Schellenberg that he could count on their full support. They'd even actively intervene if additional force was required.

But once all the pieces were seemingly in place, the plot began to unravel. Despite the firm report that had initiated the mission, the duke and duchess apparently were in no great hurry to go hunting in Spain. They were having too good a time living the high life in Estoril on the Portuguese Riviera. Undeterred, Schellenberg went to Estoril to see for himself. With a fieldman's careful eye, he reconnoitered their borrowed home in all its palatial splendor, and then had his local agents gather up more detailed intelligence—the number of entrances, the location of the duke and duchess's bedroom, the number of servants, and the size and deployment of the British security detail. In anticipation of the abduction, he arranged for a car with an engine souped up by the automotive wizards in the SD (as the Reich Security Service was commonly known) to be shipped to Estoril.

But Schellenberg found himself still hesitating. His informants' latest reports were one reason for pause: while the duke was disappointed by His Majesty's government's recent decision to ship him off to the backwaters of Bermuda to serve as governor ("a third-rate colony," the duke pouted), he had even less desire to live out the war in either a neutral or an enemy country. And as for the hunting trip to the Spanish forest, that was a whim that had passed—which meant Schellenberg would need to fight his way past the British security guards protecting the Estoril house, grab the duke and the duchess, and then figure on a running battle all the way to the safety of Spain. What would Hitler do, Schellenberg could not help but worry, if the mission ended with the duke, or perhaps the duchess, being killed in the cross fire? The likelihood of success, Schellenberg had come to realize, had dwindled from small to none.

Still, an order was an order. On the night before the mission was to be launched, Schellenberg, feeling "tired and beaten," met in a quiet restaurant with a well-placed Portuguese asset to work out the final operational details. Reconciled, he announced, "Tomorrow I have to bring the Duke of Windsor across the Spanish frontier by force. The plan has to be worked out tonight." But when the two men launched into the specifics, they both came to the conclusion that it would end in disgrace. Not only would it undoubtedly fail, but the Reich would be ridiculed for the madcap scheme. In the unsatisfying aftermath, the search for blame would begin. Schellenberg had little doubt that the admonitory fingers would all be pointed directly at him. Nor did he wonder about the punishment Hitler would inflict on the man responsible for the death of either the duke or the duchess; a firing squad would be the kindest end he could wish for.

In their shared desperation, the two men came up with a plan to circumvent Hitler's order. They set it in motion that night. On Schellenberg's command, his local assets began to circulate the rumor that a Nazi plan was afoot to whisk the duke and duchess off to Germany before they sailed to Bermuda. As Schellenberg had anticipated, this "secret" quickly reached the ears of the army of Allied agents camping out in Portugal. In quick response, the British security detail, already impressive, was fortified by an additional twenty men, all now on high alert.

Schellenberg sent a flash cable to Berlin reporting the increased security surrounding the couple. He had no choice but to call the mission off. Two days later the duke and duchess sailed to Bermuda, and Schellenberg, quaking with fear, returned to Berlin to find out his fate.

Ribbentrop delivered the news. But first he let Schellenberg stand in his office at mute attention as the foreign minister made a big show of going about other tasks. When he finally got around to speaking, he made no attempt to disguise his regret over the verdict. "The Führer," he announced with a cool disdain, "asks me to tell you that in spite of his disappointment at the outcome of the whole affair, he agrees with your decisions and expresses his approval of the manner in which you proceeded."

For the first time since he had left Portugal, Schellenberg's heart stopped racing. He had outsmarted both Hitler and Ribbentrop. The mission had come to nothing, but he had survived.

THEN THREE HECTIC YEARS LATER—in wartime, the years an instant—he found himself wondering if he'd soon be pressured by his masters into another fanciful version of Operation Willi—and whether he'd need to conjure up another scheme to escape from an even more consequential disaster.

Schellenberg's concerns were prompted by the identical intelligence that had caused Mike Reilly's recent fears (though of course neither man knew of the other's apprehension). A transcript of the August 31, 1943, radio address Winston Churchill had made at the conclusion of the Quebec Conference had crossed his desk. He had started reading with only small interest. It rambled on with a full-throated optimism predicting the Allied victory that he found particularly painful since he, too, had become increasingly convinced of the same inevitability. But midway through the pages, he was suddenly caught short. "Nothing is nearer to the wishes of President Roosevelt and myself," he read with a new alertness, "than to have a three-fold meeting with Marshal Stalin."

A meeting of the Big Three!

Schellenberg recognized at once that this would offer a tempting trio of targets that the Oberkommando der Wehrmacht (the German armed forces high command) would find hard to resist. True, only the most ardent Nazis—Hitler or Goebbels, he imagined—would dare to believe that these deaths could affect the final outcome of the war; Germany's defeat was a grim certainty. But with Roosevelt, Churchill, and Stalin out of the picture, there might very well be a different peace. It would be possible to negotiate an end to the war before the Allies launched their invasion of Europe, before the armies of this second front marched into Berlin. And it could be a reasonable peace, not one that vindictively insisted on an unconditional surrender. In all the recorded history of war, Schellenberg realized, only the Romans had made such a brutal demand on an enemy—and in the end Carthage had been leveled. He understood the desperate logic that would be calling for a mission to eliminate the Big Three.

But just as abruptly, he realized his musings were absurd. With a veteran intelligence agent's careful perspective restored, he saw things with a sobering clarity. There was no chance of launching such a historic mission. Other than the fact that Churchill and Roosevelt were urging Stalin to meet with them, he had no hard facts. He did not know when the meeting would occur, or, for that matter, where it would take place. In the absence of those two essential pieces of intelligence, drafting as much as a preliminary action plan would be impossible. He had even less to go on than when he'd set off on his hapless attempt to kidnap the Duke and Duchess of Windsor.

And he was certain: the location and date of the conference was an intelligence treasure that would be forever beyond the Reich's grasp. It would be one of the most closely held Allied secrets of the entire war. There was no point in giving the assassinations further thought. Besides, he chided himself, the security surrounding the duke and duchess had been sufficient to scare him off. The precautions the Allies would take to protect their leaders would be more intense, a different category altogether. It would be a suicide mission, one without even the slightest chance of success.

Resigned, Schellenberg instead turned his attention to finalizing his plans for a more feasible stealth operation. He went back to completing the arrangements for a series of covert parachute drops into Iran. These sabotage missions were, he fully acknowledged, targeted at a distant and unimportant corner of the war, a sideshow, and a small one at that, to the major battles that would soon be fought. They would play no part in shaping the peace. Nevertheless, full of a soldier's sense of duty, he told himself he would make the best use of the dwindling resources he still could muster. He would fight on as best he could.

8

THE OPERATIONAL GENESIS OF THE covert parachute missions into Iran had occurred months earlier during a morning canter through the Tiergarten bridle paths. At that hour, not long after the sun had risen over Berlin, the rough smell of cordite would often still be strong; the antiaircraft batteries pounded away through the night, the antsy gunners starting in as soon as they heard the distant dins from the engines of the approaching RAF bombers, and they kept firing long after the planes were gone. Nevertheless, in December 1942, as the war raged, the 520-acre Tiergarten (the name an artifact from a halcyon time when the park was a royal hunting preserve; "animal garden" is the literal translation) still remained an improbable oasis in a sullen, wintry city.

Its pebbled paths twisted through neglected patches of lawn bordered by walls of evergreen hedges, skirted icy ornamental ponds where fierce statues stood guard, climbed to small hills gone brown in the cold, and ended at the approach to dense, dark copses of substantial ancient trees that rose high in the leaden winter sky. An earthen riding trail sufficiently wide to allow two horses to proceed side by side circled the circumference of nearly the entire park, past the open heathland and through the Grimm-like expanse of deep forest. And on two or three mornings a week, a calming prelude to the inevitable chaos of the looming day, the two spymasters who ran cloak-and-dagger operations for the rival German foreign intelligence services, General Walter Schellenberg, the head of Section 6 of the SS's Reich Security Service, and Admiral Wilhelm Canaris, the director of the Abwehr, the military espionage organization, would set out together in a convivial ride over the Tiergarten's trails.

THEY WERE AN UNLIKELY PAIR, their differences apparent at a glance, and the distinctions ran even deeper beneath the surface. Canaris, a creaky fifty-six, was old enough to have been Schellenberg's father. Added to that, he had pale skin and soft pale hair, stood barely five feet, three inches in his polished bespoke shoes, would go about cuddling his two adored wirehaired dachshunds, Seppel and Kaspar, to his warm chest, and seemed not just slight but insignificant when measured against the granite-jawed, youthful Schellenberg. True, Schellenberg was not a big man (a molehill when compared with the mountain that was Mike Reilly) but in his coal-black SS uniform with the visor of his general's cap pulled low, leather cross belts strapped across his chest, tight riding breeches and high riding boots—"dashing and elegant" he preened after staring at his reflection—he cut a fearsome military figure.

The reality, however, was something quite different, but it, too, accentuated the polarity in their lives. Canaris, despite his modest appearance, was a genuine warrior. He had served on a light cruiser in the thick of the Battle of the Falkland Islands during the First World War, escaped from a Chilean internment camp after his badly damaged ship had been scuttled, managed against all odds and obstacles to make his way back to Berlin, and finished the war commanding a U-boat that had prowled the Mediterranean with a lethal cunning; even the kaiser had praised Canaris for his skill in ambushing and sinking enemy ships. In recognition of his brilliant war, he was awarded the Iron Cross First Class. Two years after Hitler took control of the German government, in January 1935, he was given control of the Abwehr, Germany's hoary, tradition-bound military intelligence organization.

In background, breeding, and disposition, the admiral was a fitting choice for the job, an upper-class spymaster—"Intelligence is a gentleman's job," he'd say with an acid hauteur—who was representative of the men under his command. They, too, were military veterans, sons of wealthy, often aristocratic lineage, and deep thinkers who went about their intelligence responsibilities with a professional objectivity that was rare in the politicized Reich. Basking in the glories of their venerated predecessors, they saw themselves as derring-do players of the Great Game, gentlemen spies working in the shadows to restore the Fatherland's past glory. They were a select, proud, and often self-important army: fifteen thousand officials and agents on the job in more than five hundred cities across the world.

Schellenberg's biography told another story. Yet like Canaris, he, too, was in many ways a mirror of the men with whom he worked, and the more makeshift espionage organization he served, one that had not existed before September 1939. He had risen up from barely middle-class roots; his father struggled to sell pianos, dragging the family from the crushing poverty of French-occupied Saarbrücken to Luxembourg, where things proved not much better. The majority of the SD's recruits had come from similarly rough-and-tumble backgrounds, and it was a social distinction that did not escape the well-bred Abwehr operatives who peered through their monocles with haughty disdain at the proletarian spies who were their new competitors.

Further, unlike Canaris and his staff, who had won their spurs in demanding covert missions, Schellenberg had no previous intelligence training. And while he possessed a nimble mind and would quickly learn on the job, growing comfortably into his spymaster's role, few of those with whom he worked would ever possess the subtle qualities of thought and the slow-burning cunning necessary for mounting foreign intrigues and running agents. They had been recruited for the SD, a proudly Aryan, race-based espionage service controlled by the SS, after passing a single ideological test—a pledge of commitment to a fanatical anti-Semitism and anti-Bolshevism. All other credentials were largely irrelevant. As a result, their stultifying narrowness of mind, their taut adherence to a preconceived xenophobic Nazi ideology, made it impossible for the rank-and-file SD operatives and analysts to conduct intelligence operations with either creativity or objectivity. Blinded by their dogma, they solved any mystery at once: the Jews and the Communists were to blame.

Lastly, and not least, Schellenberg was hardly the squared-away, lantern-jawed soldier he appeared to be. He had never seen combat; a stomach ailment had prevented him from passing the SS physical required for frontline service. It was a malady for which, he would confess, he'd be forever grateful; he had no illusions about what would've been required of him. His brother SS officers who had done tours in war zones and the occupied territories were not a rough-edged elite. They were mass murderers.

The foreign-duty logs of the senior officers in the SD would one day be read, Schellenberg was convinced, as counts in war crimes indictments. Dozens of his colleagues, including officers on his own Section 6 staff, had served with the Einsatzgruppen— genocidal execution units—on the northern Russian front and in Poland. Their hands dripped with the blood of tens of thousands of civilians. Schellenberg could find no justification, no instinct, for such hate in his own practical heart. His father had many customers who were Jews and they had always, he had said, dealt with him honestly. Yet at the same careful, restraining time, Schellenberg could not summon up the courage to condemn either his SS brethren or their ideology. So what if he had only to walk through the long corridors at 22 Berkaerstrasse, the headquarters of the Foreign Intelligence Section of the Reich Security Office, to imagine in his reproachful mind the gang of thugs sitting at their desks breaking out into the Horst Wessel song? He was a pragmatist, not a moralist; and that, he told himself, was the only stance one could take if he wanted to survive in the wartime Reich.

STILL, IT WAS SCHELLENBERG'S STRONG distaste for the retinue of mass murders with whom, out of administrative necessity, he was forced to rub shoulders in the course of his day that had helped make the early-morning interludes with Canaris so appealing. The admiral, with his dissembling charm and courtly old-world manners, would share daring gossip about Hitler and his henchmen, suggest a variety of medical treatments for Schellenberg's queasy stomach, and still find time to school his riding partner on the qualities of the vintages that he'd stored in his cellar in anticipation of the war. "Schellenberg," he would advise as they cantered through the Tiergarten, "always remember the goodness of animals. You see, my dachshund is discreet and will never betray me. I cannot say that of any human being." How could he "not help liking the admiral," Schellenberg would gush, whose "attitude toward me was always kind and paternal"?

There was more, however, that pushed both spymasters to make the time for their morning rides. While friendly, neither was sufficiently naive to presume that they were friends. Their relationship was one between the best of enemies, a foxy mutual dependence fueled by mutual suspicions. Both men understood that Schellenberg had his eye on Canaris's job. His long-held ambition was to absorb the Abwehr into his Section 6, for the new espionage service to gain control of the older one. The larger his fiefdom, Schellenberg had decided with a ruthless practicality, the more irreplaceable he'd be if the long knives that were always lurking about Hitler considered coming after him. With the tradecraft of a diligent fieldman, he used his time with Canaris to take measure of his opponent, gathering the intelligence that he'd use when he made his case to Himmler and finally launched his coup.

As for the admiral, he was not fooled. An old pro, he was playing, too; the bonhomie was all disguise. A veteran of the cutthroat Reich, he understood the mistake it would be to turn his back on his enemy. Better to keep him close.

THEIR EARLY-MORNING RIDES BECAME AN institution. The rule
was that business would not be discussed, and with the same firm
resolve that it had been made it was also invariably broken. The
propitious moment was announced, Schellenberg recalled, always
in the same theatrical fashion. Without prelude, the admiral would
abruptly pull hard on his reins. Then, after his horse came to a full
stop, Canaris, as triumphant as any magician reaching into his top
hat, would reveal what he'd kept hidden since they had set out from
the stable.

That morning in December 1942, he announced that the Abwehr
had "received a jolt from the blue." The Japanese intelligence service had passed on a cable that had been sent from Iran. The four
German agents who had been dispatched under deep cover to Tehran two years earlier, operatives who had not been heard from since
the successful British-Russian invasion of Iran in 1941, had suddenly signaled that they were alive and well.

Both services had harbored a sense of shame over the cavalier
way they'd abandoned these brave spies behind enemy lines. This
was further compounded by a shared sense of powerlessness; Germany, besieged on many fronts, rushing pell-mell into the demanding Russian campaign, had no resources to spare on a handful of
stay-behind agents who had been forced to take to ground in some
unknown corner of the Peacock realm—if that, indeed, was what
had occurred. Their long silence had only reinforced the logical
conclusion that they'd been swept up by either the Russian or British invaders. If they weren't dead, then they were in a prison camp
baking under the hot desert sun. But now, against all odds, word
had come that the network, with a miraculous Dickensian resil-
iency, had been "recalled to life."

9

I N TRUTH, WHILE SCHELLENBERG IN the course of that portentous morning ride took care not to reveal his ignorance to his rival, he had known very little about his service's previous history in Iran. Nor, for that matter, did he have more than a passing—and quickly passing, at that—knowledge of the Fatherland's past political and diplomatic machinations in that far-off corner of the world. Yet these gaps, he told himself as he struggled to find a justification that wouldn't leave him feeling a total fool, were understandable.

He had taken control of Section 6 only less than a year earlier, in March 1942, after his inept predecessor, Heinz Jost (or, as his contemptuous staff officers sneered, Frau Jost), had been sacked and then quickly banished for his sins to the Baltic states, where he took command of the villainous Einsatzgruppe A. And no sooner had Schellenberg begun to settle in than his boss, Reinhard Heydrich, was murdered in May by Czech partisans. Just like that, he found himself having to answer to a new head of the Reich Security Office, Ernst Kaltenbrunner.

In keeping with the way things frequently played out in the dog-eat-dog Reich, the two men's relationship swiftly deteriorated into a nasty, truculent feud. Kaltenbrunner saw his underling as a careerist, a striving bounder on the make who, worst of all, was not a true believer, neither the fanatical Nazi nor the Hitler worshipper an SS general should be. Schellenberg, for his vituperative part, could not stop himself from summoning up a catalog of unpleasant images at just the thought of his new chief: "From the first moment he made me feel quite sick" with his "thick neck," "eyes of a viper," "bad teeth," and "hands of an old gorilla." And to this mean-spirited (and arguably subjective) appraisal, he could add one hard fact: Kaltenbrunner was a drunk, showing up at the office hungover and bleary eyed, constantly bellowing from his desk for his beleaguered orderly to bring another bottle of champagne or brandy. It was an open secret that on several occasions Himmler had dispatched the RSHA head to a Swiss sanatorium to dry out.

Therefore—new to the job, taking over a complex, clandestine war being fought in the back alleys of Europe while at the same time fending off no less dangerous enemies at home—it was small wonder, Schellenberg could have confided to Canaris, that he had not gotten around to focusing on the department's far-flung operations in Iran. Plus, they were no longer active missions, but very much dormant ops, if not flat-out dead. Yet Schellenberg was enough of a professional to realize his excuses, however firmly enumerated, would have been dismissed as little more than defensive rationalizations. He should have known.

When he arrived that morning at his office on the Berkaerstrasse, Schellenberg called for all the files on Iran. He wanted not just his own service's archives, but also, after the necessary token assurances of future mutual cooperation in the region were pledged, any that could be culled from his rivals at the Abwehr. The files kept arriving at his office throughout the day, bulging volumes as well as suspiciously thin ones, and on his order they were piled high on his mahogany desk. He pored over them through the night.

IN INTELLIGENCE WORK, THE DETAILS more often than not can make all the difference, but since Schellenberg would be dusting off decades of reports, he'd have had little choice but to make do with the operational summaries. Nevertheless, even these capsule histories offered quite an education.

Like sepia-colored photographs, the origins of Germany's *Orient-*

politik were dispatches from a bygone era—a buccaneering tale of a naively adventuristic time. At the dawn of the twentieth century, when the last gasps of the Imperial Age still gripped the world, Iran—then called Persia, the name bestowed by its Greek conquerors more than three hundred years before Christ was born—had caught the predatory attention of both Russia and Great Britain. Although a backward, primitive land, its days of glory under Xerxes Ancient History, it nevertheless had been blessed by nature with two salient qualities that made the powerful players on the world stage pay close attention.

A glance at a map revealed the first. Persia was an ideally situated buffer state, squeezed between the Russian Empire to the north and the British Raj, which ruled to the east in nearby India. A self-protective strategy, therefore, had both the Russian bear and the English bulldog casting their eyes covetously toward the Peacock Throne.

The second attribute was less obvious. It required—literally—more digging, yet it proved well worth the effort. Persia was sitting on vast subterranean oceans of oil. But leave it to the British to swoop in and figure out a way to take what hadn't been allotted to them by divine right. In 1901, the Anglo-Persian Oil Company was formed, with the Anglo faction of the ostensible partnership making out like the bandits they were. It was only natural given the greed and competing ambitions of nations that Germany, too, wanted to elbow its way in.

Kaiser Wilhelm II's assault on the Middle East was largely diplomatic, but it shrewdly succeeded in winning Persian hearts and minds. In 1898, the young kaiser barnstormed through the Middle East, attracting adoring multitudes. A constant talking point, one that was as calculated as it was apparently heartfelt, was his love and respect for Islam. There was even the widespread rumor—the Abwehr did its manipulative best to keep it buzzing—that he had concluded his journey by converting. While that wasn't the case, the reality was only slightly less ardent. "If I had come there without any religion," he revealed in a letter to Tsar Nicholas II, "I would certainly have turned Mahommeten." It was the kaiser's phenomenal popularity in the Middle East that greased the tracks for the visionary agreements that were signed (although never fully acted on) to build a railroad stretching from Berlin to Baghdad—a line that would have gone straight through Tehran, as well as through the heart of a British sphere of influence. Similarly, his star power allowed the Hamburg-America Line to challenge British nautical hegemony by launching commercial and passenger service between Germany and the Persian Gulf. Even a decade after his grand tour, Persians continued to be flattered by the kaiser's seeming fascination with life in the Middle East. Although the hard evidence was scant, many powerful Persians had started to believe that Germany offered their little kingdom the chance to align with a benevolent world power rather than the nakedly opportunistic Russia or Britain.

Then with the start of the First World War, the files took a new turn, telling the improbable yet for once true story of a new German legend who had won firm hold of the country's affections—Wassmuss of Persia. Posted as a lowly vice-consul in Būshehr, near the southern Gulf coast, Wilhelm Wassmuss had become enamored of his exotic new home. Unlike the other silk shirt diplomats who largely hobnobbed with one another, he took the time to learn the language and actually went into the dusty city streets and hiked to the hardscrabble mountain encampments to talk to the people. And when the fighting started, thanks to his feats of bloodcurdling personal courage and inventive tactics, Wassmuss succeeded in reinventing himself as another Lawrence of Arabia.

In fact, the case could be made—and the Abwehr files proudly did—that his actions were more consequential than Lawrence's. He engineered a stunningly effective outbreak of tribal insurrection against the British, forging alliances between traditional adversaries, convincing previously pro-British chieftains to turn against their longtime sponsors. As a result, the already thinly stretched

British army was forced to redeploy a substantial number of troops from elsewhere in the Middle East to protect its suddenly vulnerable oil fields and pipelines in Persia. And the sly Turks took quick advantage. They pressed their siege of the British garrison at Kut al-Amara, south of Baghdad, and inflicted one of the war's worst defeats on the Allies. Major General Charles Townshend along with twelve thousand bedraggled British troops were taken prisoner—and Wassmuss of Persia was heralded as making it all possible.

After the war, during the shaky Weimar period, the flurry of dispatches in the files on Schellenberg's desk gave cheery reports on the budding prospects in Persia. The Germans had begun to arrive by the boatfuls and they found it sympathetic territory, largely because the country had a new, unabashedly pro-German leader. Reza Khan, an illiterate shepherd boy, had joined the Persian army as a youth, and with a determination that was as fierce as it was ruthless bulldozed his way up the ranks. Starting as a lowly rifle-toting infantry grunt, he rose to brigade commander, then to prime minister, to become, triumphantly in 1925, Reza Shah Pahlavi, the Shadow of the Almighty, the King of Kings, the Vice Regent of God, and the first shah of, as he boldly declared at the moment of his investiture, the Pahlavi dynasty.

His guiding ambition was to bring the country into the modern age, and the more his bewildered people kicked and screamed in protest, the more the hardheaded shah doubled down. He blithely challenged the conservative Muslim clergy, banning the veil and giving women the right to vote. When one mullah had the effrontery to criticize his wife's European attire, the shah, accompanied by an intimidating entourage of bruisers, wasted no time showing up at the zealot's mosque. There was no attempt at discussion. Instead, as his henchmen restrained the suddenly silent crowd, Reza, with a systematic fury, beat the offensive mullah to within an inch of his life. And with overflowing reservoirs of oil money to bankroll even his most grandiose dreams, he set out to transform Tehran into a twentieth-century city—a little bit of Paris, he promised, in the Middle East. He more or less kept his promise. A little bit—the emphasis on "little"—of Tehran soon had wide, tree-lined boule-vards, honking cars, cafés, even electricity and dial telephones. A decree prohibited camels from entering the city gates (same as in Paris, the shah assured his incredulous critics). Yet take a short stroll beyond the newly refurbished government quarter, and the disso-nance was immediate: enter a city of squat, weather-beaten stucco houses and faded tents, of chaotic bazaars offering the trinkets and rugs turned out by tribal craftsmen. Here Tehran was crisscrossed by a maze of narrow alleyways, still very much gripped by the heart of a nomadic darkness: a sand-strewn, dusty world of yapping packs of mongrel dogs, ditches filled with filmy water, of mangy horses and flea-bitten donkeys. There was no sewage system, no electric-ity. Beyond the shiny new boulevards, the past had not yet become past.

Still, Persia, both the old and new, was a good place to be Ger-man. The shah, who felt bullied by the autocratic Russians and cheated by the British oil magnates, rushed to embrace Germany. He did not look too deeply at the Fatherland's long-range inten-tions. Germany loomed as an alternative to the two powers that had picked away at his kingdom for their sport for generations; that was all that mattered. And so the Germans arrived. It was German engi-neers who helped build the railroad that stretched from the Caspian Sea to the Persian Gulf, as well as the new docks and paved roads. German educators took control of the school system. German air-lines flew from Tehran to Berlin, with stops at Baghdad, Damascus, and Athens along the way. During the same heady time, Germany's share in Persian foreign trade, a meager 8 percent in 1930, quickly started to grow significantly. Heavy machinery and chemical dyes were coming in from factories across the Fatherland, and cotton and wool—an astonishing 90 percent of the annual crop—were going out to Germany in return. And all the while a proudly ethnic German community—"Little Berlin," it was called only partly in jest—began taking root in Tehran. There were German bookstores,

German-language newspapers, German schools, German clubs, German riding schools, German hotels, and even shops where a decent Weisswurst could be had for an exorbitant sum.

Then Hitler came to power, Weimar fell, and the files on Schellenberg's desk grew thicker, the dispatches filled with a new urgency.

10

HOW CAN ONE EXPLAIN THE deep mutual attraction between Reza Shah and Adolf Hitler? Two strongmen, prone to fiery tirades, who held on to power with an unforgiving, take-no-prisoners vengeance? Two egotists hell-bent on realizing their personal ambitions under the pretense of the national interest? Two would-be dynastical rulers convinced their legacy would resonate for the next thousand years? Certainly, the commonalities ran deep. But the files Schellenberg perused contained little that wandered into such nuanced, personalized realms. There was no gloss. Instead, they told the story of the relationship between the Nazis and the Peacock Throne in more concrete, politicized terms.

Clearly, race was a shared rallying cry. Reza Shah proudly howled whenever he got the chance that his people were not lowly Semites like their Jewish or Arab neighbors, but pure-blooded Aryans—same as the Germans. He made sure the world got this message, too. In 1935 he issued a proclamation to the League of Nations that "henceforth" his country would be called Iran—the name reaching back in time to the country's ancient roots and the Sanskrit phrase *Airyanem Vaejah*, or "Home of the Aryans."

In quick response, Germany bestowed its seal of racial purity on the kingdom: the pernicious Nuremberg Laws that had made anti-Semitism the law of the land were amended. Iranians, the Nazis' racial nitpickers formally adjudicated in 1936, were to be considered as Aryan as any full-blooded German.

This happy kinship received further cultural staying power from the fact that the swastika was emblazoned all over Germany, from the flag to the uniforms of its goose-stepping battalions. It was the iconic emblem of the Third Reich. Yet millennia before the criss-crossed geometric design was designated as the calling card of the Nazi Party, it had been a commonplace good luck symbol in Eurasia; the word "swastika" can be traced back to sacred Sanskrit texts. The swastika had decorated Persian art since the time of Zoroaster, carved into ancient stone columns, etched into tribal pottery. Now, however, this historical accident was deliberately seen as something more—further proof of the deep-seated Aryan ties between the people of the Reza Shah and, as the German chancellor was called with deference in Iran, Hitler Shah.

But Reza Shah's affection for the Nazis had other deep roots, too. An emperor setting out to do nothing less than establish a dynasty, he was by necessity a practical statesman. He wanted, needed, to be on the side that was winning. In the opening years of the war, the Nazis had not only blitzkrieged across Europe, but seemed poised to take control of the Middle East. The Reich's far-reaching talons were firmly hooked into Morocco, Algeria, Tunisia, Lebanon, and Syria. Waves of German paratroopers had dropped like mythic omnipotent gods from the sky to seize the oil fields and refineries at Mosul, in northern Iraq. And the Afrika Korps was still on the march. It seemed inevitable that German panzers would roll victoriously through Palestine, Egypt, and Iran as the unstoppable battalions rumbled toward India. Reza Shah was convinced he was backing the winning side.

And Hitler? Schellenberg, who knew the Führer only too well ("highly developed political instincts which were combined with a complete lack of moral scruples," he'd succinctly judged), found himself wondering what Hitler wanted from his admirer, the Reza Shah. He did not put much stock in Hitler's falling for the widely disseminated claptrap of "Aryan brotherhood." That the Führer with all his ardent proclamations about the inherent racial superiority of the German *Volk* would now complacently accept the

backward Persians, even if they were now calling themselves Iranians, as blood brothers—well, the likelihood, Schellenberg would
say, struck him as "absurd."

The files did go on with some puffery about the natural resources Iran had to offer the Reich. There were papers confidently
predicting that once the Trans-Iranian Railway was completed in
1938, freight cars loaded with iron and copper would begin to make
their long way to Germany. Other reports envisioned the inevitable day when rigorous German expertise would take charge of the
backward country's agricultural production, and previously unexpected rewards would follow; there was much speculation, albeit
vague, about newfound "medicinal plants." One dispatch, though,
helpfully pointed out that castor oil plants had only recently been
proved to be a source of an efficient aircraft lubricant, and vast fields
of the plants could be grown in the wastelands of Iran. This suggestion was quickly followed by another that was even more grandiose:
German agricultural communes would one day pop up across Iran,
providing Lebensraum for an ever-expanding Reich.

To Schellenberg's critical mind, these dispatches were dutifully
spouting Nazi Party dogma rather than realistic ideas. Glued to his
desk, he continued his journey, searching with a growing impatience through the fanciful proposals.

BUT THEN THE FILES FOUND a new preoccupation—oil. And with
that came a new intensity. All at once the rapaciousness seemed to
leap off the page. Reading the analysts' explanation of how Iran's
endless oil reserves would lubricate the Reich's durable strategy to
win the war, Schellenberg felt, he'd say, as if at last he'd gotten to
the heart of the matter. Hitler's courtship of the Reza Shah no longer seemed quixotic, but part of a carefully reasoned master plan:
Iran would be the Nazis' gateway to the entire Middle East.

This stepping-stone strategy was laid out, albeit in typical long-
winded Germanic fashion, in Hitler's War Directive No. 32, issued

in June 1941. "The possibility of exerting strong pressure on Turkey and Iran," the Nazi war planners wrote, "improves the prospect of making direct or indirect use of the countries in the struggle against England. . . . The struggle against the British positions in the Mediterranean and in western Asia will be continued by converging attacks launched . . . through Iran."

In self-assured conversations with his generals and ministers, though, Hitler had shared his grand plan—and how it was shaped by a shrewd lust for oil—more directly. "For a long time I have had everything prepared," he revealed in one such discussion. "As the next step we are going to advance south of the Caucasus and then help the rebels in Iran and Iraq against the English. . . . Then the English will run out of oil. In two years we will be on the borders of India. Twenty to thirty elite German divisions will do. Then the British Empire will collapse.

"By the end of 1943," the Führer promised, "we will pitch our tents in Tehran. . . . Then the oil wells will at last be dry as far as the English are concerned."

But until the glorious day when the tents were finally pitched, it had been the job of both the Abwehr and the SD, same as it had always been for intelligence services throughout history, to facilitate the long-term strategic policy. Spies would help pave the way for the columns of troops that would soon arrive.

Three undercover operatives, Schellenberg now read, had been sent into Iran. Just as Canaris had told him.

THEY WENT IN BAREFOOT, to use the jargon of the trade. Which meant that they had no operational support, no backup personnel in case the roof fell in, and no predetermined escape route. A rudimentary radio transmitter was their only lifeline to Berlin, but it was, at best, a problematic device. They were behind enemy lines, the whiff of danger always in the air, and they were completely on their own.

Max and Moritz, the names borrowed from the heroes of a

German folktale that celebrated the misadventures of two mischief-
making lads, were the code names of the two young Section 6 spies
of the SS Reich Security Service. And as if playing the roles of
scamps in a far-fetched children's tale, the two novice secret agents
arrived in tandem at the hectic port city of Pahlevī (now Bandar-
e-Anzali) in November 1940, carrying identical leather suitcases
the SD had provided, wearing identical white linen suits issued in
Berlin, and hiding behind the identical thin covers of "commercial travelers." Their shared sense of boyish bewilderment as they
ambled down the gangplank to begin their first covert mission in
a jarringly alien, sun-bleached land was no doubt compounded by
their troubling realizations that they didn't speak the language, had
no previous knowledge of the Middle East, let alone Iran, and had
only cursory training in the sinister art of intelligence. Before being christened into the secret world, Max had been Franz Mayr, a
law student recruited from a signals platoon in Potsdam. Moritz, in
his not too distant overt life, had been Roman Gamotha, a veteran
Hitler Youth street brawler who had made the easy transition to
black-uniformed Waffen-SS legionnaire.

Still, Max "with his black hair, black eyes, and black fanatical
moustache," could have blended into the flow of people jostling
their way through a Persian bazaar. Moritz, however, would have
stuck out in any crowd. Blessed with a "blond film-star type of
masculine beauty," he made his way through life in a "princely"
strut. Or that was the irritated, dismissive appraisal of the two hapless boy spies by Julius Berthold Schulze-Holthus, the generation-
older Abwehr professional who, under more substantial diplomatic
cover, was also plying his covert trade in Iran.

"A man has to be born for the intelligence service," Schulze-
Holthus would say, and the unspoken corollary was that he had
been. His biography made a convincing case: the proud scion of an
upper-class Bavarian family; decorated World War I officer; scholarly attorney (who became famous defending the rights of "nat-
uralists" to parade around on beaches; the astonishingly convivial

Nazi Bathing Law of 1942 was a direct result of his impassioned advocacy); rigorously trained Abwehr spook who had done a preliminary undercover stint in Iran while tagging along with a contingent of officials from the German Ministry of the Interior who'd been taking stock of German schools; and finally returning with his wife in 1941 under the pretense of serving as the vice-consul in Tabrīz. But what truly made him the born espionage agent, as if he'd been selected at birth for the shadowy trade, was the way he instinctively lived in the world. He had a romantic, swashbuckling dedication to the infinite complexities of the Great Game. He just loved being a spy.

Not that either his instincts or his carefully acquired tradecraft could do him much good in Iran. Like the Section 6 boy spies, he'd been burdened with a perplexingly vague mission. "Let's make mischief. Bring it on!" is the devilish refrain of the two characters in the children's tale that had inspired Max and Moritz's code names. The operational instructions both the Abwehr and Section 6 spymasters had dished out to their agents before they sent them across the world might as well have been the refrain from a similarly naughty, happy-go-lucky tune.

Only a few sparse sentences had been offered: They were to plant the seeds for an irrepressible fifth column. They were to ensure that Iranians would welcome the Afrika Korps with open arms when they came storming in. But how the spies were to accomplish this impressive political feat—well, that was left unsaid. Further complicating the task, once the three agents had been sent to Iran, they'd been abandoned by the Berlin deskmen of their parent services. No messages—neither a reassuring pat on the back nor a scolding call to action—had ever been received by any of them. They had been left entirely on their own. And all these superspies had to do was win the allegiance of an entire nation. Somehow.

As Schellenberg read the exasperating pages, his mind could not help traveling back to the time when he, the novice fieldman, had been sent on his first clandestine mission. It was the autumn of

1938, and Reinhard Heydrich had dispatched him to Dakar, the chief French naval station in Africa. Traveling under the cover of a Dutch diamond merchant's son, a carefully doctored Dutch passport attesting to this identity, armed with a specially designed Leica camera, he was given the mission to find out all he could about the French harbor installations. Now, years later, he was comfortably seated at his desk in Berkaerstrasse, but in his galloping thoughts the transformation was complete. Once again, he'd recall with a quiver, he was living like a fugitive: "Nervous in the streets and in the glance of every casual passer-by I sensed the sharp, searching eye of a Sûreté agent." The nights had been worse. "This apprehension, the climate, and the unfamiliar surrounding completely exhausted me," he remembered without shame. "Each night I lay awake pursued by all the mistakes I had made during the day. In the end, my thoughts would weave themselves into a restless, dream-laden sleep, for which I would awake towards dawn unrefreshed and bathed in sweat." Yes, Schellenberg could very well imagine the accumulating apprehensions that had plagued the abandoned agents in Iran, the what-ifs that had paraded in a constant unnerving stream through their thoughts.

Then, as the files made painfully clear, every spy's worst fears suddenly came true. On August 25, 1941, British and Russian forces launched Operation Countenance. Germany's three covert operatives were no longer just barefoot in Iran. Now they were running for their lives on burning coals.

"I WAS NOT WITHOUT SOME anxiety about embarking on a Persian war, but the arguments for it were compulsive," Churchill would later explain with a politician's usual smooth justifications. Yet in this instance his logic was difficult to dispute. The risks of Allied inaction were too real, as well as too alarming—the rupture of Britain's crucial pathway to its empire beyond the Suez Canal; the forfeiture of the supply lines carrying the much-needed war matériel the Russians were receiving by the trainload from the Americans; the loss of oil reserves that could fuel the Allied war machine till the end of time, or, if it came first, the end of the war; and, if German U-boats were allowed to nest in the Persian Gulf and Indian Ocean, possibly even the forced abandonment of India. Better to strike preemptively in Iran than to wait idly until Germany got around to making its play.

There wasn't much of a fight. The British forces, about 19,000 men, marched in from the west, crossing the Iraqi border. And from the north, hurling down from Central Asia, the larger Russian force, nearly 40,000 troops, invaded. The Iranians could mobilize nine divisions, an army of more than 125,000 soldiers backed by a powerful force of Czech-made tanks. But except for a few brave pockets of resistance, they swiftly threw up their hands with a tame bewilderment. The hostilities were pretty much over in four days.

The German spies quickly went to ground. Reza Shah held on a little longer, but that was probably because he had more bags to pack. On September 27, accompanied by eight members of his family and a mountain of luggage filled with all the glittering treasures that they could stuff inside, he sailed off on the SS *Bandra*. He would never return to Iran. His heady dream of a dynasty, however, still had a chance to survive. He was immediately succeeded by his twenty-two-year-old son, Crown Prince Mohammed Reza Pahlavi, who no less immediately wisely pledged his full support to the Allied cause.

It was at that point that the long-running story contained in the files on Schellenberg's desk ground to an abrupt and mystifying end. For nearly two long years, there had been no word, no sign of life, from the three German agents.

ONLY NOW, OUT OF THE BLUE, they had resurfaced.

Or at least two of them had. The message that had been relayed to the Abwehr via Japanese intelligence stated that the resourceful

Schulze-Holthus had found refuge with sympathetic Qashqai tribes-men in the remote hills of the western provinces. Max—Franz Mayr—had been hiding in plain sight, gone to ground somewhere amid the hustle and bustle of Tehran. As for Moritz—Roman Gamotha—there was no word. Also hiding out? Perhaps captured by the British, and shipped off to a bleak prison camp in Australia? Caught by the Russians, who would've just as readily hanged him by the neck as sent him off to Siberia? Or maybe he'd simply had the misfortune of being mortally shot by the invading forces, a not-so-innocent bystander hit by a stray bullet? Nearly anything was possible, Schellenberg realized, and so guessing was pointless.

Yet despite all the unknowns crowding his thoughts, even in those first excited moments as he began to mull the miracle that two German agents were in place behind enemy lines, the spymas-ter in him knew he wanted to leverage this unexpected gift. Swiftly the broad outline of an operational plan began to take shape in his mind. It would take time to work out the tactical details. Yet it was nevertheless a fact that at the very beginning, in his initial rushes of inchoate inspiration, he already had a fundamental vision of how to make the most of the covert resources that had been left behind, one that would set into motion a bold mission that targeted the new realities on the ground in Iran, as well as one that acknowledged the new, no less dismaying realities of the war.

11

I N THE DAYS THAT FOLLOWED—the cruel wartime spring and summer of 1943—both the Nazi spymaster who headed Section 6 and the Secret Service agent in charge of the American president's security unknowingly shared a common preoccupation: airplanes.

For Mike Reilly, the habitual worrier, his sudden interest was prompted by, not surprisingly, the president's safety. He had not yet been made cognizant, to use the service's word, of where, when, or even if the much-discussed meeting among the Big Three would take place, but it was his job to be prepared for any eventuality. The Casablanca Conference had taken FDR halfway across the world—"Africa?" he could still hear himself echoing dumbly after the Boss told him the news—and one of the largest concerns in a trip that had been jam-packed with valid reasons for distress had been the flight across the Atlantic. They had made do with one of the Army Air Force's lumbering four-engine C-54s, an efficient cargo transport plane that'd been seeing a lot of wartime action. It offered a steady-enough ride as long as the pilot kept below 22,000 feet; the cabin wasn't pressurized. The range, another asset at 3,900 miles, was good enough to allow a takeoff from Washington and a nonstop landing on the other side of the Atlantic. And while the seats were rudimentary, fashioned from a rough canvas, there was room for fifty soldiers, a space that could generously accommodate one commander in chief and a handful of the president's men without any of the distinguished passengers sitting shoulder to pin-striped shoulder. Still, for Mike, who, as he emphatically put it, was "charged with the President's safety and comfort," the C-54 left a lot to desire. And even more to fret about.

One problem was that "the Boss couldn't use normal steps." A ramp, therefore, had to be built for the president's wheelchair before the plane landed. But at the first signs of construction, enemy field agents or German analysts peering at aerial reconnaissance photos would have a telltale clue identifying the mystery traveler who'd soon be arriving. "An absolute giveaway," Mike griped.

Another concern was that the Boss, stuck in his wheelchair most of the time, unable to wander willy-nilly about the cabin, grew quickly restless. Except for conferences with his aides or reading state papers, there wasn't much for him to do but look out the window. Only the window was tiny, a porthole really, and high enough up so that FDR, strapped down tight, had to keep his head raised at an awkward, unnatural angle to steal just a glimpse. Still, Mike would've preferred that the Boss didn't do even that: the window wasn't bulletproof.

The resounding bottom line, though, to Mike's list of negatives was that the plane was simply not grand enough for any American president, and certainly not for one who had been born and bred in patrician splendor. The C-54 was a satisfactory flying machine for hauling Army grunts from one place to another, but nothing more. It hadn't been designed to transport a jaunty swell who liked his dry martinis chilled just so, or who rakishly puffed away using an enamel-tipped five-inch cigarette holder.

So, "with those things in mind," a determined Mike left Washington and made the long trip across the country to meet with the engineers and designers of the C-54. Of course he could've telephoned. Or, if the security of the phone lines had been too great a fear, he could've put his thoughts into a detailed memo, stamped the pages top secret, and had them hand-delivered by an armed Secret Service agent. But Mike wasn't looking for shortcuts. He wanted to hear everything the experts had to say in response to his suggestions, and he also wanted to work with them, to apply his firsthand knowledge, and then be on hand to help think through the inevitable problems. He knew he didn't begin to have all the answers, but he also wasn't about to let any pointy-headed engineers cut corners where the Boss was involved.

The Douglas Aircraft Company was spread across Culver Field in Santa Monica, California, just down the road from Los Angeles. Arriving from the wartime White House, a tense, cramped world of endless intrigues and monumental decisions, he quickly felt that he'd entered unfamiliar yet at the same time exhilarating territory. It wasn't just the harsh sunshine that baked the rows of hangars in a radiant glow, or the breeze coming off the incredibly blue Pacific stretching off to the west, or the very air itself, redolent of the fresh salt of the ocean. What was most affecting was the unexpected vastness of the enterprise at Culver Field, larger than the Montana town where he'd been raised, for sure, and all devoted to the making of the aircraft needed to win the war. He saw women zipping by on roller skates, and when he asked what that was about, he learned that the facility was so huge that they had to skate from one end to the other to deliver the mail. In Washington it had been easy to fall into the trap of believing that only a handful of diplomats and politicians had formed a battle line on the home front to fight this war, but out there he understood for the first time that the entire nation, men and women, had rolled up their sleeves to get the job done.

He met in an office hidden away in a corner of a mud-colored hangar with a businesslike group of Douglas officials, and they listened to what he had to say with an attention he found flattering. Later, he'd realize that was just the way engineers worked; they liked to get a handle on problems, "gather the relevant facts" was how they put it, and then they'd go to work to solve them. Unlike the daily dramas at the White House, where all the players pushed and shoved simply to maximize their own fiefdoms, out here, he couldn't help feeling, everyone was predisposed to cooperate. If there were egos or personal agendas involved, Mike couldn't detect them. They just wanted to get the job done.

The plane that was finally delivered looked like the old C-54, but at the same time was very much something different. On the assembly line, workers had welded onto the standard body a new, longer set of wings that provided space for four auxiliary fuel tanks; if weather prevented the scheduled landing, the plane could circle for hours or easily make it to a fallback destination. There was a compact, battery-powered elevator at the rear of the craft so that a ramp was no longer necessary; with just the pull of a lever, the president sitting in his wheelchair could be raised or lowered. He also got, as he'd lobbied for, an expansive bulletproof window thoughtfully positioned so that the Boss while seated could easily enjoy the view. And the accommodating engineers had taken heed of Mike's stern rants about security: from the outside the plane didn't look any different from a run-of-the-mill C-54 transport. Both the abnormally large window and the elevator attachment had been artfully concealed. An enemy agent checking out the plane from across the landing field would have no clue that this craft was carrying the president.

Inside, however, was another story, and for Mike a completely gratifying one. As he had requested, the designers went to town bringing the interior up to the Boss's high standards. There was now "an executive conference room" with an ample desk befitting a president, sofas that concealed fold-down beds, and a private presidential lavatory. Best of all, or so FDR would see it, Mike suspected, there was an electric refrigerator and freezer in the galley that could chill the presidential gin to a pleasingly numbing cold. The people at Douglas had christened the special craft with the tail numbers VC-54C, and had given it the lofty official title of "the Flying White House." The press pool wags called it the "Sacred Cow" since its pilots had the license to do whatever they—or the president, more often than not—wanted, and that was the name that stuck.

Mike felt a sort of proprietary pride in the gleaming aircraft that had come to life from the wellspring of his many worries. He thought that if the Boss was soon required to go to some distant corner of the world to huddle with Churchill and Stalin—Newfoundland was the chosen site, according to the latest White House scuttlebutt—the Sacred Cow would undoubtedly make the trip safer and more comfortable.

But even as he found this small measure of reassurance, another notion took hold. All it would require was for one enemy fighter to penetrate the cordon of protective planes flanked around the huge VC-54C, one Nazi fighter's cannons to get the craft centered in its sights, and if the aircraft was hit, if it crashed in flames—well, there was no engineering feat that would enable this president to crawl from the wreckage.

SCHELLENBERG, FOR HIS PART, had not been thinking about safety, and comfort was even further down his list. His concern was purely operational: Was there a plane that could accomplish the mission he'd begun envisioning? Before he could take his plan any further, he realized that this fundamental question needed to be answered.

When he'd left his desk after his long immersion in the Iran files, his cluttered musings kept returning to guilty thoughts about loyalty and betrayal. Both services, the incriminating record had made clear, had let their agents down. They had sent them off, and with an obliviousness that he found astonishing, left them pretty much on their own. Then when things had gotten sticky after the Allied invasion, both the Abwehr and the SD not only didn't rush to the rescue, but shrugged off their fieldmen's fates with an Olympian detachment. And the agents? They had stayed behind up to their necks in risk, always certain of their duty, still convinced that the Fatherland's ultimate victory would be reward enough for their unswerving loyalty. The entire sad episode filled Schellenberg with shame.

He was determined to write a new ending.

He went to work on an operation that would use these loyal, experienced agents and their networks. A mission that would demonstrate that their sacrifice had not been in vain. And the parsimonious spymaster in him also wanted a return on his service's long-term investment; it would be good business, after all.

But once he began to tackle the problem he found himself glumly conceding that since the three spies' arrivals in the East too much had changed—in Iran, and, more consequentially, in Germany. Their original mission had two components. The first had been intelligence gathering: identify the oil fields ripe for the taking, scout for possible locations for German airfields. The second had been political: stoke the fires of discontent, make sure that when the Nazis pitched their tents in Iran, the natives would enthusiastically help them pound in the stakes. Only those ambitions were now hopelessly out of date. Two long years ago Germany had lost its opportunity to gain control of the country. Russia and Britain had invaded Iran to pitch their tents, and more than thirty thousand American troops had come in their wake, largely to facilitate and protect the invaluable carloads of US Lend-Lease matériel traveling across the country by rail toward the Soviet Union. And the Afrika Korps marching to Iran? After the demoralizing defeat at Stalingrad, Schellenberg had come around to conceding that the Allies' savagely pouring into Berlin seemed not only more likely but destined.

So, what could be realistically done? And would it be worth the effort? Those two indelicate questions rumbled through Schellenberg's harried mind.

Yet in the course of this ruminative exercise, his operational goals began to clarify. What if, he asked himself with a growing sense of satisfaction, he could delay the ineluctable Allied march to victory? Help persuade the enemy that it was high time to negotiate a reasonable peace? And in the process earn new honor for the service, as well as for the gritty agents in Iran who had never been broken, who had maintained their loyalty during their years in isolation, had paid every price and never called it sacrifice? That would be a mission he'd be proud to launch, and one that the lofty Canaris would endorse, too.

Methodically, these questions led him to the tactical conclusion that had been gnawing at him even as he'd first read the files. But just to make sure—to recheck his sums, he'd say—he backtracked through the latest analysts' reports. And he found the hard supporting evidence: the Americans had been shipping forty thousand tons every month of much-needed Lend-Lease war supplies, and the amount was predicted to keep growing—tanks, trucks, engines, guns, machine parts—on the Trans-Iranian Railway across the country and over the borders into the Soviet Union. Meanwhile, the British were taking all the Iranian oil they could grab; it was helping to keep their war machine rolling.

And now he had it! He would put an end to all that. He'd send in commando teams who, working hand in hand with the veteran agents already in place in Iran, would launch an audacious sabotage campaign against the railroad, against the oil fields. The operation would be more than a last-gasp gesture. The Allies would bleed. It would hurt.

But before he focused on the task of recruiting the teams, he needed to assure himself that the mission was feasible. Could commandos be inserted into Iran?

He summoned to his office Werner Baumbach, the interim commander of KG 200, the elite Luftwaffe squadron that provided air support for all clandestine missions. The fate of his bold plan would hang on what the much-decorated bomber pilot had to say.

ORIGINALLY, PRIOR TO ITS BEING confiscated by the Gestapo and its residents summarily transported to the walled ghetto at Łódź, the building on Berkaerstrasse had been a Jewish old age home, and Schellenberg's large office on the fourth floor had been the director's. He had kept much of the previous inhabitant's tasteful decorations—the deep carpeting, the oversize mahogany desk, and the gracefully carved antique wooden cupboard that served as a bookshelf. But he had also added his own personal touches to the room, and these more directly reflected his spymaster's job, as well as his very real fears about becoming a victim of the internecine vendettas that often swept through the upper echelons of Hitler's Reich.

Crowded on a trolley table within easy reach of his desk was a row of telephones. Direct lines could connect him in just an instant to the Führer at the Chancellery, Himmler's office on Prinz-Albrecht Strasse, as well as his own apartment in Berlin and his country house in Herzberg; if the Gestapo long knives came after him, a last-minute appeal for mercy, or for that matter a hurried warning to his family, might make all the difference.

As an additional precaution, the entire office was wired for sound. Lodged in the walls, under the desk, in the telephone consoles, in the base of a lamp—microphones were hidden everywhere. The system was always on; it picked up every conversation, every grunt or laugh. He wanted to be sure he had an irrefutable record. The best defense, Schellenberg had come to learn as he'd mutely watched a procession of heads go on the block, would be ironclad proof that the charges were fabrications.

He'd also made sure that tampering with the evidence, or, for that matter, stealing his voluminous files filled with all sorts of useful dirty little secrets, would be impossible. Each night before he left, he flicked a switch that activated a strategically arrayed system of photoelectric cells. Anyone climbing through the window, fiddling with his safe, or just opening the door would be greeted by an ear-piercing alarm. Within thirty seconds, if not sooner, a squadron of guards would have their rifles leveled at the intruder.

And woe to him who tried to sandbag the master spy while he was sitting with apparent nonchalance hunched over his work. "My desk was like a small fortress," he'd bragged without exaggeration.

As soon as a visitor entered the room, he was automatically tracked by the muzzles of two guns discreetly built into the desk's ornate mahogany woodwork. With the press of a button within easy reach, Schellenberg could spray his guest with a hail of bullets. If he was in a more forgiving mood, another button on the desk could be tapped: an alarm would sound, guards would surround the entire building, blocking every exit, while the unwelcome guest would be shuffled off at gunpoint. After the rigorous questioning, though, the captive might have preferred that Schellenberg had simply fired away.

It was these two hidden guns that automatically fixed Oberst-leutnant Werner Baumbach in their sights as the acting commander of the KG Luftwaffe command sat opposite the head of Section 6. Quite possibly they were aimed at the Knight's Cross with Oak Leaves and Swords that the veteran pilot wore with pride around his neck. And no less a possibility, as the frustrating conversation proceeded it was also likely that the spy was tempted to press the deadly button; at least it would've put a merciful end to the discussion.

For no sooner had Schellenberg explained that he needed a plane that could transport commandos to Iran than the pilot began to hurl his objections. Sure, Baumbach offered, his Junkers Ju-290s had the range. A couple of the big, four-engine planes were parked out of sight of Allied bombers in a secret base in the Crimea, and they could make the trip to Iran and back without refueling (in size, engine configuration, even cruising speed, the craft were nearly identical to the C-54 that Mike had focused on in Santa Monica; but, of course, neither man knew what the other was up to). The problem, Baumbach proceeded to make clear, was that he was not prepared to risk one of the valuable planes in Iran. There was no way to guarantee that once it touched down in the desert, a heavily armed contingent from the Allied occupying force wouldn't swoop in and capture the craft. In fact, that was the likely scenario; their radars would be tracking the plane every foot of the way as it made its descent. Of course, there was also the chance that their eager gunners wouldn't wait for it to land. They'd shoot it out of the sky as it was coming down over Iran. Either way, though, the result would be the same.

Schellenberg didn't argue, because he knew there'd be no point. The pilot was right. The Ju-290s were too valuable to lose. And there was not much likelihood of the factories churning out a replacement at this desperate stage of the war. So much for his mission, his chance at making a difference, at repaying old debts, at redemption. Unless—

Suppose, Schellenberg now suggested with an offhandedness that belied the fact that everything hung on the answer, the plane didn't land. Didn't descend below twenty thousand feet until the end of the mission. Kept out of the range of the Allied antiaircraft guns.

Paratroopers, Baumbach said, completing the thought.

The word hung in the silence for a long moment, by all accounts.

Then: Yes, Baumbach agreed at last with a flat certainty. A paratroop mission could work. His pilots could certainly get a team to the drop point. The rest would be up to them.

12

WITH A SENSE OF ANTICIPATION, as well as a renewed urgency, Schellenberg drove his gray Audi north from Berlin on a morning not long after his heartening meeting with the Luftwaffe commander. "The Game intrigues me," he liked to say, as though he felt it was necessary to justify his boyish enthusiasm for his chosen trade, and that morning his spirits were indeed running high. Part of his mood could be explained by the relief he always experienced when he had an opportunity to escape the Section 6 headquarters, its four floors overrun with savage SS executioners back from the front and now pretending to be reflective intelligence officers; with each passing day he spent cataloging their furtive glances, he grew to feel more like a staked-out lamb as the wolves closed in. And he was buoyed, too, by the prospect of spending the day with genuine German heroes, soldiers who had truly earned the Fatherland's praise, even reverence. But beyond all else, the spymaster in him was charged by the purposeful thrill of the approaching battle, the exhilaration that came when a new mission was about to be launched.

He drove quickly, as if he were in a great hurry, but in truth he simply liked pushing the souped-up SD car to its limits and discovering how it would respond. The journey north from his headquarters in Berlin's Wilmersdorf district, a neighborhood of grand, old apartment buildings on the edge of the Grunewald forest, took him out of the city and into the country. The road climbed up a small hill and he saw an ancient church with a high steeple. Then there were fields, and more fields and, to his surprise, smoke rising from what seemed to be a bustling factory nestled in the crook of a valley. The road leveled and he followed it, still keeping his foot pressed down on the pedal. There was, he knew, no sign indicating where he should turn, but his memory from his last visit a year earlier was still strong.

After a while, he recognized the junction. He turned off the road and drove up to a high brick wall. Two soldiers, fit and hostile, studied his credentials, then saluted. A gate opened and he drove through.

A long allée of tall chestnut trees flanked the drive like sentinels, and he continued on past a barn, a stable, and several smallish outbuildings. The road dipped and he was led along the periphery of a shimmering blue lake, only to follow it to a car park that fronted an impressively large house. The house had been painted an immaculate white, and two long brick wings flew off at sharp right angles from the modest entryway; the front door, in fact, was a remnant from the original wooden farmhouse that, generations earlier, had been perched on this idyllic lakefront site. Schellenberg parked, and as he walked to the threshold of the house he was suddenly surrounded by about a half-dozen men, all in civilian clothes, aiming their weapons at him.

THEY HAD CAUGHT HIM BY surprise, and by the way they were grinning they were very proud of the trap that had been sprung.

This was Lake Quenz, officially the Abwehr's "special training course for special assignments." In plainer language, though, it was the service's elite commando school for saboteurs and assassins. Its trainees had been carefully selected from the tough-guy volunteers in the Brandenburg Division, resourceful men who had gone behind enemy lines in Belgium, Holland, and the Balkans, executing one bold mission after another as the vanguard of the invading Nazi armies. At Lake Quenz, the most promising Brandenburgers were immersed in a course of rigorous training designed to make them even tougher than the tough. They would become the archetypal Nazi supermen.

In and out of the classroom, they learned all the black arts. They could kill with their bare hands without making a sound. They could hurl a knife with lethal accuracy at thirty paces, or, if battling hand to hand, neatly sever a jugular with a flick of the wrist. They were marksmen trained in a variety of guns, able to turn on sudden command and empty a Luger with lethal accuracy, or they could hunker down in a concealed perch to put a bullet right between the victim's eyes with a Mauser sniper rifle from seemingly impossible distances. They could pick door locks, get a car motor running without an ignition key, and no pair of handcuffs would restrain them for long. They could plant powerful TNT devices that'd detonate with a lighted match or by remote control, and if dynamite wasn't handy they could fabricate a bomb in a jiffy from items that could be foraged from a kitchen; a short railroad line running adjacent to the lake had been constructed to give the trainees a hands-on education in how to plant their explosives to do the most damage to locomotives, freight cars, or the track itself. They were up at four a.m. running ten miles with loaded rucksacks in the predawn darkness, then spent grueling hours performing calisthenics in the gym to make their bodies hard as brick walls, and only when the frigid waters of Lake Quenz had completely iced over were the three-mile swims canceled. Drop them anywhere and they would never be lost; map training and navigation were drummed in through extensive field exercises. Yet for Canaris and his Abwehr subordinates the most valuable operational talent taught to the Lake Quenz recruits was the ability to slip into an enemy country and—presto!—blend in. They were taught to speak, act, dress, even think like the people in the countries where they would be sent. Reviewing the Quenz team heading off on a mission to sabotage enemy supply and troop trains before the main advance on Moscow, their Abwehr handler gloated, only partially in jest, that "they even had learned to spit like Russians."

Now a team of Quenz commandos had their weapons trained on Schellenberg. There was no possibility of springing free, of fighting his way out of this predicament. Days ago he'd informed Canaris of his impending visit; a joint Abwehr-SD mission into Iran, he'd suggested, seemed appropriate since both services already had their agents on the ground. The admiral, affecting his customary avuncular charm, had seconded the idea. But now Schellenberg wondered if Canaris had sent him off with a smile into a trap. It was either the moment he'd been preparing himself for since he'd risen to the head of Section 6, the one when all the enemies he'd made in his youthful ascent to the top of the ladder demanded their revenge for prior insults, for his success at their expense. Or it was something else.

As THINGS TURNED OUT, it'd been a mistake. He'd been the wrong general in the right place. Earlier that morning the commandos had been deployed on a training exercise. The challenge was to get past the guards and then somehow make their way into the headquarters building. The man in the general's uniform, they'd assumed, was part of the game, and they'd been eyeing his arrival as soon as his Audi pulled into the parking area. Quickly, they'd improvised a plan in which the "general" would be the ticket they needed to get them inside. That's when they'd pounced.

There were a few tricky moments before they finally came around to believing Schellenberg was not an instructor trying to pull a fast one, that he was who he claimed he was—a genuine SS general who had arrived for an appointment scheduled by no less than Admiral Canaris. But once that explanation stuck, there were deferential salutes and embarrassed apologies. In turn, Schellenberg, his authority established, found the professional grace to manage a compliment on their stealth. Yet when he entered the headquarters, his apparent calm was all disguise: his insides were precariously close to heaving.

The man he'd come to see, Major Rudolf von Holten-Pflug, was in the midst of delivering a lecture to a classroom of attentive trainees. The subject was assassination. In other circumstances, Schellenberg would not have had any qualms about peremptorily summoning the major from his students. But that morning, still grappling with the unnerving aftershocks caused by the half-dozen or so weapons aimed at his head by professional killers, he decided to sit mutely at the back of the room. The lecture would offer some much-needed time to gather his wits.

In his second surprise of the day, it offered something more. As the formal lecture finished, a discussion began between the teacher and his young charges. One exchange in particular had him following along with close attention. Over the weeks that followed, the conversation would continue to stick in his mind, the precise words summoned up time after time. And in the recurring process, they gathered a new energy, as well as an intractable persuasiveness. But at the time, he had no inkling of their ultimate impact. He'd simply listened attentively, intrigued.

After the class had been dismissed, his business with the major went quickly. Holten-Pflug was old Abwehr, a monocle-wearing aristocrat who had found his way into espionage because he'd been seeking a romantic and dangerous trade in which a patriotic gentleman might have some fun. He had not been disappointed. He had lived by his cunning with genial conviction for nearly a decade before being put out to pasture as an instructor at Lake Quenz. His adventurous career over too soon, he'd spent every day of his tenure at the school mourning its loss. And now Schellenberg was offering him an opportunity to return to the Great Game. His specific operational assignment was still to be defined. Whether he'd personally jump with the first commando team parachuting into Iran, or simply be the talent spotter and handler—that is, the officer in charge of team selection and mission training—while he waited for his turn to come, that would be up to Canaris. But either role, Holten-Pflug recognized at once, was preferable to his having to drone on day after stolid day in a classroom. He did not hesitate to sign on. And without prompting, he volunteered to scout the Brandenburg training schools for the native Persians who had come to Germany to offer their services when it still had looked like the Nazis would be marching into their homeland. It wouldn't hurt to have a few people along who could speak the language, he advised the general.

After that, there wasn't much more to say. As the general and the major exchanged salutes, the deal was struck: Holten-Pflug would begin putting together an Abwehr insertion team.

13

I T WAS STILL THE SAME long day, and Schellenberg's next stop
was only a short distance away. Although the countryside he drove
through was no less pleasant, sectioned into large, verdant fields
and attractively dotted with irregularly shaped ponds, the journey
brought him none of the anticipatory pleasure he had experienced
on his way to Lake Quenz. As he grew closer to his destination, he
imagined the familiar telltale odor was already permeating the car.

The locals, he had heard, had complained several months back,
and the Gestapo had supposedly complied: they would no longer
burn bodies in the mobile crematoriums they'd been testing for use
on the eastern front. But whether they'd actually stopped or not
he did not know. All he knew was that he couldn't help but feel he
was inhaling the fetid smell of death. When he drove through the
iron gates of Sachsenhausen concentration camp, passing beneath
the sneeringly ironic words ARBEIT MACHT FREI ("Work Sets You
Free") the rancid smell of burnt and burning flesh, whether real or
imagined, traveled down through his nostrils and lodged deep. He
felt as if he were suffocating. His appointment was waiting in the
far eastern corner of the sprawling camp, but it was not far enough
away for him.

He had come to meet Captain Otto Skorzeny. Whenever he
thought of Skorzeny, Schellenberg thought of their first meeting.
Himmler, stoking the growing rivalry with the Abwehr, had decided that the SD should have its own version of Quenz Lake—a
training school for derring-do commandos who could be sent off

on impossible missions. Yet there'd be a fundamental difference—the SD recruits would all be SS veterans, men whose commitment to the dogmatic Nazi racial and political ideology was unwavering. The new Oranienburg unit—the name, with a sensitivity that was rare for the SS, referred to the town rather than the concentration camp where it was based—would be under the immediate command of Section 6, and so it had fallen to Schellenberg to interview Himmler's candidate to head the group.

The Reichsführer's choice had been Skorzeny, but when Schellenberg reviewed the man's military records he had found little to recommend him. It was, on paper at least, a rather lackluster career. Rejected by the Luftwaffe as "much too old" at thirty-one, Skorzeny instead had served as an engineer assigned to an SS combat battalion that had advanced without incident into France, and then had the fight of their lives when they penetrated into Serbia, Poland, and Russia. In the six months before being summoned to Schellenberg's office, Skorzeny had been mired in the tedium of barracks duty in Berlin as an engineer assigned to an SS armored division. What Himmler had seen in this veteran soldier, what qualities the Reichsführer had perceived that suggested this old-guard SS man could be the head of an innovative school for special action commandos, were not at all apparent to Schellenberg as he reviewed Skorzeny's file.

His reservations, however, had quickly dissolved in the course of their first meeting in his office. The man sitting across from him was broad and powerful with a dueling scar etched into his surprisingly boyish face. Skorzeny was at least a head taller than the SS general, a handsome man with alert brown eyes. He held himself with a deadly stillness that suggested confidence, as well as, Schellenberg grew to recognize, an even deeper streak of arrogance. When he spoke, the words came out in a bellow, like a drill sergeant's.

But what most impressed Schellenberg was their conversation. Skorzeny had conceded that he did not possess either the prior knowledge or experience that would have prepared him for the job. So Schellenberg, who was too much of a politician to think about rejecting Himmler's candidate, patiently suggested he'd have to "beg, borrow or steal all the information" he could get and "then go full speed ahead."

Skorzeny considered this, taking his time. For a rough moment Schellenberg feared he'd turn down the offer, and then how would he explain that to the Reichsführer? But when Skorzeny finally answered, the words came out in his previous assured bark. "Live dangerously," he said thoughtfully, quoting Nietzsche, and that's what he would do. He would serve his country "in an unusual way in its hour of need."

It was this firmly articulated commitment, full of zeal, full of a sense of the uniqueness of the mission, the words spoken with a grave formality, that had convinced Schellenberg that the Reichsführer had been correct after all—Skorzeny was the right man for the job.

In the months that followed, Schellenberg had not been disappointed. Skorzeny had brought many innovative ways to the special course, including specialized sabotage instructions and language classes. And he'd taken particular pride in making sure his men were efficient killers. He was unhappy that the training facility was housed in a fenced-off corner of a dreary concentration camp, and with Schellenberg's approval he was in the midst of making plans to move the group at the end of the summer to a large and very grand eighteenth-century *Schloss* nearby. Yet he also was quick to take advantage of the practical opportunities Sachsenhausen offered for training purposes. He had his men testing the efficacy of newly manufactured poisoned bullets and gas grenades on camp inmates until they'd mastered the lethal know-how necessary to get the job done. And he used inmates for demonstrations on first aid techniques such as amputating legs and resuscitating drowning victims; even if the subject didn't survive the lesson, Skorzeny's feeling was that the trainees would have at least learned something in the process. After only a few months, the SS had a commando school that could turn out agents who were as ruthless and efficient as the Quenz supermen.

These were the recollections that came back to Schellenberg as he made his way to the SS captain's office at Oranienburg. As with his meeting with Holten-Pflug, things proceeded quickly. No sooner had he outlined his plan than Skorzeny agreed that it could be done, and he would personally make sure that it succeeded. Although he was a different sort of soldier, as well as a different manner of man, than the aristocratic Abwehr major, he was no less hard charging. He, too, was driven by a gladiator's raw courage.

It was agreed: a team of SS commandos would begin training for a sabotage mission in Iran.

THERE WAS ONE LAST BIT of business. It was simply good tradecraft, Schellenberg believed, to have an ace hidden up his sleeve, to deploy assets who would keep a covert watch on all the moving parts of an operation. That way there'd be no surprises. He called these supervisory operatives his "hand-picked special agents," and with repetition their employment in the field became part of what those in the intelligence business referred to as his "handwriting." The Iran missions would be no exception.

As preparations were continuing at the two commando schools, he summoned Winifred Oberg to his office. He didn't like Oberg or, for that matter, trust him. But he knew he could control him. In his office safe he had photographs of the former lawyer enjoying what was apparently a very good time in the bed of Ernst Röhm, the onetime leader of the SA or Brownshirts, the Nazi Party's original paramilitary force. And while Oberg's homosexuality would have caused little more than a raised eyebrow or two among the Nazi ruling elite, it was this vivid proof of his friendship with Röhm, who had been executed on Himmler's command, that was the "sin" that could not be ignored: it would have undoubtedly resulted in his own death sentence. Oberg had long ago resigned himself to obeying Schellenberg's orders.

Oberg's new assignment, he learned as he sat across from the SS general, was to make his way to Iran, then initiate contact with Mayr, code name Max, the SD agent who had stayed behind in Tehran. Once he hooked up with Max, Oberg was to monitor the success of the sabotage commando missions. He was to send weekly reports marked "for Schellenberg's eyes only" to Berlin.

Oberg was overwhelmed. You realize I don't speak Farsi? he asked.

Schellenberg shrugged as if it were no consequence.

Well, can you provide Max's address in Tehran? he went on.

I'm afraid I don't have it, Schellenberg explained flatly.

It's a big city, Oberg tried. He had no previous knowledge of Tehran.

About three-quarters of a million people, Schellenberg said, agreeing. But he expressed his assurance in Oberg's ability to find his man. When Oberg with a newfound stubbornness started to protest, Schellenberg rose from his seat and stepped toward his huge safe. For further effect, he began to spin the dial.

Oberg got the message. How will I get to Iran? he wondered with a weary resignation.

Now Schellenberg was on firmer ground. He responded that he'd given the matter some thought. He had ruled out Oberg's parachuting in with one of the commando teams; even if he could survive the jump, it'd be better if the squads didn't know he'd been sent to spy on them. Which left, the general continued, only two other possibilities. He could go in disguised as one of the many pilgrims on their way to Meshed in the northeast of the country, but since Oberg didn't speak the language he'd never be able to pull that off. In the end he'd decided Oberg should enter on a neutral ship sailing from a Turkish port. Of course, he'd need a convincing cover story to explain his journey. He told Oberg to give the matter some thought, and when he'd settled on his legend (as background stories were called in the spy trade), he should report to Section F4. They'd provide him with all the travel documents for his new identity—passport, ration card, even a driver's license.

With that, the improbable meeting was suddenly over. In the busy weeks and months that followed, Schellenberg did not give it another thought.

He would regret this mistake.

THE HOUSE IN THE WANNSEE suburb of Berlin was large and stately. Whether it was the absurdly pretty Villa Marlier, where a little over a year earlier Reinhard Heydrich had convened a conference to decide the Final Solution to "the Jewish Question," remains today a matter of historical debate; evidence can be found in the SD records that is both supportive as well as more problematic. But if the site wasn't the Marlier residence, it was certainly one of the villa's equally grand neighbors. And there is no dispute that a historic celebration took place.

It was a farewell party. It was about a week before the first group would parachute into Iran, and the two dozen or so Abwehr and SD commandos had been assembled in anticipation of their missions. Schellenberg was there, as was his dreaded boss, Kaltenbrunner. Himmler had sent a message conveying his deep regret at not being able to attend, along with the announcement that all the commandos had been promoted one rank higher.

As the festivities grew more raucous, as the beer and schnapps continued to flow, Hauptsturmführer Martin Kurmis, an SS man who'd be jumping into Iran with the first team, made a public vow. "We're going to hot the place up a bit," he promised. The words were offered almost casually, the sort of boastful, confident remark soldiers are prone to make at public gatherings, especially when alcohol helps reinforce the prebattle resolve.

But they struck a chord in Schellenberg. In the weeks that followed, these words, a soldier's spontaneous pledge, would rumble about in his mind until they pushed his thoughts toward the contemplation of even greater possibilities.

14

FIVE O'CLOCK WAS TEATIME AT the elegant Eden Hotel bar on Budapester Strasse in Berlin, and in wartime the *Eintänzers*—taxi dancers—did a brisk business. They were young men, teenagers and often barely so, who earned a few marks by dancing with the lonely women whose husbands or boyfriends were off fighting for the Reich. On an evening late in July 1943, Schellenberg found himself making his way through a flutter of well-dressed women studying with great intensity the row of boys young enough to be their sons seated along the periphery of the dance floor. He continued on to a dark corner at the rear of the gold-gilded room to an unmarked door, and to his own intrigues.

He entered a wood-paneled salon. There was a table in the middle surrounded by chairs, but Canaris, a drink in his hand, had already chosen one of the leather club chairs that were arranged in a small circle near the far window. The window offered a view across the busy city street toward the incongruous spectacle of the Elephant's Gate—a bright red pagoda with a green-tiled roof flanked by two colossal stone elephants marking the entrance to the Berlin Zoo. Seated across from the admiral was Colonel Georg Hansen, the service's deskman in charge of the Abwehr's overseas field stations (and who, a year later, would be one of the planners of an assassination attempt on Hitler). Schellenberg took a seat with his back to the window, staring straight into Canaris's soft, pink face.

He was exhausted. The afternoon had started with a routine meeting with Kaltenbrunner, which would have been ordeal enough. But then his boss insisted Schellenberg accompany him to Himmler's office to greet the grand mufti of Jerusalem. It was not a convivial discussion. The mufti was enraged. He had recently learned that the Muslims in Germany's Bosnian division were receiving alcohol and pork rations same as other soldiers fighting for the Reich. This must stop, the mufti insisted. It was a violation of Allah's precepts. Elaborate apologies were offered, as well as fawning assurances that suitable rations would be issued to the Muslim troops. And that should've been that, Schellenberg had thought. But to his dismay, the conversation with the valuable Middle Eastern ally dragged on and submissively on. All Schellenberg could do was sit in weary frustration, a pleasant smile fixed on his face, while keeping the contrarian thought to himself that no one had forced the Bosnian soldiers to drink the forbidden beer or eat the offending ham.

And now it was the evening after a weary day. Schellenberg was sitting in a pleasant private salon at the Eden, a glass of Canaris's carefully selected wine in his hand, the odious Kaltenbrunner nowhere in sight, and he felt he could at last begin to relax. He'd come to the hotel at the admiral's invitation, and he waited patiently to hear what the Abwehr chief had on his mind. The wine was delicious; he was in no hurry.

Canaris, playing the polite, genial host, allowed the conversation to ramble for a while before he came to the point. The Abwehr radio room had received a transmission from Iran, and it was very good news: the first stage of Operation Franz—the code name of the Oranienburg mission—had been successfully completed. Four Skorzeny-trained SS commandos had parachuted into the hill country near the rural village of Siah Kuh. The next day they would begin to make their way to Tehran to track down Mayr—code name Max. If all went according to plan, the attacks on the Allied railway shipments would soon begin.

And there was more. Operation Anton, the insertion of the Abwehr team into the mountainous tribal region to rendezvous with Schulze-Holthus, the admiral announced with some ceremony, was ready to be launched. It would be only a matter of days before a Junkers Ju-290 took off from the Crimea with the Lake Quenz commandos aboard.

Schellenberg listened, and just like that, all his previous fatigue vanished. He tried to make sense of his emotions. This had been his operational vision. He had carefully nurtured the incipient idea and then set the plan in motion. And now it was moving successfully forward! One team was in Iran, another would soon be heading out. He was elated. After suffering through the daily downward spiral of this wretched, losing war for so long, Schellenberg at last had something to celebrate. It would be a vanity to believe these commando missions would alter the doomed trajectory of the war. He was no starry-eyed true believer; he read the frontline intelligence reports that arrived with an increasingly mournful solemnity each day at his headquarters on Berkaerstrasse. But tonight he could not help himself. After seeing things one way for so long, he was filled with a sense of pride, of accomplishment, even, rarest of all in these dark days of the Third Reich, of possibilities.

THE SPYMASTERS TOASTED THEIR SHARED success. A bottle was drained, and, on Canaris's haughty command, another promptly appeared.

But later—no one was looking at his watch; time had its own careless tempo that evening—Colonel Hansen took control. Schellenberg had been wondering why Canaris had brought him; Hansen had no role in the Iranian missions. He waited with interest as the Abwehr colonel reached into his briefcase and removed a thick file.

These are cables, Hansen said, according to several accounts of that memorable evening, from our agents in the field. Each one authoritatively reveals the exact day and location of the meeting among Churchill, Roosevelt, and Stalin to plan the Allied invasion of Europe.

The colonel paused theatrically, and Schellenberg waited for the inevitable punch line.

They're all different, Hansen finally revealed, not at all pleased. He went on: According to the definitive—the word bristling with irony—information we have received, the conference will take place in Alaska. Or Newfoundland. Or Africa. Perhaps Egypt. It will happen in August. Or September. Maybe October. Or possibly not at all. So much for our vaunted networks, he complained with exasperation.

Then, as if the two Abwehr men were working from a prearranged script, Canaris made his move. "It is a priority for Hitler," he said. "The Führer does not want to be surprised—again."

Hitler had received no advance knowledge that Churchill and the American president would be meeting at Casablanca, the admiral revealed. And he never had expected Roosevelt to announce his demand for an unconditional surrender. "Why was I not warned? What good is my intelligence service?" the Führer had ranted accusingly for perilous weeks on end to Himmler and anyone else who happened to be within his circle.

Canaris fixed his gaze lavishly on the young SS general. Then he spoke: Hitler has ordered the Abwehr to discover where and when the meeting of the Big Three will take place. And if we cannot? The Führer has made it clear that failure is not an option he will tolerate.

I need Section 6's help, he implored, as several accounts of the conversation confirm. We worked together on the Iran missions. We put competition aside. I'm asking you to work with me once again. Section 6 has agents all over the world. Give them the order. Tell them to beg, borrow, or steal. Work with me to obtain the intelligence the Führer demands and that Germany needs—the date and the location of the Allied summit.

How can what transpired next be explained? No doubt Schellenberg was still basking in the reassuring boost to his spirits the news of the successful launch of the Iranian mission had provided; the war might be lost, but there were still battles that could be won. It can also be assumed with a similar persuasiveness that Canaris's beseeching request, the specific intelligence that he had just demanded, played its part in directing the path Schellenberg's mind began to take. Then, too, his trip to Lake Quenz had not been that long ago; the entire experience was still fresh, the tides of memory still running strong. And perhaps the celebratory alcohol played a part, the wine encouraging fanciful thoughts. But while Schellenberg never shared what prompted his reminiscence, what he said was noted and remembered.

He related with a fieldman's precision the dialogue between teacher and pupil that he had overheard while sitting in the back of Holten-Pflug's classroom at the Abwehr training camp. (At the time, he'd been catching his breath, trying to climb back up to steady ground after his unnerving experience with the gun-pointing commandos, but Schellenberg decided it was not necessary to share this, too.) Without prelude, then, he plunged into his account. He told it mildly, and slowly. It was as if he was trying to convince not just Canaris, but also himself.

"Fifty men! That's all I need," Holten-Pflug had said, according to the tale Schellenberg told (as well as the memory, still indelible years later, of the very student he had been lecturing). "Fifty men who are able and willing. Men who have the courage and the know-how to storm their way into the right places, the places where the orders come from—Washington, London, Moscow. One small bullet from one small revolver can do more damage than a whole regiment of artillery. What would the common Russian soldier do if Stalin suddenly disappeared? Would he go on fighting, do you think?"

The student, skeptical, challenged his teacher. "You don't think that if Churchill or Roosevelt disappeared others would come forward to fill the gaps? How about the generals? After all, they do the actual fighting."

Holten-Pflug did not back down. "The generals?" he had repeated scornfully. "Don't make me laugh! Theirs are no better than ours. They just sit on their backsides at the card table all day, safe and sound in their own quarters. Have you ever seen a general on the actual battlefield?"

When he finished recounting the conversation, Schellenberg offered no further comment. There was no persuasion, no coercion. The challenge was out there, and its historic implications filled the room.

THEN SCHELLENBERG OFFERED HIS OWN operational critique of the mission he had not yet even dared to articulate. He laid out the obstacles with the dispassionate objectivity of a veteran intelligence analyst, and each was an irrefutable fact.

Fact: Neither the Abwehr nor Section 6 had any idea where or when the meeting of the Big Three would occur. And this knowledge, as Canaris had already conceded, would be difficult, if not impossible, to obtain.

Fact: Even if Germany somehow managed to learn in advance the date and location of the conference, the three leaders collectively controlled the largest military machine in the history of the world. They would be protected by an immense security force.

Fact: If a commando team attacked, if they found the courage to attempt to plow past the guards, they would be mowed down before they could get near their targets. A frontal assault would be a suicide mission. And stealth would be impossible.

Once he had laid it all out this way, flatly, with a professional's neutral judgment, not even Schellenberg was prepared to put much stock in his own wild thoughts and the heights to which they had initially led him. The two Abwehr men were also adamant. The conclusion was clear: It could not be done. There was no possible way to assassinate the Big Three at their summit.

But nevertheless, on that evening in July the first seeds had been planted. The possibility, however remote, of Germany's bringing the war to a conclusion with a reasonable peace, a settlement without the vengeance of an unconditional surrender, had entered these intelligence chieftains' minds with a sudden jarring thunder. And despite all his misgivings and doubts, Schellenberg could not repress a goading memory: a commando bravely promising against seemingly insurmountable odds to "hot it up."

In Washington, Mike Reilly's world, too, was filled with thoughts about, to use the Secret Service's deliberately detached language, "high-priority targets." In fact, he had "made a rather exhaustive study of the history of assassination." With the war, he'd say, "the Reilly interest in the ancient art of assassination increased considerably."

There were many ways to kill a man, he'd discovered, and presidents were like other men—only they had more enemies. But his "intensified research into the history and technique" of presidential murder had led him to focus on the two most effective methods—by gun or by bomb.

Statistics made a convincing case for the effectiveness of gunfire. "To date," Mike had found, "we Americans have shot and killed one out of every ten men we have elected president." Count the close calls, and the numbers were even more disheartening: "We have fired with intent to kill upon one out of every five men who have lived in the White House."

But a bomb was, potentially, an even more dangerous weapon. "The business of protecting a man from gunfire is complicated enough, but it is the very essence of simplicity," Mike knew, "compared to outwitting bomb experts who can throw, hide, or mail their deadly weapons with ease."

In the end, though, either a gun or a bomb could get the job done.

And Mike had no doubt that the Nazis had teams of expert marksmen, and laboratories filled with inventive bomb makers.

These were his constant fears as the complicated diplomatic negotiations continued to arrange a meeting among the Boss and Churchill and Stalin. The date, the location—nothing had been resolved. For Mike these were merely operational details. Every bone in his being was alert to the prospect that wherever the summit occurred, whatever the date, the Nazis might very well be coming after the man he had vowed to protect with, if it came down to that, his own life. The enemy could come with guns, or with bombs, but no matter what they chose, he would make sure they failed.

15

I T WAS TESTIMONY TO THE tentativeness as well as the secrecy
with which the spymasters proceeded that their next conversation about a mission targeting the three Allied leaders occurred
once again at a meeting ostensibly convened to discuss the progress
of the Iranian expeditions.

It was three weeks later, a sultry August in Berlin, and this time
it was just Canaris and the Section 6 head, and they met in Schellenberg's office. For the session, Schellenberg revealed to his guest
that he'd turned off all the microphones; there would be no tapes
of their conversation. He presented this as a courtesy, one spymaster
showing respect to the head of a fraternal intelligence organization.
But both men were shrewd enough to grasp the tacit message—
they could talk freely about anything, and without fear of repercussions. The teams on the ground in Iran were given short shrift, and
the two spies plunged without much delay into the matter that had
been occupying their thoughts since their initial oblique discussion.

It was not a time for illusions. Or for faith in miracles. Both
men had no false hopes about the many difficulties—no, the
impossibilities—that surrounded the sort of mission they were at
last daring to discuss in earnest. They also realized that failure, especially in the backbiting Reich, always cast an opprobrious shadow on
those responsible, and in its aftermath the consequences could turn
decidedly more dire. Yet they were professionals who understood
that the intelligence service that refused to take risks, that walked a

narrow, smoothly paved path, was not doing its job. And they both loved their country. They detested the rapidly approaching inevitability of Germany's being completely broken, brought to its knees, by the Allied demand for an unconditional surrender. If there was a way, however unlikely, for the Fatherland to avoid such a devastating outcome, honor and duty demanded that it be explored.

In this way, the heads of Germany's two intelligence agencies became, in effect, the case agents for the plot to murder the Big Three. Their first practical steps, therefore, were to get the bureaucratic preliminaries out of the way: the terms of their intra-agency co-operation needed to be formalized. This was accomplished after surprisingly little negotiation. "With a view to the extreme importance and absolute priority of the plan in question," they agreed:

One: The Abwehr and Section 6 of the RSHA would exchange all available information and make every effort not to block the other service's intelligence-gathering activities.

Two: Both organizations would alert their field agents and assets that information about the timing and location of the tripartite meeting was of the highest priority.

Three: Members of the teams would be selected from both the Lake Quenz and Oranienburg special-action duty lists, and merged into a separate unit.

Four: Since it was likely that the conference would occur in either Russian-, American-, or British-controlled territory, commandos fluent in either Russian or English would be essential.

Five: The tactical departments of both organizations would work together to provide, and if necessary create, the optimal weapons and explosive devices required for the mission.

Six: The selected commandos would begin training without being informed of the specific nature or aim of their mission. Further, the identity of the targets would not be revealed until the operation was launched.

With the broad parameters in place, one more bit of housekeeping remained: the operation needed a code name. Oddly, this task proved the most contentious. Canaris, a stickler throughout his long career, took the position that secrecy must be paramount, and that sensible, if not self-evident, concern became the backbone of his argument. The Iranian ops, he began, had originally been referred to as simply *Ferneinsätze*, or "long-range operations." And what is the one fact we know with certainty about the Allied conference? That it will take place beyond Germany's borders, he said, politely answering his own question. The assassination mission, therefore, will undoubtedly be a long-range enterprise. In the interest of the strictest operational security, the admiral argued with gusto, the preparations should be designated as Ferneinsätze Alpha.

Schellenberg understood the admiral's caution. As the war teetered toward disaster, loyalties had grown more pragmatic; he had no doubt double agents lurked in the ranks of the SD, perhaps even in the offices at Berkaerstrasse. Nevertheless, Schellenberg, who had his showman's side, could not find any sympathy for such a lackluster code name. The mission being considered was the most audacious intelligence operation of the entire war, arguably in history. He was not willing to have it branded with such a pale, downright banal code name.

It was, he countered with a vehemence that threatened to turn uncharacteristically aggressive, something more than a mere long-range operation. It was much, much more ambitious. It was—and he appeared to find the word in a moment of spontaneous inspiration—a long jump (*Weitsprung*).

And the name stuck. From that moment on, the mission to assassinate the three Allied leaders was officially called Operation Long Jump.

BUT IN THE HIGH CHURCH of espionage, a christening did not signify that an enterprise had been brought to life. It still required, both spymasters readily conceded, a long jump of the imagination to believe the mission would be anything other than stillborn. The familiar obstacles remained very much intact, and there was not the slightest prospect that these formidable walls could ever be scaled: an unknown location, on an unknown date, and three targets who were the best-protected men in the world. They weren't just pessimistic about Long Jump's prospects. They were resigned to its failure. And in their secret hearts, both men believed it was more likely than not that the entire endeavor would never get out of the training camp.

Nevertheless, in the aftermath of that meeting, Schellenberg took one further step that had not been discussed with the admiral. It was motivated neither by security nor tradecraft, but by self-preservation. All he would need, he feared with sound reason, was for Canaris, or for that matter anyone in the Abwehr, to mention, however casually, Long Jump to Kaltenbrunner before the self-important chief of the SD had been informed of the discussions by his own underling, and Schellenberg's head would be on the chopping block, perhaps literally. Taking care to downplay the endeavor, presenting his efforts as merely exploratory workings, he gave his boss an oral report on how far things had progressed. Schellenberg might have been a scientist sharing a wild hypothesis that, while compelling, could never be proved.

To his consternation, the always mercurial Kaltenbrunner was intrigued, even, albeit in his guarded, political way, encouraging. Still, Schellenberg had not anticipated that the SD head would pass the information up the chain of command to Himmler. Or that the Reichsführer, in turn, would brief Hitler. And not only was the Führer bursting with excitement at the prospect, but he proposed a new mission objective: rather than liquidating the three Allied leaders, he wanted to kidnap them.

When Schellenberg heard this, his reaction was pure fury. The Long Jump commandos would have sufficient challenges in getting close enough to their targets to put a bullet between the eyes or a bomb under a desk. How could Hitler give any serious thought to the possibility of a team swooping in right under the noses of the Allied guards, grabbing the three men, and then racing back to Germany with their captives—all with a few divisions or so of Allied soldiers hot on their trail?

A talk with Canaris brought his overheated temperature back down to normal. This was just another of our beleaguered Führer's wild proposals, a priority one day and then forgotten the next, the admiral promised.

Schellenberg thought about that. Then, as if conceding the admiral's point, he shared the tale of Hitler's sending him off to kidnap the Duke and Duchess of Windsor. With the passage of time, he managed to turn the entire mission, as well as his own seesawing mood, into something farcical.

Exactly, Canaris shot back. In the end the Führer had let that foolhardy scheme flutter away. Sit back, keep your mouth closed, and this bit of grandiosity will die its natural death, too, he counseled with solid confidence.

Now lifted from his doldrums, Schellenberg made another stab at humor. He shared a fantasy of FDR, Churchill, and Stalin locked in a cage and forced to listen to a stream of the Führer's histrionic tirades.

The two spies shared an illicit laugh.

Yet both men were unaware that another of Hitler's impulsive schemes—a kidnapping plot, too—was already in the works. Or that before long they would be following in its large operational footsteps.

16

MONG THE MANY COINCIDENCES THAT can be found in the files of the covert history of Operation Long Jump are the parallel events that occurred on July 26, 1943. For it was on the very day when the two spy chiefs had their first meeting at the Eden Hotel that Adolf Hitler also began to tread in similar territory. He, too, had inaugurated the planning for an adventurous, and by all reasonable expectations, impossible mission. Further, in what would prove to be an even more significant concurrence, in his opening move that summer afternoon Hitler had reached out, just as Schellenberg had when he'd started, to the head of the Oranienburg special action school—SS captain Otto Skorzeny.

"COULD IT BE CONNECTED WITH Operation Franz?" Skorzeny would recall wondering in the first moments after he'd received the perplexing news that he'd been summoned to the Wolfschanze, Hitler's secluded headquarters deep in the woods of East Prussia. But he swiftly dismissed the notion; it seemed implausible that the Führer would want a personal briefing on a run-of-the-mill mission like the one in Iran. Instead, his "brain was plagued with useless queries," and no good answers. And on that sunny late-July afternoon when he boarded the Junkers Ju-52 parked at Templehofer airfield, he was gripped by a nagging fear: in the Reich the bill for past sins, whether real or merely perceived, might be presented at any moment.

There were twelve seats on the plane and no other passengers, and he had no idea whether that was reason for encouragement or not. But there was a cocktail cabinet at the front of the aircraft, and he helped himself to a glass of brandy. Then another for good measure. Skorzeny's nerves began to soothe, the plane lifted off, and he tried to prepare himself. He would be standing for the first time face-to-face with Adolf Hitler, the Führer of the Reich and the supreme commander of the Wehrmacht.

A big Mercedes was waiting when the Junkers touched down. A drive through a thick forest led to a checkpoint, and after credentials were presented the car continued along a narrow road edged by birch trees. Then a second barrier, another demand for identification, and a short drive to a tall barbed wire fence. When the gate opened, the car followed a winding drive surrounded by low buildings and barracks; the structures were covered with camouflage nets, and trees had been planted on the flat roofs of many of the buildings for additional concealment. From the air, it would look like just another Prussian forest.

It was dark when he arrived at the Tea House, a wooden building where, he was told, the generals took their meals. Skorzeny was brought to a drawing room spacious enough for several wooden tables and upholstered chairs. A bouclé carpet, dark and plain, covered the planked floor. He was made to wait, but in time a Waffen-SS captain appeared. "I'll take you to the Führer. Please come this way," he requested.

Another building. Another well-furnished anteroom, and this one bigger than the previous one. On the wall was a pretty drawing of a flower in a silver frame; he guessed it was a Dürer. Then he was led through a hallway into a large, lofty space. A fire burned in the hearth and a massive table was covered with piles of maps. A door abruptly opened, and with slow steps Adolf Hitler entered the room.

Skorzeny clicked his heels and stood at attention. Hitler raised his right arm out straight, his well-known salute. He was dressed in a field-gray uniform opened at the neck to reveal a white shirt and black tie. An Iron Cross First Class was pinned to his breast.

When he finally spoke, it was in a deep voice. "I have an important commission for you," Hitler announced. "Mussolini, my friend and our loyal comrade in arms, was betrayed yesterday by his king and arrested by his own countrymen."

Skorzeny quickly tried to recall what he had read. Benito Mussolini, the Fascist dictator who ruled Italy with a heavy hand, had arrived for an audience with King Victor Emmanuel of Italy. No sooner had he sat down than Victor Emmanuel had bluntly announced that the Supreme Council had asked the king to command the army and take over the affairs of state, and he had accepted. A shaken Mussolini left the palace, only to be confronted by a captain of the carabinieri, who directed him to a Red Cross ambulance. The rear door opened—to reveal a squad of police armed with submachine guns. At gunpoint, the now former Italian dictator was shoved inside. The ambulance drove off, its destination a secret, as was Mussolini's fate.

Back in the present, Skorzeny listened as the Führer grew more animated. "I cannot and will not leave Italy's greatest son in the lurch. . . . He must be rescued promptly or he will be handed over to the Allies. I am entrusting to you the execution of an undertaking which is of great importance to the future course of the war. You must do everything in your power to carry out this order. You will need to find out where Il Duce [literally, 'the Duke,' the title the Italian Fascist movement had bestowed on Mussolini] is, and rescue him."

At attention, Skorzeny kept his eyes locked on Hitler. He felt himself being drawn in, carried along, he'd remember vividly, by "a compelling force."

The Führer went on without pause. "Now we come to the most important part," he said. "It is absolutely essential that the affair should be kept a strict secret."

The longer Hitler spoke, the more Skorzeny fell under his spell.

"At that moment," the SS captain would explain, "I had not the slightest doubt about the success of the project."

Then the two men were shaking hands. Skorzeny bowed and made his exit, and as he walked out the door he could still feel Hitler's eyes boring into him.

YET ONCE HE WAS BACK alone with his thoughts in the Tea House, Skorzeny's previous confidence turned to sand. His nerves were "in a pretty bad state" and hundreds of questions seemed to be screaming in unison in his head. So he forced himself to concentrate, to think like a soldier. "Our first problem," he told himself as he worked to regain control, "was to find out where Mussolini was." Only no sooner had he focused on that problem than another immediately rose up. "But if we managed to find him, what next?" he asked himself. "Il Duce would certainly be in some very safe place and extremely well-guarded. Should we have to storm a fortress or a prison?" His ranging mind "conjured up all sorts of fantastic situations," and none of them were consoling.

Still, he reined himself in. Drawing on years of discipline, he started to make a list. He'd need fifty of his best men, and they all should have some knowledge of Italian, he began. Set them up as nine-man teams, that would be manageable. Then he considered weapons and explosives. Since it was a small force, it would need the greatest possible firepower, he told himself. But in the next moment he ruled out heavy artillery; they might have to drop by parachute. Instead, he decided, they'd have to make do with only two mounted machine guns for each team. The others would be armed with just light machine pistols, but that was a lethal-enough weapon when fired by a marksman. And explosives? Hand grenades, of course. And while thirty kilograms of plastic explosives should be plenty, he also made a note to get the British-manufactured bombs that the SS had scavenged in Holland; they were more reliable than anything distributed to the Wehrmacht. All sorts of fuses, too, both long and short running, would be needed; there was no way of predicting the battle plan, so they'd better be prepared for any eventuality. Then they'd need tropical helmets and light underclothing; you wouldn't want to be traipsing around Italy under the burning summer sun in long johns. And food, of course, had better be requisitioned. Rations for six days and emergency rations for three more should keep the men going. If that wasn't enough, well then, the chances were that they would be on the run from the Allies in enemy territory, and eating would be the last thing on any of their minds.

When Skorzeny had completed his list, he found the radio room so he could send it off to his headquarters in Berlin by teletype. Then he returned to the cot that had been made up for him in the Tea House. It was well after midnight, the end of an exhausting day, but he could not sleep. "Turning over and over in bed," he'd say, "I tried to banish thought, but five minutes later I was wrestling with my problems again." The more he picked away at the mission, "the poorer seemed the prospect of success."

Unknown to Skorzeny, on that same long night across the Reich in Berlin, Schellenberg tossed restlessly in his own bed as he mulled remarkably similar tactical problems. He, too, could reach only a despairing conclusion.

IT WAS A DEMANDING TIME. He left it to his adjuncts to keep the force in fighting trim, ready for whatever physical demands the mission might require. As for himself, Skorzeny concentrated on a single objective: finding Mussolini. There was no point in planning an assault until they knew where Il Duce was held captive. He needed to solve one mystery before he could even begin to grapple with the next.

"All sorts of rumors were flying about as to where Mussolini could be found," he discovered, and he had no choice but to chase after each of them. A grocer had heard there was "a very high-ranking

Howard Blum

prisoner" on the remote penal island of Ponza. An Italian sailor turned informant was certain he was interred on a warship cruising off the port of La Spezia. A postman sighted Il Duce in a heavily guarded villa on the island of Sardinia. And Canaris had gotten into the hunt, too, insisting the Abwehr had received reliable intelligence establishing that Mussolini was being kept in a makeshift prison on a thin strip of an island off Elba. But none of these panned out. After three futile weeks, Skorzeny fumed, "we were back at the beginning." And when Hitler summoned him once again to reiterate that "my friend Mussolini must be freed at the earliest possible moment," his already low mood nose-dived even deeper. For an egotist like Skorzeny, failure was the worst fate that could be imagined.

But as he was preparing to give up all hope, he received an intelligence report detailing a car accident involving two very high-ranking Italian officers in the Abruzzi mountains. What were they doing up there? Skorzeny wondered. It was a long way from the fighting, or, for that matter, from any military installation.

When he followed this trail, Mussolini drew closer. And at last a plan for his rescue started to take shape.

THERE WERE TWELVE GLIDERS, and the idea was that they would swoop in for their soft landings as if on cat's feet, and that way the teams would have the benefit of surprise. It wasn't a carefully worked-out plan, and there were too many uncertainties, too many unknowns, a dozen things that could easily go wrong. Skorzeny knew his chances of pulling it off were "very slim." He doubted that his men could overpower the guards before Mussolini would be executed. But he had considered all the other possibilities, and this was the only one that held even a trace of promise.

Il Duce was being held, he had finally verified to his satisfaction, in a ski resort perched on top of a nearly seven-thousand-foot Apennine mountain. A single cable car ran from the valley up to the summit, and a detachment of heavily armed soldiers stood guard around the station, while carabinieri had blocked off the approaching road. The Hotel Campo Imperatore, where Mussolini was being held, might just as well have been a fortress: solid brick, four stories, and at least a hundred rooms—and Il Duce could have been in any of them. Added to that, about 150 soldiers, as best as the intel reports could estimate, had dug in on the mountaintop and were guarding the hotel and its only guest. With a nod of professional praise, Skorzeny had to give the Italians credit. If he had wanted to keep someone safely hidden away, this was what he might've done. No, he conceded, this was even better.

His admiration for the Italians' shrewdness grew as he tried to work out a rescue plan. He quickly ruled out a ground assault. Making their way up the steep mountainside would be a running battle, and with the enemy firing down from fortified positions, a losing one. Surprise would be the first casualty. There'd be such a racket of gunfire and explosions, he imagined, that it'd be heard in Rome. The Italians would have all the time they needed to scurry off with Mussolini, or, equally likely, shoot a bullet straight into his head.

The more he thought it through, the more the element of surprise became essential. The mission would be a gamble, and this would be, he said, his "trump card." So he had considered a parachute attack, his commandos jumping from planes. But the Luftwaffe experts ruled it out. At that altitude, in the thin air, the men would drop from the sky like lead weights, slamming into the ground. And those would be the lucky ones—jagged rock formations lay scattered all about the mountaintop, projectiles as sharp as swords.

By default, gliders would have to do. Only that required a big, level landing field where the craft could come down after their towing planes had cut them loose. The closest thing the surveillance photos offered was a foggy glimpse of a triangular meadow not far from the hotel. The Luftwaffe wise men quickly vetoed that, too. A glider landing at this altitude without the assurance of a well-prepared landing ground was sheer folly, they insisted. At least

80 percent of the troops, according to their prediction, would be wiped out when the light craft careened about the rocky meadow. There wouldn't be a sufficient force remaining to storm the hotel.

Skorzeny took his time before responding. "Of course, gentlemen," he said at last with a careful politeness, "I am ready to carry out any alternative scheme you may suggest."

In that way, the decision was made. And on September 12, 1943, at about one in the afternoon, the gliders began to drop out of the sky and come down in a rush, the wind shrieking. A gust caught one of the craft, and it fell as if shot out of the sky, pounding into a rocky slope and smashing into pieces. Another two were blown far off course. And Skorzeny's glider came down in a nose-first crash that bounced the shattered machine about as if it were a stone skimmed across a pond. But when he pulled the bolt and climbed out of the exit hatch, he saw that he was only about twenty yards from the hotel.

Of the fight that ensued, there's not much to say, because it was not much of a fight. The shocked sentries put up their hands in surrender on Skorzeny's command, and the team rushed into the entrance hall. On instinct, Skorzeny chose a staircase and leaped up it three steps at a time. He started flinging doors open, and on the third try he found Mussolini guarded by two Italian soldiers, who were hustled out of the room. The entire assault had taken four minutes at most.

A small Fiesler Storch plane, with its single propeller and long wings, had landed on the now secured mountaintop, and Mussolini climbed into the only rear seat. There was no room for another passenger, but Skorzeny was not about to abandon his charge (or the triumph that would be his when he presented his hard-won prize to Hitler). He somehow managed to fit himself into the cramped space behind Il Duce. The overloaded plane had to struggle to rise into the air, but just when it seemed that it had reached the end of the plateau and was poised to nose-dive into the gully below, it caught a gust and climbed high into the blue sky.

Three days later Skorzeny and Mussolini were having midnight tea with the Führer at the Wolfschanze. Hitler awarded the SS commando the Knight's Cross and promoted him to major (Sturmbannführer). "I will not forget what I owe you," the Führer promised him in a burst of emotion.

Paul Joseph Goebbels, the Reich minister of propaganda, made sure that the world, too, would not forget what Skorzeny had accomplished. The front pages of newspapers throughout Germany offered up suspenseful accounts of the daring mission, and for once the Nazi reporters could stick to the facts, because the truth was sufficiently extraordinary. A short newsreel film was produced, widely shown to applauding audiences, and Skorzeny's handsome smiling face became quickly known all over Germany. Even the papers in the United States and England had to admit that the Nazis had pulled off a remarkable success. Their headlines announced that Skorzeny was "Europe's Most Dangerous Man."

But arguably it was Goebbels himself, writing in his diary, who best caught the full impact of the moment. "This action has made the deepest impression throughout the world," he wrote. "There has not been a single military action since the outbreak of the war that has shaken people to such an extent or called forth such enthusiasm. We may indeed celebrate a great moral victory."

OF COURSE, SCHELLENBERG ALSO FOUND himself contemplating what Skorzeny—the very man he'd selected to train the SS commandos for the Iran missions—had accomplished. In his mind he followed a direct line that led from a raid on an impregnable Italian mountaintop to the assassination of the Allied leaders. And it left him filled with hope. He now had the evidence that encouraged him to feel that despite all odds the impossible could indeed be accomplished. If Skorzeny could manage to pull off one miracle, well, why not another? For the first time Schellenberg found himself believing that it could be possible to kill FDR, Churchill, and

Stalin in a single covert operation—and in the process alter not just the outcome of the war, but also the peace.

Yet before too long, all his usual misgivings attacked. The imponderables were enormous: He had no idea where the three-party conference would take place. Or when it would occur.

Without this crucial intelligence, nothing would ever be possible. If he didn't know the time, if he didn't know the place, if he didn't know any of the specific operational pitfalls that lay in his path, then no team of commandos, even one led by the likes of Skorzeny, would have a chance. If, if, if. A litany of ifs, each one a question without an answer.

17

IN THE EARLY AUTUMN OF 1943, as the leaves in Washington and Berlin began to turn, the identical mystery consumed both Mike Reilly's and Walter Schellenberg's thoughts: Where and when would the meeting among the three Allied leaders take place? The answer would help determine whether the fate of mankind would be handed over to statesmen—or to assassins. To complicate the matter, the frustrating truth was that the three Allied leaders still had no idea of the answer, or if, in fact, they would ever have one. "No one who did not live through it," Churchill would complain, the memory turning him petulant even years later, "can measure the worries and complications which attended the fixing of the time, place, and conditions of this, the first conference of what were then called the Big Three."

The agenda to be discussed was nothing less than the grand design for the final push of the war—where and when the United States and Britain would launch their invasion of Europe. And while the three leaders all acknowledged how consequential this decision loomed, there was little agreement on how to proceed. Roosevelt envisioned a bold, sustained push through France, but at a propitious time, only after a fearsome invading army and an armada of ships and landing craft had been assembled. Churchill favored caution, a strategic toehold in Italy and then a methodical drive up into the heartland of Europe. And Stalin, whose country had been locked in a remorseless life-and-death struggle against the Nazis for years, one in which the scale of the suffering was vast and unconscionable, with a death toll that had already climbed into the millions, and whose troops continued to fight on heroically, demanded that his allies move with speed to alleviate the pressures and burdens weighing on his homeland. And as if this was not enough to resolve, FDR had a visionary (if not recklessly wishful) scheme on his mind, too. He felt he could put an end to future chaos by reaching a personal understanding with Stalin that would reconcile Western democracy with Communism. Basking in this warm spirit of fellowship, the two superpowers of the future would work together to keep the world's rascals in line.

With such historic stakes, it might have seemed as if the logistics of the meeting were minor matters, mere housekeeping tasks that would be expeditiously ironed out. FDR, who on his sunny days glowed with a hail-fellow optimism, certainly started out feeling that way. With a winsome confidence he cabled Stalin, "I am placing very great importance on the personal and intimate conversations which you and Churchill and I will have, for on them the hope of the future of the world will greatly depend." But Stalin was in no rush to sit down with the two leaders, and, more of a hurdle, he wanted the meeting on his own terms.

Was his obduracy driven by the demands of the war, by his having to keep close watch on the battles on his western front still being fought? Or was it motivated by a deeply ingrained conviction that the American president and the British prime minister were no less his philosophical enemies than his former ally Hitler, and they deserved to be treated with capriciousness? Then again, as some have suggested, perhaps it was simply that he had a profound fear of flying and was determined at all costs to avoid a long flight from Moscow. In the end, it might just as well have been the dictator's self-possessed nature; he was, after all, a man accustomed to getting his way. Yet whatever the strands of reason and character that weaved together to form Stalin's mercurial moods, the result was clear: Stalin was set on putting FDR and Churchill through their paces.

A prolonged courtship began to play out.

LIKE EAGER SUITORS, FDR AND Churchill first tried genial accommodation to sway a reluctant heart. The American president was a wide ocean away from the European continent, unable to walk, and, although the youngest of the three at sixty-one, hardly in robust health. A wartime journey promised to be a fatiguing hardship, and it might very well take an even more profound medical toll. For Mike, whose job was to ensure the president's well-being, the mere contemplation of such a trip was a holy terror. But as much as he would have liked to have the final say, it was not his decision to make. And the Boss was stoically game. After Stalin had tersely dismissed Alaska and London as sites, FDR quickly sent a cable offering up what he thought was a more than generous compromise. "I personally could arrange to meet in a place as far as North Africa between November 15 and December 15," he cabled the Soviet leader early in September.

Stalin was not persuaded. He had his duties, he explained with a sentinel authority. There was, he pointed out as if his were the only troops deployed in active combat, "the situation on the Soviet-German front where more than 500 divisions are engaged in fighting in all, and where the control on the part of the High Command of the USSR is needed almost daily." He followed this up with a suggestion that he undoubtedly knew would infuriate those who were courting him. "It would be expedient to choose as the place of the meeting the country where there are representation of all three countries." "For instance," he went on mischievously, "Iran."

Iran? A journey of more than six thousand miles from Washington across oceans and continents, and in wartime, when every mile held unpredictable dangers? FDR for the first time fully realized he was negotiating with a deliberately cantankerous principal. Nevertheless, still the avid suitor, he tried to placate Stalin with a calming reason.

"The problem of my going to the place you suggested is becoming

so acute that I feel I should tell you frankly that, for constitutional
reasons, I cannot take the risk," he began smoothly. "The Congress
will be in session. New laws and resolutions must be acted on by
me after their receipt and must be returned to Congress physically
before ten days have elapsed. . . . The possibility of delay in getting
over the mountains—first, east bound and then west bound is insurmountable."

At this point, a man of lesser patience might have switched tones,
curtly reminding Marshal Stalin (or Uncle Joe, or more simply UJ,
as Churchill and Roosevelt had, like naughty schoolboys, taken to
calling their worrisome ally) that the site he had proposed was four
times as far from the White House as it was from the Kremlin. But
FDR, his eyes fixed on all that needed to be done, clung to the high
road. As helpful as any travel agent, he obligingly threw out alternative destinations, each one holding the promise of a swell time.

"In many ways Cairo is attractive," he wrote with a hearty enthusiasm, "and I understand there is a hotel and some villas out near
the pyramids which could be completely segregated."

Or perhaps the marshal was looking for something less exotic,
free of supercilious distractions? "Asmara, the former capital of Er-
itrea, is said to have excellent buildings and a landing field—good
at all times," the president offered.

For that matter, sea breezes could be quite restorative: "There
is the possibility of meeting at some port in the Eastern Mediterranean, each one of us to have a ship. If this idea attracts you we could
easily place a fine ship entirely at your disposal."

Then again, roughing it had its charms, too: "Another suggestion is in the neighborhood of Baghdad where we could have three
comfortable camps with adequate Russian, British and American
guards."

And while the president waited with a weary yet dignified silence for Stalin to reply, Churchill chimed in, and had some whim-
sical fun in the process. "I have a new idea about EUREKA [the
code name for the proposed conference]. . . . There is a place in

the desert. . . . We could put up three encampments and live comfortably in perfect seclusion." There was, he went on with a vicar's pedantry, precedent for such a distinguished gathering. "See also meanwhile St. Matthew Chapter 17 Verse 4," he pointed out helpfully.

The president's wranglers broke this code, and conscientiously added the plaintext as a footnote to the cable: "Then answered Peter, and said unto Jesus, Lord, it is good for us to be here: if thou wilt, let us make here three tabernacles: one for thee, and one for Moses, and one for Elias."

But the Soviet dictator was not tempted by alternative locations. He would not budge, and he left it to Vyacheslav Molotov, his foreign minister, to relay his thoughts. "The question of any other place than Tehran was a most difficult one," he announced, taking a diplomat's refuge in understatement.

In case either the president or the prime minister hadn't caught the inflexible point he was making, Molotov, still playing the straight man, drove it home with a subtle bit of troublemaking. It might be possible, he threw out, "to postpone the meeting until next Spring . . . at which time Fairbanks might be an appropriate place."

Which was the identical location Roosevelt had suggested four months earlier—and that had been summarily rejected.

IN BERLIN, SCHELLENBERG HAD NO knowledge of the push and pull of these negotiations. But he remained determined to find out what he could: Long Jump's only operational hope depended on his discovering the date and location of the Big Three's conference. With so much at stake, Schellenberg, like FDR, was willing to swallow a bit of pride, as well as his usual common sense. When Himmler announced he had a plan to ascertain what the Allies were up to, he listened, bottled up all his instincts to declare it preposterous, and instead agreed that it was worth a try. It was, after all, a time in the Reich when desperation held sway over reason. Menace was in the air.

An order, therefore, was sent to the commanders of several concentration camps and then read to the inmates in German, French, and Russian:

"The SS Reichsführer and the chief of the German Police seek experts in occultism, palmistry, and radiesthesia [a process, like dowsing, that attempts to locate buried objects] for a confidential mission highly important to the security of the Reich."

There were about eighty volunteers culled from the camps, and it was a ragtag collection—scheming charlatans, wily professional entertainers, as well as true believers who had convinced themselves they possessed a gift. Himmler personally selected the most promising and called them into his office for the final test.

"A few people are about to meet," he asked according to an interview Jean-Jacques Beguin, a French hypnotist, gave after the war. "Who are they? What are their names?" Himmler demanded, the questions his first test.

There were deep, ruminative silences, which were invariably followed by wild guesses about the identities of the "few people." Through luck or inspiration, several of the participants managed to deduce that the question involved the Allied leaders. The others were summarily removed, and then the Reichsführer moved on. "Tell us where and when the meeting is about to take place," he asked with an unmistakable eagerness.

In response, an eclectic variety of answers, some nothing more than nebulous clues, others boldly specific, were offered.

Himmler, impressed and keen, passed this heaven-sent intelligence on to Schellenberg, and one by one the spy chief ruled out each location. In the end, he came to the dismal conclusion that he had no idea where the Big Three would meet. And without this necessary intelligence, he was in the same frustrating position as Mike: he couldn't do his job.

The difference, however, was that while one man's aim was to protect the Allied leaders, the other's was to assassinate them.

AS THE NEGOTIATIONS CONTINUED ALONG the same tedious and discouraging path, FDR's suppressed anger began to rise until at last it welled over. He had had enough. He was done kowtowing to Stalin. He could no longer see the point of demeaning himself—or his republic—to satisfy the overreaching whims of the Russian dictator.

"I am deeply disappointed in your message received today in regard to our meeting," the president began in a long, testy letter delivered to Stalin. The communiqué built to a firm and definitive conclusion: "The possibility of Tehran is out because I find the time risks are flatly impossible to take."

And with that, not only was Tehran once and for all dismissed as a site, but the very possibility of a meeting of the Big Three also went up in smoke.

18

A s the negotiations among the Allied leaders continued to play out contentiously in the shadows, the Most Dangerous Man in Europe was busy searching for a golden gun. Otto Skorzeny, basking in the hero's acclaim he'd won for liberating Mussolini from his mountaintop prison, had returned to his duties at the Oranienburg SS commando school only to find himself quickly wrapped up in the practicalities of procuring a solid-gold Walther PPK pistol. Except now the man Hitler had applauded as a "magician" was having a difficult time working his magic.

The gun itself was easy enough; the semiautomatic pistol, an accurate and menacing weapon, was standard issue throughout the German military—even the Luftwaffe's pilots carried a PPK in a holster dangling from the belt around their waists like American cowboys. But the manufacturer, Carl Walther firearms, had patiently explained that even if gold bars were delivered to its factory for smelting, its makeshift wartime workers weren't alchemists. They simply didn't have the machinery or the expertise to fabricate a solid-gold pistol. And prying the gold out of the SS's coffers was also no easy task. It didn't matter that a mountain of gold had been confiscated from the treasuries of the conquered territories, from the jewelry and life savings of deported Jews and other undesirables, and even from the fillings yanked from the teeth of the dead who had been murdered in the camps. The SS hierarchy was set on holding on to its tainted fortune; its leaders were already thinking about funding the new identities and new lives they'd need once the victorious Allies began hunting them down. After knocking on too many doors throughout Germany and having little to show for his efforts, Skorzeny realized he had no choice but to swallow his enormous pride. He reached out to Schellenberg for help.

Schellenberg had not earned his general's stars on the battlefield, but rather in the trenches of the SS bureaucracy, and as a veteran of this barbarous combat, if he knew anything, he knew how to get things done in the Reich. With an efficient alacrity that left Skorzeny filled with admiration, Schellenberg issued a flurry of edicts, then reinforced those commands with succinct written orders, and the result was a clicking of heels followed by a snappy chorus of "*Jawohl, Herr General.*" The vaults opened wide and gold was provided. Next, the craftsmen (aided, according to one report, by an expert found in the Sachsenhausen concentration camp) of Section 6's F4 unit, the makers of all sorts of inventive SD spy gadgets, put their ingenious minds and skills to the problem. About two weeks later an SS staff car delivered a solid-gold Walther PPK to the grand, turreted eighteenth-century *Schloss* that Skorzeny had recently christened as his new headquarters, just down the road from the original SS commando school.

The Most Dangerous Man in Europe weighed the pistol's heft in his hand, admired its bright yellow sheen, and was filled with delight. He had his gift fit for a king—or, more precisely, a tribal chief.

The chief was Nasr Khan, the mighty ilkhan of the Qashqai, arguably the most powerful man in Iran, leader of 600,000 nomadic tribesmen, commander of a standing army of 20,000 warriors, and beyond doubt the richest man in the country, his Aladdin's treasure trove of gold, silver, and precious gemstones making the shah a pauper by comparison. Since the days of Genghis Khan, the Qashqai had sat around fires in their tribal compounds across southern Iran and listened to tales glorifying the courage and fighting spirit of their cherished ancestors, brave and skillful horsemen who had charged into battle and, against all odds, brought Timur and the Mongol hordes to their knees. And now as the European war crossed the borders into their land, the campfires rang with a new tale calculated to excite the hero's blood coursing through their veins—the story of a poisoned razor.

It was a tale of betrayal, and the British were the masterminds of the deceit. According to the story every Qashqai knew by heart—and whether it was the whole truth or spun from embroidered cloth no longer mattered; repetition had bestowed an impeccable imprimatur—Reza Shah had extended an invitation to the illustrious Ismail Khan, the ruling ilkhan's father, to the palace. He never left alive. The shah, acting on orders from the British, who feared Qashqai raiders would terrorize their oil fields, locked Ismail Khan away in a remote dungeon. The British, however, were not placated; as long as he was alive, the ilkhan remained a threat. And so they conceived a plot that would ensure his death. Ismail Khan, even in the dank, dark depths of the shah's prison, remained fastidious, as a man of his station should be. He demanded a razor so that he might attend to his toilette. His jailer consented—only the razor provided had been embedded by the perfidious British with a fast-acting poison. Ismail Khan died before completing his shave.

In retaliation, his vengeful son was waging a guerrilla war against the British soldiers who occupied southern Iran. High-pitched war yelps echoing across the desert sands, rifles blazing, scimitars slashing, Nasr Khan's army had left a British force of 1,900 soldiers in tatters, the shaken survivors retreating in panicked disarray.

A warrior who rode to the sound of the guns, Nasr Khan was a man after Skorzeny's own heart. And he was a chieftain who would wage Germany's fight in Iran. The Abwehr agent Schulze-Holthus, after he'd been forced to go to ground when the Allied forces had marched into Iran and put a price of 5 million tomans on his head, had taken refuge with the Qashqai. He had been serving as a sort of military adviser and confidant to the khan, and, with his reports back to Berlin, he had helped plan the first Anton mission.

But that had just been a preliminary operation, and one without any strategic accomplishments. Now a new parachute drop—Anton Two—was being planned. Both Schellenberg and Skorzeny envisioned that these SS commandos would at last launch the sabotage attacks against the Trans-Iranian Railway carrying the invaluable American Lend-Lease shipments to Russia. And they wanted Nasr Khan and his fierce men on horseback, brothers in the struggle against the Allies, to lead the way.

The leader of the mission, SS captain Martin Kurmis, would jump out of the Junkers Ju-290 with a rucksack strapped securely to his back containing 200,000 British pounds and a golden Walther PPK. These would be gifts from Hitler Shah to Nasr Khan, homage that would hopefully cement the ilkhan's allegiance to the Reich. The British banknotes were counterfeit, the handiwork of the busy Operation Bernhard (an SD project that originally had been designed to undermine the British economy, but after 1942 had been scaled back to simply provide funds for Section 6 missions) engravers interned at Sachsenhausen. But Schellenberg and Skorzeny, reportedly sharing a snide laugh, figured the chief would never notice; and anyway, where was he going to spend the money? Besides, the golden gun was genuine, and that should be sufficient to win any warrior's heart.

IT WAS THE SECOND-HAPPIEST DAY Schulze-Holthus had experienced in the past two very difficult years. The happiest had been back in May 1941, when the Abwehr agent, full of schemes and dreams, had begun his residency in Iran under the diplomatic cover of vice-consul in Tabrīz.

Today, though, in his hideout in the foothills of southern Iran, he felt nearly as triumphant, and for the first time in years, optimistic. Nasr Khan had brought wonderful news.

"Four Germans were dropped in our region by parachute," the chieftain announced. "They have brought gold and dynamite, and a message from Hitler Shah to Nasr Khan." Then, pausing as he searched for the right words, he added, "and funny poles." It was a moment before Schulze-Holthus realized, to his considerable joy, that these were radio-transmitting antennas.

The unexpected news ran through the customarily constrained veteran spy, he'd recall, "like an electric shock." The timing was a godsend. It had become increasingly apparent that the ilkhan was growing disenchanted with the Reich, openly questioning whether the Nazis would ever march into Iran to wrest control out of the Allies' hands. "Do you think that the outbreak of an armed rebellion in the Qashqai region," the chieftain had recently challenged in a low growl, "could hasten the German invasion? Could it be the spark to set off a decision of the German Army Command to invade Persia at once?"

At that moment the spy could have added one more lie to a career in which falsehoods were the occupational currency. But for reasons he couldn't easily identify—whether the cascade of German battlefront losses had drained him of hope, or he had simply lost the deceiver's art during his years with the tribe—for once this ruthless man who had spent a lifetime in a ruthless profession found himself blurting out the truth.

"Your Highness," he replied gravely, "I do not think that a local event such as the revolt of the Qashqai would alter the basic plans of the German General Staffs."

But today the Germans had come! How foolish he'd been to give up hope. This was the invasion he'd no longer dared to anticipate. He mounted his horse and drove it hard. Twenty or so miles away he found the camouflaged German camp. Tents had been pitched in a nook of a rock outcropping, a clandestine site shaded by the long, dense shadow cast by a steep cliff.

The proud Abwehr captain who'd never abandoned his post vaulted from his horse and, with some ceremony, introduced himself to his countrymen. The conversation did not go well at all.

It did not take the old spy long to realize that these SS men were nothing more than thugs, head bashers by temperament and training. They possessed neither the careful instincts nor the subtle tradecraft required for a dangerous, secret life behind enemy lines. Kurmis was a captain, yet he was in the weary veteran's eyes just a child, in his early twenties, at least half Schulze-Holthus's age. But if he'd been a decade, even two decades, older, the Abwehr spy would have had no patience for a lout like him. What can you say to a man like Kurmis when he solemnly tells you "an order is an order, and Reichsführer-SS Himmler looks after our conscience"? How can you respond to him when he brags, "We've had special training with Skorzeny in Oranienburg. We've been very well trained in blowing up oil pipes and pumping stations"? Didn't the SD realize that "playing it that way," these sort of strong-arm tactics, was a mistake? That their ambition was too narrow, wildly shortsighted? Where were the professional fieldmen, the agent runners who could inspire the tribesmen? Men who could win over their ancient souls, get them to pledge their reckless courage, and instill the new faith needed for an all-out rebellion? "I was disappointed and depressed," the old-world Abwehr agent recalled, more crestfallen than when his day had begun. He rode away from the doctrinaire SS men even faster than he'd ridden toward them.

Time proved Schulze-Holthus right. The commandos' bullish ways and swagger alienated the Qashqai from the start, and on Nasr Khan's orders they were kept under close guard by thirty stony tribesmen, each armed with a sword and rifle. The SS men spent their time doing endless calisthenics, cleaning and recleaning their weapons with a scrupulous Germanic attention, and drinking rivers of arrak. The tedium of tribal life was too much for Kurmis: the doctrinaire SS man committed suicide.

On its operational merits alone, then, Anton Two might have escaped from even a mention in this history of events. But in its small, seemingly inconsequential wake, there were several accomplishments that only later would claim Schellenberg's attention and be given their full due. For one, the mission had demonstrated that a Skorzeny-trained commando team could be successfully inserted into Iran. For another, the Germans had succeeded with their "funny poles" in setting up a radio transmitter; it was now possible for Berlin to communicate with Schulze-Holthus. And equally significant as things would work out, Nasr Khan was very grateful for his golden gun. And he was a man who always repaid a kindness.

19

THEN THERE WAS THE FRANZ TEAM. From the tribal encampments in the foothills of the South, it was a four-day camel ride across harsh country to the bustling capital city—nearly a million inhabitants and growing—of Tehran. It was in this lively metropolis, as a disillusioned Schulze-Holthus waged his prickly verbal war with the SS brutes, that the other remaining German stay-behind agent tried to infiltrate the Operation Franz commando team into his clandestine world. But while there had been a procession of problems, Franz Mayr—the SD agent code-named Max—had not anticipated that he'd wind up chopping the body of one of the saboteurs into pieces, stuffing the arms, legs, and torso into a couple of valises, the head into a rucksack, and then burying the remains in an overgrown field outside the city, just off Varamin Road.

The Franz mission—Schellenberg's and Canaris's initial wildcat insertion scheme—had seemed doomed from the start. They came in blind, as the parachutists would say, on a moonless night without bonfires blazing to illuminate the landing site or a welcoming party to help them make their way. Mayr had sent a message through German sources in Turkey suggesting a drop at the foot of the Siah Kuh hills, a vast, congenial expanse of flat, green fields about sixty miles from Tehran. The six parachutists missed the drop zone by tens of miles. And straight off they were fighting for their lives.

They had landed in black mud. The twisting shoreline of Kavir

Masileh, a great salt lake, seemed at first glance hospitable, a silty mix of sand and salt that would guarantee a soft landing. But directly beneath this cushion lay a deep, dark primordial ooze that could swallow camels whole and then, for good measure, devour their engulfed riders. The natives called this quicksand-like morass "black mud."

It was only teamwork, as well as a surge of desperation, that got them through. As one of the commandos began to sink, mud up to his knees, then suddenly reaching his waist, then climbing up to his shoulders, the others, who had somehow managed to extricate themselves, formed a human chain. With a great tug, one final exertion of will energized by sheer panic, they at last pulled their comrade to safety. The fate of their supplies was not as fortunate.

The Junkers Ju-290 crew had shoved a bountiful payload out of the cargo door of the high-flying plane. It was an inventory carefully designed by the owls in the Section 6 planning section to sustain a sabotage campaign in enemy territory: nine machine pistols, six revolvers, one sniper's rifle, more than fifty pounds of gelignite, four long-range radio sets, one receiver, four generators, about $20,000 in American currency, 600 gold francs, and, a fortune that could if necessary pave the way out of most any jam, about 2,200 gold sovereigns. The black mud had claimed the lion's share of this trove, and what had survived lay scattered for miles across the adjacent desert.

But the commandos were alive. Now they could confront the next daunting problem: they needed to rendezvous with their control, Franz Mayr. After consulting maps, they realized that they'd landed not just off course, but bafflingly off course; Tehran was perhaps two hundred miles away. A scorching desert stretched between them and the city. And if they could somehow survive the journey, there still was the challenge of finding a single furtive spy in a city of one million. They had no idea where Franz Mayr had gone to ground, or how to contact him.

Yet they were soldiers, and they had no choice but to forge on.

They'd head off across the desert as a team; as the black mud travail had demonstrated, when unexpected problems occurred, it'd be a godsend if they were in it together, able to work in unison to handle things. As their first night in the wilderness dragged on, a more thoughtful discussion killed this rash scheme. It was pointed out that there were six of them and that would mean buying or, if it came to it, stealing, six camels, and that was bound to attract attention in any village; the locals would rush to the authorities, eager to claim the reward they'd undoubtedly get for reporting a group of German-speaking soldiers. Provided, of course, that the British, Russian, or American troops scattered about the country didn't spot them first. In wartime the soldiers would shoot before asking questions; that's, after all, what they'd do.

Ultimately, only one possible plan made any sense. And for once luck seemed to be on their side. There was a man on the mission who could speak Farsi, had already mastered the cumbersome skill of riding a camel, had spent time in Tehran, and, although a Sudeten German, could pass in a pinch as a Persian. Corporal Karl Korel at thirty-eight was the oldest of the team, a rail-thin string bean of a man with a clerk's unassertive, diffident demeanor, a man who listened carefully and then took his time before answering in a voice hardly more than a murmur. But he was a veteran Abwehr agent, and his natural quiet had been good cover for a daring secret agent in the course of several sticky situations; he was the last man anyone would suspect as a spy. Add to this that he'd done an undercover stint in Tehran before the war, and, more good fortune, had spent some time years earlier with Franz Mayr—well, the plan, despite the weight of all the imponderables, seemed to write itself.

As the sun rose above the salt lake of Kavir Masileh, Corporal Korel set out in the new day's early light to make the long journey across the desert. His fanciful goal was to arrive in Tehran and then find one man among the million.

On grand boulevards and tucked into cobbled alleyways, Tehran was a city of cafés, some sprawling spaces, others just a single narrow room, but all deliberately shadowy haunts crackling with the energy of intense conversations, the stolid air at any hour wafting with hookah smoke and the pungent aroma of the nerve-jangling local espresso. Over a bowl of *dizi*, the bracing mutton stew thickened with chickpeas that the natives seemed to consume with gusto for at least one meal each day, or a glass of arrak with its sharp licorice bite, an afternoon could be pleasantly passed sitting on the terrace of the Naderi Café, sheltered by the red-and-white awnings that circled round Lalehzar Street. Or there was the Café Ferdowsi, with its murals celebrating ancient Persian heroes and where in the evenings there'd be readings of the *Shahnameh*, the kingdom's great epic tale, that'd continue on relentlessly despite the unremitting clamor at the tables. And for those wanting something more cosmopolitan, there was the Continental, with its glamorous, well-heeled crowd of dark-suited diplomats and self-satisfied Iranian officials, peddlers of influence and information, fingering their worry beads and sucking on their opium pipes.

Franz Mayr would spend a good part of his days and most of his nights floating in and out of the city's many cafés. They were his command posts. Experience had taught him that a secret spoken in public in a conversational tone would more likely go unnoticed than a confidence whispered during the course of a clandestine walk-and-talk on a deserted street; there was no telling who might wander by and what suspicions would then be sparked. Every spy who's played the game long enough settles on the tradecraft that becomes his handwriting, his routine for getting things done. It was across the tables in these crowded haunts, in full view of anyone who cared to notice, that the agent code-named Max would invariably schedule meets with the soldiers in his army of secret sources.

For Max had been busy. Although on the run, in hiding from the authorities since the Allied invasion, he'd not abandoned his secret life. Rather, with diligence, his charmer's skills, and a thick wad of foreign currency (albeit counterfeit, but that was his and his Berlin handlers' secret), he'd recruited an impressive collection of assets, or "Joes," as the old hands called them with a comradely fondness. He was as wired into what was going on in Iran, he'd boast, as the shah.

He had Ernst Merser, a steady Swiss businessman, the well-respected representative of a wide collection of American and European firms that did business in Iran, with his big Mercedes sedan and an impressive two-story villa on tony Kakh Street staffed by a collection of servants. Merser was a bachelor, short and portly, but he had impeccable manners, held his liquor, and could talk about anything with a fetching charm, and so he was invited everywhere. Even better, he had the gift of remembering whatever he heard. Whatever his motive—Money? Allegiance to the Reich? A daredevil need for danger?—he offered up a steady stream of intelligence product, some of which even had the added blessing of turning out to be true.

For muscle, there was Misbah Ebtehaj and the ragtag gang of hard cases who followed faithfully in his wake. Ebtehaj was one of Tehran's celebrities, a shrewd, iron-chested hulk who had won his fame as a Pahlevani athlete, the wildly popular brand of traditional hand-to-hand combat that demanded both a wrestler's brute force and a sufi's soul-searching spiritualism. Flocking around him, ready to spring into action on his command, were a motley legion of the *tsharukeshes*, who, as the word accurately conveys in translation, were quite literally cutthroats; the *garden koflot*, or street brawlers; and, always good for tantalizing gossip or working a honeypot operation, the *luty*, the city's pimps.

But Mayr's most cherished conspirator was Lili Sanjari. She was Iranian by birth, and when her widowed mother had married a prosperous German named Lange she had gone off to Berlin. By the time she returned to Tehran as a teenager, she was the well-educated product of both cultures—fluent in several languages, versed in history, physics, chemistry, and mathematics, could play

oompah on the accordion or concertos on the piano, and, as everyone she met couldn't help but notice, had grown up to be a doe-
eyed, raven-haired, fun-loving beauty. Working in tandem with
her friend Lucille, her assignment was, as she'd put it, to promote
"the propaganda angle," to flit about town spreading earnest tales
about how glorious life would be once the Germans came marching in.

Beyond Lili's operational value, however, there was something
else stoking the spy's interest in the twenty-two-year-old: she was
his mistress. But their long-running affair was more than just an
unbridled romp. Mayr wanted to marry her. He loved her. And Lili
loved him, too—in her fashion.

Whether it was because the spy talked of marriage but didn't
act, whether the prospect of being his bride had left her unsettled,
or whether perhaps her covert life simply had left her accustomed
to betrayal remains another buried mystery in this tale. But what is
known is that while Lili was spending nights with the SD operative, she was also spending afternoons in rented rooms around the
city cuddled next to a twenty-three-year-old American sergeant,
Robert J. Merrick.

Merrick, who was a transport clerk, played in a dance band, and
it was at a concert that the two music lovers had met. But while romances are often set in motion by fortuitous events, there are no ac-
cidents in the secret world. Merrick was also a spy, an Army Counter
Intelligence Corps (CIC) agent. His mission that first night was to
bump into Lili, strike up a conversation, and see where it might lead.
It led to rented rooms, double beds, and his conscientiously passing
on typed summaries of their pillow talk to his intelligence superiors.

Lili had no idea of the rippling pools of betrayal in which she
was swimming. And Mayr had even less of an inkling.

It was into this simmering world of spies, assets, and duplicitous lovers that Corporal Korel arrived. Straight from his marathon
camel ride across the desert, he walked into the Café Ferdowsi,
glanced about the room, and then, with a triumphant smile on his

sunburned, unshaven face, took a seat across the table from an astonished Franz Mayr.

KOREL WAS NO LESS ASTONISHED. In the course of his arduous journey across the broiling desert, he'd settled on a strategy. He knew Mayr's handwriting and so had made up his mind to visit every café in the city until he crossed paths with his handler. At the same time that he'd worked this out, he also realized that it was little more than a wild gamble. What were the odds of his showing up at the right café at precisely the right time? It was just as likely that their paths might never cross. But in the first café out of the dozens spread across the city that the corporal had decided to investigate, he found the man he was looking for.

Both men told themselves that their reunion was a harbinger of the larger successes Operation Franz's commandos would soon celebrate. And this prediction seemed accurate when the corporal, now driving a truck one of Ebtehaj's cohorts had rustled up, headed into the desert, found his comrades pretty much where he'd left them, and then brought them into Tehran without incident. On Mayr's instructions the commandos split up into groups of two, and each pair was shuttled off to a separate safe house around the city that had been scrounged by his network of agents; it would be more secure that way, he explained. And more careful tradecraft, he also insisted that they go slowly. Get a feel of the city, learn to move around and blend in as he had done; time spent on preparation is never time wasted, he lectured. Only after all the pieces were in place should they start watching the railroad, discover when the American shipments occurred, and make the important decisions about where to place their bombs and when to detonate them.

Then, just as they were preparing to move into action, to strike the first blow for Germany in Iran, Korel was struck down with typhus. At first it seemed like only a cold, but as if in an instant it grew into something more horrifying, the corporal wasting away before their eyes. Lili managed to find a doctor they could trust, but the doctor took one look at the ghostly pale man soaking in a river of his own hot sweat, and threw up his hands in despair. Without medicine, what can I do? the doctor pleaded, as agonized, Mayr felt, as if he were the condemned patient.

When Korel died it was no surprise, but still a shock. Mayr and the others were left reeling. Once again the mission had turned on them. Once again they began to live with the dispiriting suspicion that Operation Franz had been doomed from the start.

Before they could regroup, a new concern pushed their spirits lower. It was brought about by nothing more sinister than the prudent realization that unless they disposed of the body, either through cremation or a burial deep in the ground, a deadly typhus plague would spread with relentless determination across Tehran. But for spies behind enemy lines the tasks would be challenges. There was nowhere in the city they could set a match to a corpse without attracting attention. Nor could they cart a body out to the desert without the fear of being stopped by the police and being pelted with questions that they didn't dare to answer. Mayr resigned himself to the only feasible solution, and Lili, with a cold-blooded practicality, agreed to help.

Mayr did the lion's share of the hacking. He couldn't find a saw, and so he had to make do with a machete. It was gruesome, tedious work. There were so many pieces that Lili had to hurry home at the last minute to forage in her uncle's closet for an additional valise. But finally the dismembered corpse was ready for transport.

There was a deserted field out by Varamin Road just beyond the city where the spy and his young mistress had once lain together in the tall grass on a languid summer's afternoon, and now it became a burial ground. All the surviving commandos assembled to pay their respects. There was no ceremony; the fear of attracting curious stares was very strong. Their mute presence, they hoped, would demonstrate sufficient respect.

The team returned to their hideouts. The plan was to regroup, and then strike. But they could no longer find the will; it was as if part of themselves, whatever had remained of their fighting spirit, had also been buried in that lonely Iranian field. Two of the commandos headed off to the tribal areas; they had no plan beyond an eagerness to flee the city. The other three survivors spent their time being ferried from one safe house to another, shepherded all the time by the protective attentions of Mayr's network.

For weeks the commandos talked among themselves and to the others about the attacks they would launch, but they lacked conviction. No one was surprised when their shallow schemes never came to anything.

Ernst Merser, who once had great hopes for the Reich, for the crucial role he would play as a gentleman spy, grew resigned, too. In the anticlimax of the saboteur's plots, he decided it was his sad destiny to live on the far periphery of events, outside the flow of history. "Tehran was the last place in the world where I would have wished to bury myself till the end of the war," he complained to Mayr, who by then shared the identical belief. "Whatever happens or doesn't happen in Tehran, the fate of the war isn't likely to be decided here."

FOR THE MORE PRACTICAL SECTION 6 deskmen in Berlin, however, it was not so much the actual deeds as the long-term lessons that measured the success of a mission. They were willing to trade many losses for the prospect of a single stunning victory. Operation Franz, same as its brother expedition Anton Two, had established important capabilities, field experiences that could one day come in handy: a commando team had made its way to Tehran and managed to hide out in a labyrinth of safe houses without the authorities being any wiser. In addition—and this was a genuine accomplishment by any standard—a reliable network of capable, resourceful agents was already up and running in an enemy city. Schellenberg considered all this, and while he hadn't done all he'd set out to do, he nevertheless had a high sense of achievement. He had learned a lot, and now he carefully filed it all away, not knowing whether a day would ever come when he might have a reason to put this hard-won knowledge to some clandestine use. Espionage, Canaris had lectured in the course of one of their convivial morning rides through the Tiergarten, is a game like chess: you must always think several moves ahead. For the first time, Schellenberg was beginning to appreciate that wisdom.

Mike Reilly, on guard in the lower right-hand corner. In a single horrifying moment, he watched as a dagger flew straight across the platform toward the president. *Universal History Archive/Contributor*

Mike, the student of assassinations, and the commander in chief he was determined to protect. *Bettmann/Contributor*

Walter Schellenberg, the young SS general who headed Section 6 of RSHA. He knew the war was lost, but he had a desperation plan for winning the peace. *Bundesarchiv/Bild 101III-Alber-178-04A*

Ernst Kaltenbrunner, the head of the Reich Security Office. "From the first moment," Schellenberg wrote of his superior, "he made me feel quite sick." *Bundesarchiv/ Bild 183-H03554*

Franz Mayr, code-named Max, the Section 6 spy who went to ground in Tehran. *National Archives/KV2/1481*

Mayr and a commando team that had parachuted into Iran to "hot things up." *National Archives/KV2/1481*

Hitler Shah sends his greetings to Reza Shah, both proud Aryans setting out to build dynasties. *Truth Seeker, Fawiki*

The "Sacred Cow," the president's specially designed C-54. Mike wanted a plane that could fly through war zones—and provide the boss with a chilled martini. *Courtesy of the National Museum of the U.S. Airforce*

The Secret Service shooting range in the subbasement of the Treasury building. Mike insisted on frequent practice sessions, yet he knew that if the enemy came at the boss they'd be professionals, too. *Bettmann/Contributor*

Otto Skorzeny, the "Most Dangerous Man in Europe." *Popperfoto/Contributor*

Skorzeny's commandos had swooped in on gliders, landed on the summit of an Apennine mountain, and rescued Mussolini—a daring mission that paved the way for Operation Long Jump. *Bundesarchiv/Bild 101I-567-1503A-07*

Elyesa Bazna, the valet to the British ambassador in Ankara—and the German spy code-named Cicero. Or, Schellenberg wondered, was the walk-in a double agent? *Кашак/WikiCommons*

Roman Gamotha: the Nazis had sent him under deep cover into Iran, but when the spy returned to Berlin, he was secretly working for the Russians. *Bundesarchiv*

Below: Number 76/78 Tripitzufer, on the banks of Berlin's Landwehr Canal, was home to the Abwehr's technical wizards. *ullstein bild Dtl./ Contributor*

The versatile Gammon bomb. Mike Reilly had always feared the challenge of "outwitting bomb experts who can throw, hide, or mail their deadly weapons with ease." *CC BY-SA 3.0*

As a wily teenager, Gevork Vartanian headed the "Light Cavalry" that roamed the nighttime streets of Tehran for the NKVD. *Capital Pictures*

Flying from a secret base in Crimea, the long-range Junkers Ju-290s transported the Nazi parachute commando teams into Iran. *Bundesarchiv/Bild 141-2472*

With Nazi assassins on the loose in Tehran, FDR took refuge in the Russian Embassy. Only now, Mike worried, the brutes dusting the furniture had Lugers on every hip. *Imperial War Museum*

The Big Three seated on the steps of the Russian embassy—proud, imperious, with victory in their grasp. Or were they sitting targets? *Courtesy of the Roosevelt Library*

A *zurkhaneh*, a gymnasium where Pahlevani wrestlers trained—and Nazi assassins hid. *Pascal Mannaerts/Alamy Stock Photo*

November 30, 1943, Churchill's festive sixty-ninth birthday party. The celebration that Schellenberg hoped would become the night of the assassins. *Imperial War Museum*

20

SCHELLENBERG MOVED FORWARD ON MANY fronts. He did not allow his focus to be confined to the commando missions unfolding in Iran. Nor did he let his ignorance of where and when the Allies would be meeting hold him back. Instead, with an impressive steadiness of purpose, he continued all the while to push ahead with the planning for Operation Long Jump. Whether the scheme would ever amount to anything more than a preposterous project that would be filed away without ever breathing its first breath of operational life, he was not ready to predict. But the possibility it held remained staggering: the shape of the peace would be transformed. And hand in hand with a new postwar reality, his own foreordained future would be rewritten, too.

What choice, then, did he have? The Allies' demand for an unconditional German surrender had left no room for mercy. He had only to imagine the hard edge to the charges that would be hurled at him as he stood, subservient and deferential, in the dock before a scouring military tribunal: General Schellenberg had invested his life, had squandered his humanity, in the service of the Reich. How would he respond to that? Claim he was merely a witness, as much a victim of the madness as a perpetrator? Come Judgment Day it wouldn't matter to the victors that he had spoken up against what he'd branded the "excesses"—a timid word, he'd later concede—of the Einsatzgruppen on the eastern front. How could the hands of an SS general be anything but dripping with blood, they'd sanctimoniously argue (and not without reason, he knew in his secret soul). For his own sake, to keep the conqueror's hangman from tightening a noose around his own neck, he must try, he implored himself. And with that awareness, a grave and untenable fear rose up inside the spymaster: inaction would be death. Germany's only hope, his only hope as well, was to eliminate the three uncompromising Allied leaders.

Sitting in his stronghold of an office on the Berkaerstrasse, he decided there was no point in wasting more time on what he didn't know; this intelligence, for the time being—perhaps forever, he acknowledged in the next moment with a pang—remained beyond his grasp. With a brisk practicality he turned his thoughts instead to what he did know, to what he could anticipate with a reasonable certainty would occur when the three Allied leaders met.

He began, logically enough for a man planning an assassination, with security. An army would be assembled to protect the three principals. Armed to the teeth. On war footing. But no sooner had he locked this foreboding image in his head than he corrected himself: there'd be three armies.

And that got him thinking.

The politicians would be running things, not the security professionals. They'd have the final say on how their head man would be protected. Allies or not, it would run deep in their jingoistic blood to insist that *their* army, elite squads culled from *their* military, protect *their* commander in chief. Each of the states would cling to the patriotic credo that its own soldiers could do the job best. Which meant that the guards deployed would be as multinational as the leaders assembled around the conference table.

It was an arrangement that could only foster confusion. None of the three security teams would have previously worked in tandem. They wouldn't recognize one another; they'd be unable to tell at a glance if the armed soldier in the unfamiliar uniform across the room was an impostor or the real thing. Communication would be a problem, too. Things come crashing down, the ensuing ruckus would be a veritable Tower of Babel. The Americans and the British wouldn't be able to figure out what the Russians were saying, and vice versa. And from what he knew of these matters, despite their speaking the same mother tongue, English cockney or an American southern drawl could be just as incomprehensible to the uninitiated. These were elements, Schellenberg decided in a rare burst of confidence, he could exploit.

And with that, a first tentative scenario began to take shape. His initial thought was that he'd ferret through the Brandenburg rolls hunting for battle-tested Germans who spoke either English or Russian. Outfit them in the uniforms of the Allied armies and then get them up close to their targets. They could go in heavily armed, without even concealing their weapons, and it wouldn't raise an eyebrow; what could be more natural than gun-toting soldiers? How he'd get them to the conference room, well, he'd just need to deal with that later when—or if, he corrected himself—he discovered where the meeting would be held. So much was if, he silently groaned, and not for the first time.

Still, there was precedent, he knew, for that sort of false flag operation. Back in the beginnings of the war, in May 1940, commandos dressed in the uniforms of Belgian and Dutch frontier guards had led the way when the Low Countries were overrun. And he had been one of the masterminds of Operation Himmler, in which 150 German operatives disguised in Polish army uniforms stormed the Gleiwitz radio station, providing the transparent excuse the Reich legions required to goose-step into Poland.

Yet even as he worked to flesh out this initial notion, he found himself walking away from it. American, British, and Russian impostors? The sheer scale of his scheme compounded the problems. First he'd need to find soldiers who could convincingly pass as citizens from three separate nations. And, a heavier concern, he'd need men who could be counted on to get the job done when the guns started blazing; you go off to shoot the Big Three and only a fool would doubt that he was heading into a suicide mission. Not everyone had that manner of steely, fatalistic courage. Yet by casting a

wide net, looking for soldiers fluent in different languages, different national mores, impostors who could pass for the real thing,
he would increase the likelihood that he'd haul in men of dubious
quality. Add to that the need to infiltrate three separate teams in
the uniforms of three separate nations into the conference, and the
entire mission began to grow shaky under the weight of all the many
components.

Slowing down, he allowed his thoughts to regroup. He began
to reconstruct things, and in the painstaking process that followed
he found himself playing with new questions. Were three teams of
assassins truly necessary? he wondered. Would a multinational force
of impostors create more problems than operational benefits? Once
he raised those challenges, his mind began to wander in another
direction. And then he knew he had it.

ANDREY VLASOV MAY BE A traitor, but he was now our traitor.
That had been Schellenberg's unswerving professional assessment
since the day the previous March when the Russian general, after
his capture on the eastern front, had turned his back on the Bolsheviks and declared his willingness to lead an army of Russian defectors into battle against his homeland. The spymaster had blithely
accepted this conversion with an unjudgmental shrug; in a profession whose stock in trade was betrayal, absolutism had no standing.
And there was often much to gain. Years of experience had taught
him that changes of heart were the great romances of the secret
world; one nation's turncoat was another's secret source.

In fact, he'd already been sending Russian defectors back into
the fray as part of Operation Zeppelin. For the past year special
squadrons of the Luftwaffe had been inserting these newly recruited
deep-penetration agents along the entire length of the eastern front.
Their covert mission: "sabotage, subversion, and the collection of
information." Time after time, their exploits behind enemy lines
had Schellenberg admiring their courage and resourcefulness. "On

one occasion," Schellenberg would boast with a deskman's proprietary pride, "an agent succeeded in reaching Vladivostok with a troop transport. There he observed and sent back full details of certain troop movements."

And now as he wrestled with the tactical problems of Long Jump, his thoughts turned to the Russian Liberation Army that Vlasov had assembled. Here was an entire force, nearly one thousand strong, all defectors, many of whom had won battle ribbons fighting for their lives. But most promising of all, the rebuttal argument he returned to whenever his misgivings began to assert themselves, these soldiers wouldn't need to pass for Russians—they *were* Russians. They wouldn't be playing a part; this was their life. They were already even wearing Soviet army uniforms. Talk about natural cover, he applauded himself. If he could select, say, fifty of Vlasov's toughest—the sort who'd slit a throat as easily as they'd shake a hand—he might, just might, be able to get them close to the Big Three. Operational control of the mission would be held by a core group—a half-dozen? more? at this preliminary juncture he was unprepared to deal in firm numbers—of experienced Lake Quenz and Oranienburg commandos. But Vlasov's Russians would compose the bulk of the fighting force.

The more he pushed this scenario along in his thoughts, looking all the time for flaws, listening for the alarm bells to start clanging, the more he grew convinced: it could work. A squad of assassins, led by Germany's best, beefed up by Vlasov's Russians, would have a chance of getting close enough without attracting attention. And they'd never back down. They'd complete the mission, or die trying.

There was just one problem—Hitler.

The Führer had no faith in battlefield conversions. And in his spiteful world, the only thing worse than a traitor was a Russian traitor. "I shall never build up a Russian army," the Führer had ranted. "This is a fantasy of the first order." He wanted nothing to do with the deceitful Vlasov and his turncoats.

Schellenberg had encountered this problem even as he was reaping the intelligence rewards of Operation Zeppelin. A stern Himmler had summoned the spymaster to rant about the reliance on "unreliable" Soviet agents. "The burdens of your post," the Reichsführer had threatened, "are obviously becoming too heavy for you." It was, Schellenberg had said, "a very rough interview." Before it could turn disastrous, however, he had found the wit to fight back: he smiled at the criticism. And that bit of insubordination won the day. "Enfant terrible!" Himmler decided with a woeful shake of the head, and that was that. His wave of anger had passed.

Schellenberg, though, had little confidence that Hitler would be so easily assuaged or his wrath so quickly defused. Especially when the Führer learned that Vlasov's men—Russian traitors—would be at the fighting core of the most consequential German commando operation of the entire war. Schellenberg wondered how he could finesse this. Did he dare not inform Hitler of the entirety of his plan? Yet if he divulged the role the Russians would play, he knew it would take more than a smile for him to win this argument—and to save his job, perhaps even his life.

Then, as Schellenberg was weighing the risks of his rashness, Himmler ordered him to report. He went not knowing, as always, what to expect; either a medal or a bullet was always looming in the capricious Reich. One time the Reichsführer had handed over a photograph of Schellenberg's fiancée, but only after he had used a green pencil to circle her lipstick and eyebrows; "Exaggerated" he had written as his lone, yet brutal, accompanying comment. But there were no photographs this time. As things turned out, the Reichsführer wanted to talk about Skorzeny.

The Führer, he explained in his usual Bavarian twang, had grown to appreciate Major Skorzeny's capabilities. The rescue of Mussolini, of course, was miraculous, a triumph that brought glory to the Reich. But the Führer was also impressed with the Anton Two mission. Major Skorzeny had inserted a team into Iran. It was confirmed that the Führer's personal message to the tribal chieftain had been delivered. Correct?

Schellenberg agreed that this had been accomplished. But at the same time he wondered what Himmler was building to. Infuriatingly, his manner was rarely direct.

The Führer has a new mission for the major, Himmler revealed at last. "'There is but one man in the world who can carry it off,'" he quoted Hitler as proclaiming. He wanted Otto Skorzeny to command Operation Long Jump.

Schellenberg left the meeting convinced he had won two victories. The first was the more obvious: If anyone could get the job done, accomplish an impossible mission, it was the ambitious, daring, and ruthless Skorzeny. He'd be equal to the assassin's task. But, second, Schellenberg had also scored a personal triumph. The SS major now would be the focus of Hitler's mercurial attentions. The Führer would not press with questions about the composition of the rest of the team, and Schellenberg certainly would not bring it up. If Long Jump succeeded, if Roosevelt, Churchill, and Stalin were killed, it would be Skorzeny's name in the historic headlines. And if it failed, the fact that a crew of Russian traitors had also been on the ill-fated mission would be the least of his problems.

Yet Schellenberg also was very much aware that the risks he faced were unpredictable. "To decide to continue one's own line of policy in these circumstances required some courage," he would say, "for Hitler's sensitivity and pathological suspicion rose in direct ratio to the deterioration of the general situation." It would be wise, he knew, to be on guard.

21

THE TEN COMMANDMENTS," MIKE HAD wanted to call it, but by the time he was done, he'd wound up with thirteen rules, and "the Thirteen Commandments" struck him as sacrilegious, maybe even unlucky. So he'd given up on a title. Besides, once he reread what he'd written, he decided that a glib title would be a distraction. This was a serious topic, about as serious as anything could be with the world at war.

Like Schellenberg, he'd been giving some thought to the manner of men he'd need if the meeting of the Big Three finally happened. And while the German spy chief would be dispatching soldiers to do his bidding, Mike's concern was more direct: he was grooming agents who'd be at his side, men he'd need to count on should things turn bad.

It had taken Mike the good part of a week to enumerate all the criteria. First he'd written it all down in his loping cursive, finding the moments whenever he could grab them. When he'd finished, he went to the cubbyhole of a room where the White House's chief porter had a typewriter he often let Mike use. The room was just off the front door to the mansion, and so there were always a lot of people passing by, but Mike paid them no mind. The hulking, broad-shouldered agent sat like a colossus at the big wooden desk—how they'd ever shoehorned it into that tiny space always left him wondering—and banged away in his two-fingered way on the ancient Remington. He'd learned to type in this awkward fashion in college, and he'd become quite good at it.

When he was done, he reviewed his work. He had not completely known his mind till then. But now he did: he was preparing his men for battle.

Sure, he'd paid a lot of attention to personal bearing and comportment; he was the head of the detail, and he felt he needed to set the tone. A vision came back to him from when he had first joined the service. He had walked into the White House with no idea how to act or even what to wear; he was just some rube from the hills of Montana, he recalled with a self-critical twinge. He remembered being sent into the Oval Office, only no one had explained how close he should get to the president. Where should he stand? The president had to breathe, had his secrets, yet at the same time it was Mike's duty to be right there. There was a thin line between being watchful and being intrusive, and on that first day he'd had trouble seeing the boundaries. But he'd worked it out (and the process had been smoother than might've been expected, because the Boss liked him, and he liked the Boss). Now that he was in charge, he would make things clear. He paid a great deal of attention to these sort of details, and he wanted to make sure his men did, too. His nature was to have everything neat and tucked away. But he also knew discipline never lost a battle. And in a pinch it could help win one.

So he laid down the law. "Chewing gum, smoking or engaging in any form of horseplay while actively participating on a protective detail is not in order." And he staked out the locations of the minefields into which his men would be traipsing. "Agents must be quiet and unobtrusive in carrying out their duties. . . . Inspection of the buildings, grounds, and adjacent areas must be made frequently and thoroughly and should be made in such a manner as will not inconvenience the occupants or cause any apprehension on their part."

Then he also made it clear that despite the WARNING! signs he'd posted, there'd be times when his men had better be prepared to rush in, damn the mines. "Their presence should be known in such a way as to give assurance to the person being protected. They should avoid an attitude of undue humility or servitude." "Laxity and indifference. . . are to be guarded against with the utmost diligence."

With that bit of housekeeping out of the way, he moved to the heart of the matter: "The President is the Commander in Chief of the Army and the Navy, and because of the present war in which our nation is engaged the responsibility of each agent . . . has increased many fold. It is a grave responsibility."

And with grave responsibilities came sober qualifications: "Excellence in the use of firearms, the ability to think and act quickly and with sound judgment. . . . We must be alert sixty seconds every minute." And woe to the agent who didn't stay in shape, who complacently put on a few pounds. Mike wanted athletes, strong, intimidating bruisers carved out of mountains of granite, same as he was. "Agents should bear in mind their continuance on such details depends upon the degree to which they possess physical ability for the duty required."

Satisfied, Mike made copies of his manifesto and personally handed the pages to the agents who had gone with him to the Casablanca Conference. If the Boss managed to work out the arrangements for the meeting with Churchill and Stalin, they would be the core team. He wanted his men to be ready—"Primed," he'd repeatedly lecture—for such an unprecedented event.

It was only later that Mike would understand there'd been no way to prepare fully for what they were heading into. Except by then it was too late.

SCHELLENBERG, FOR HIS NASCENT MISSION, had a more succinct vision of the Vlasov Russians he required: he needed killers. And so he dispatched a killer to select them.

Major Hans Ulrich von Ortel was an excitable, aggressive, unscrupulous drunk. He stormed into battle with a smug murderousness and thought about little beyond his share of the spoils. Guilt was too complex and too natural an emotion to intrude into his savage life; he never, those who knew him suggested, had to suppress even a silent scream. With him anything was possible, and nothing was too much. He was, by all accounts, a model SS executioner.

As an officer in Einsatzgruppe C, Ortel had demonstrated his remorseless efficiency in a series of "police actions," to use the deliberately oblique language of the combat reports, across western Ukraine. The wretched truth was something more: time after time, Major Ortel's gloved fist had pounded on the door as the SS prowled through the Rovno Ghetto to round up "Bolshevik agents" and "Jewish functionaries" and lead them off never to be seen again. And when the decision had been made that the piecemeal elimination of Jews was insufficient, he'd been front and center as the entire ghetto—Fifteen thousand? Eighteen thousand condemned souls? In their zeal, the executioners didn't stop to count—had been marched to Sosenki Forest and lined up to stare helplessly into a fusillade of bullets.

The Jews of Rovno had been eradicated; only the ghosts of martyrs now floated through the smoke of the ghetto. However, Ortel, their persecutor, remained stationed at Rovno, recruited by the SD because he spoke Russian like a commissar. Schellenberg had used him to train the agents who'd been infiltrated into the Soviet Union for Operation Zeppelin, and, as part of his intelligence duties, he also kept a watchful eye on the partisans surrounding Rovno who were waging a guerrilla war against the Red Army.

This was the man Schellenberg summoned to Berlin. The spy chief thought the Russian-speaking SS major had the instincts he needed. Ortel, he believed, could peruse the ranks of the Vlasov army, talk to these Russians, stare them in the eye, take a reading of their dark souls, and then identify the men who could carry out an assassination mission. As for Ortel's other, more problematic qualities, the operation-oriented case agent in Schellenberg made the decision to ignore them.

Still, Schellenberg was sufficiently wary to share only generalities about the mission he'd been planning with his new recruit (and this was made easier because at this point he had few details). He told Ortel, according to one account of the meeting, "that he was to participate in an operation of primary importance, something like Skorzeny's action." Ortel would pick the Vlasov Russians who'd play a key role in this commando mission, and he'd also be involved in their training. The session concluded with the general emphasizing that secrecy was essential. Ortel was not to reveal his new assignment to anyone. Not a word, he reiterated. *Jawohl, Herr General*, the major staunchly agreed.

In the best of circumstances, Ortel's pledge was a capricious bond. When he was drinking, however, it completely dissolved. Returning to Rovno, sharing one bottle of kummel, then another, with his buddy Lieutenant Paul Wilhelm Siebert, a wounded veteran now stuck behind a desk working for the Reich economic organization that was plundering the Ukraine, Ortel grew excited. He was gesticulating, talking wildly, first in conspiratorial whispers, then nearly shouting, only to abruptly slip back into his previous furtive voice. He wanted his friend to know that he had "a big secret."

Siebert did not press. He simply refilled his friend's glass.

Finally, Ortel could no longer restrain himself. He revealed that he had been chosen by no less than General Schellenberg to participate in an action that would "decide the future of Germany." It would "change the outcome of the war."

It was only when Ortel began waving Otto Skorzeny's name about like a banner that Siebert interrupted.

"What about Skorzeny?" his friend asked. It was the most natural of questions.

Ortel was eager to boast. He'd been handpicked to be at Skorzeny's side on this important mission, he exulted.

Siebert now abandoned any pretense of disinterest. He badgered his friend for more details. Ortel, though, couldn't provide them. He had divulged all he knew.

But it was enough. His drinking buddy was a Russian spy.

Wehrmacht lieutenant Paul Wilhelm Siebert was dead, killed in action. The First Directorate of the NKVD, the Soviet intelligence organization that directed foreign clandestine ops from its offices in Moscow Center, had recovered his papers and passed them on to Nikolai Ivanovich Kuznetsov. And the graduate from the NKVD espionage academy in Leningrad had assumed the soldier's identity.

Kuznetsov was the perfect double agent. It wasn't that he could speak, thanks to his childhood in the Perm Mountains, a faultless German. Nor was it his actor's ability to assume the character the part demanded, whether it was the embittered bureaucrat drinking his way through the remainder of the war, or the swashbuckling staff officer who walked into a German command center to conduct a surprise inspection and left with a briefcase filled with secret intelligence reports. What truly distinguished Kuznetsov was his operational intuition, his heightened sense that a shred of gossip, a stray remark, a casual rumor, held the promise of valuable intelligence.

When he returned from his late-night session with Ortel, he transcribed his conversation. Then he sent a priority cable to his handler at the First Directorate. It was in this way that Moscow Center learned that the Nazis were planning a major commando operation, one in which the dangerous Skorzeny would have a part, and one that would accomplish nothing less than changing the course of the war.

The Soviet spymasters could only guess what it might be. But they were now on alert, eager to identify the unknown danger that was taking shape.

Not long after Ortel spilled his secrets, Schellenberg had another visitor to his office—and his arrival was a cause for celebration.

Roman Gamotha—the SD agent code-named Moritz who had gone into Iran with Mayr three years earlier, only to sink without a trace—had returned. He brought back with him to Berlin a breathtaking account of his great escape.

The essence of his tale—and even the full story was scarce on details—was this: When the Allies had invaded Iran, he said good-bye to Mayr and hightailed it north. He had a plan, admittedly vague, of making his way through the Russian sector to Azerbaijan, where he had some contacts, White Russians, who'd put him up. Before he reached the border, however, he was taken captive by a Soviet platoon. They roughed him up, hurled lots of questions at him. When he didn't break, they threw him into a Russian intern-ment camp. It was a rough confinement, hard work, low rations, and the constant threat of a firing squad. But after his imprison-ment had stretched on for more than a year, his jailers grew lax. He crawled under a fence in the dead of night and eventually made his exhausted way to Turkey. The Turks had kept him interned at their Yozgat prison for three months. Finally, with the help of the German authorities, he'd won his release.

And now he was in Schellenberg's office suffering from malaria, but nevertheless in good spirits and reporting for duty.

Gamotha received a hero's welcome. The SD rewarded him with 10,000 Reichsmarks (the equivalent of about $4,000). Himmler, in an effusive letter to Hitler, proposed the valiant secret agent ("he was repeatedly in great danger of his life") for an Iron Cross First Class, and the Führer swiftly granted it. The Propaganda Ministry arranged for a flurry of radio interviews and articles in the press so that the German people would learn of the steadfast courage of their loyal secret agent. As further reward, Schellenberg not only promoted Gamotha to captain, but also put him in charge of Sec-tion 6's newly formed Iranian desk.

There was only one problem with Gamotha's inspirational story—it was not completely accurate.

His narrative, up to the moment of his capture, was true. But once Gamotha had been face-to-face with his Soviet interrogators, the spy crumbled. First he told them everything he knew. Then the

Russians turned him. And finally they fed him back to the SD as a double agent.

Moscow Center now had reason to let out a secret cheer. They had succeeded in putting a mole into the operational heart of Section 6, the Nazi Security Service office that ran clandestine foreign activities. The only cause for disappointment, the Russian spy chiefs might have sighed, was that their agent had the misfortune to have been assigned to the backwater of the Iran desk, far from the more turbulent flow of the war.

22

NUMBER 76/78 TRIPITZUFER WAS SOLID STONE, a gloomy stronghold of a building rising from the banks of a spindly stretch of Berlin's Landwehr Canal. In the first heady years of the Reich, the Abwehr had moved in, and hundreds of busy, well-bred intelligence officers had orchestrated their furtive plots behind closed mahogany doors. In the hard-pressed fall of 1943, though, the grand spaces of this sober, neoclassical espionage headquarters were largely vacant. Nowhere in Berlin seemed safe, but the building's long, red flagstone roof may just as well have been a beacon signaling the location of a nest of enemy spies to the Allied bombers. Many of the top officials, including Admiral Canaris, had decamped to the relative safety of the concrete bunkers of the Zossen military complex south of the city. But some refused to be intimidated (or simply weren't given the choice), and among these diehards were the technical wizards of Abwehr II, the sabotage department.

It was a meeting with an Abwehr II specialist that had brought Otto Skorzeny to Tripitzufer in late October 1943. He needed a bomb.

There were many ways to assassinate a man (as Mike Reilly had learned to his chagrin in the course of his troubled yet compulsive investigation). But when Hitler had anointed the celebrated SS major to lead Operation Long Jump, that meant the killing would be done as Skorzeny thought best.

As Skorzeny moved ahead to shape a tactical plan, he was not encumbered by the large gaps in his operational knowledge. It did not matter to him—at least not at this stage—that he had no idea where the meeting would take place, whether it would be in a city, in the countryside, or even on a ship at sea. Nor was he bothered about his ignorance concerning when the Big Three's meeting would occur: the next week, the next month, or, for all he knew, the next year. Regardless of the location, regardless of the time he had to get the mission off the ground, he had known from the start how he'd get the job done.

"My knowledge of pain, learned with the sabre," he had said in an attempt to explain his aggressive battlefield credo, "taught me not to be afraid." "And just as in dueling when you must concentrate on your enemy's cheek, so, too, in war. You cannot waste time on feinting and side-stepping."

He would not sidestep his way through Long Jump. Skorzeny would not sequester himself on a rooftop with a sniper's rifle, an unseen hunter stalking his prey. He would not slyly poison the food or the water. Neither would he sit impassively next to a pilot at ten thousand feet and order "Bombs away!" Nor would he call in the coordinates for an artillery attack, then watch from a safe distance as the powerful 88s blew the Allied leaders to kingdom come.

The most significant commando operation of the war, perhaps even in history, would define his legend for all times. He was determined to kill the enemy as a warrior would. It was important to him that in their last moments Roosevelt, Churchill, and Stalin know that Otto Skorzeny had come for them. He would stare into their eyes, and watch them die.

And for that he needed a special bomb.

CANARIS HAD INSTRUCTED General Erwin von Lahousen, the Austrian-born aristocrat who headed Abwehr II, to arrange to have one of his senior explosives experts available for a meeting with Skorzeny. And, of course, Skorzeny's reputation had preceded him; his personal involvement made the importance of the forthcoming operation apparent. The specialist's full cooperation was assured. But there was also a significant restraint on the discussion: Skorzeny could not divulge the exact nature of the mission he'd be undertaking. Not more than a half-dozen officials—including the Führer—in the entire Reich knew about the plot to assassinate the Allied leaders, and maintaining that secrecy was essential. The mere rumor of what was in the works would have the Allies running to ratchet up their protective measures; perhaps they'd even rethink the wisdom of the three heads of state getting together in one place. Skorzeny, therefore, could talk only in a broad, deliberately circumscribed manner and hope that would be sufficient to convey the sort of weapon he needed. He offered a riddle, but with few clues.

Skorzeny began, according to the memories of those briefed on the discussion, by explaining that he wanted to attack a group of people. At close quarters.

OK, the expert agreed, an antipersonnel device. Are you thinking a concussion bomb? That would do the most damage in an enclosed space, generate the greatest number of casualties.

No, said Skorzeny. Casualties were not an option. He needed kills. His targets must be eliminated. It was of no concern to him whether the bystanders survived or not.

A fragmentation bomb, then, the expert decided. One that had a tight kill zone. He thought a minute and said he had an idea: the Goliath. It was a remote control device that ran on treads. Armored, virtually indestructible. Carried an explosive payload that would immobilize a tank. And it was relatively light—about 150 pounds.

Skorzeny said that wouldn't work. For one thing, it was too heavy. He might parachute in to the target area. Or possibly he'd be coming in by small boat. He was not sure at this point, but he needed to be prepared for any eventuality. He needed something lightweight. Easy to transport. And, although it went unsaid, he might just as well have added that he was not a soldier who did his killing by remote control.

Will you have a long window of opportunity? Time to detonate several bombs? the expert asked.

Skorzeny said he couldn't be sure, but he hoped he'd have time to make at least two attempts before executing his escape. Perhaps he'd have time for more. Then again, he quickly corrected himself, maybe there'd be just the single chance. He sounded, he must have realized, haplessly imprecise.

The specialist, though, continued in his matter-of-fact way; there is a natural companionship when professionals talk about killing. You will require a long-running fuse? he simply asked.

No, countered the SS major. He'd prefer if the device detonated instantaneously. Then he thought for a moment and once again overruled himself. A variable fuse would be better. He could not predict how much time he'd require, he disclosed.

And the explosive charge? Would the targets be in the open? Or in a vehicle? A room?

Skorzeny conceded that at the moment that, too, remained unresolved. In fact, he might not know the location of his targets until the day of the attack. He needed, he said not for the first time, to be prepared for several possibilities.

A heavy explosive charge would increase the weight of the weapon, the Abwehr specialist worried. Which could create a problem in transport. He played with this problem in silence. Then: What if the bomb had a flexible charge, if the amount of munition could be adjusted on the day of the mission to suit the operational circumstances?

That would work, Skorzeny agreed. He might have been talking to Wilhelm Holters, his tailor on Tauentzienstrasse who sewed his bespoke uniforms. The conversation had a similar polite, earnest quality. Only now he wasn't discussing the cut of his tunic. He was planning to murder three very important men.

The expert said he had a final question: Do you require the device to be relatively silent? Would that be necessary to facilitate your escape?

Quite the opposite, Skorzeny said. The louder the better would be preferable. He wanted panic. He needed the bystanders to be running for their lives, looking for safety. He'd make his getaway in the bedlam.

The expert asked for a moment to review all the requirements. When he finally spoke, he shared his conclusion with a pedant's authority.

What you are looking for, he said, according to several of the Oranienburg commandos who'd later been briefed on the gist of the discussion, is a grenade that is not a grenade. He explained that the typical grenade was a highly mobile weapon, easy to deploy, with a short-burning fuse. A soldier could throw one after another at the enemy—if he wasn't busy dodging bullets.

All the standard grenades, however, had drawbacks that made them unacceptable for the sort of mission that Skorzeny had outlined. The standard Nazi stick grenade, the famous "potato masher," was portable enough, and the trinitrotoluene charge would let off a powerful blast in a confined space. But if the target was in a car, particularly an armored car, its effect was more problematic. And it was a very temperamental weapon: in close quarters its detonation, or often merely the heat from the initial blast, could ignite the fuses of any remaining grenades the assassin had in his pockets. Then he could forget about getting a second chance; he'd be the one going up in smoke while the targets escaped.

The expert's lecture moved on to the Allies' Mk2 grenade. The regulation "pineapple," as the cast iron weapon was called because its grooved surface resembled the textured skin of the fruit, could be refitted with a Grenite mixture specifically manufactured for this mission, he said. That would certainly give the grenade more power and the sort of loud, resounding boom the op required. But there would be a standard delay of four to five seconds between pulling the pin and the explosion. And there was no way of altering the timing. Another problem was that the fuse let off a faint hissing sound when it started to burn, and that could alert the targets, give them time to—literally—run for their lives.

The 97 grenade used by the Japanese was quieter, but its fuse had an even longer delay. And in a rough-and-tumble parachute landing, or, to choose another operational possibility, while storming through a barricaded door, the weapon became unreliable. It had a very unstable firing pin; give it a good jolt and the primer was likely to initiate the explosive sequence. You'd have seven seconds to get rid of it. Of course, if you were in the middle of a firefight, then you might not even notice that the weapon had started arming itself before it was too late.

But just as Skorzeny was growing discouraged, his usual brimming confidence for once starting to ebb, the expert found a piece of paper and produced a quick, crude sketch. He drew what at first glance looked like a Humpty Dumpty–shaped creature, wide at the bottom and hips, with a cap on its small head.

It was a Gammon bomb, the expert explained. Named after its inventor, Captain R. S. Gammon of the British First Parachute Regiment. And it was a very ingenious and very effective hand-thrown weapon.

For starters, it packed a terrific punch. It was loaded with a newly developed RDX explosive that was many times more powerful than TNT. But, as Skorzeny had requested, the Gammon bomb's charge was flexible. The amount of munition it carried could be quickly and easily adjusted. There was a fabric bag—the wide hips of the bomb—under the screw-off cap. This bag could be filled with a small stick of the RDX explosive in addition to, if you wanted to intensify the lethal force in the killing zone, razor-sharp shrapnel projectiles. It would be the perfect weapon for eliminating the enemy in a small, crowded room. But if you filled the bag completely to the brim with RDX, you could take out a tank or, say, several targets in a large space, even if they were protected by a wall of troops.

The fuse was changeable, too. The device could be set to explode on impact. Or it could be set with a delay for intervals up to
five minutes. That could conceivably give you an opportunity to
plant the device before the arrival of one's targets and then sneak off
before the fireworks.

And it was lightweight, completely portable. Even when packed
with enough explosives to put a tank out of commission, the Gammon weighed little more than a pound. Plus, the wide bottom made
it easy to grip; it could be hurled with accuracy over thirty yards,
farther with a strong throwing arm and practice.

Skorzeny listened intently, and then asked one question: How
many Gammon bombs were immediately available? He did not
know how long he'd have before he'd need to launch his mission.
The timing depended on circumstances beyond his control, he said
with a soldier's resigned battlefield candor.

The exact number? The expert said he didn't know; he'd have to
make a call before he could answer that sort of question.

When he left the room, Skorzeny used the solitude to process
all he had learned. He began to visualize the attack in his mind.
The targets would be clustered together, perhaps sitting at a table,
perhaps eating dinner. They were old men, unable to run. Hell,
Roosevelt couldn't even walk. They would never escape from the
blast. At detonation, their bodyguards would be irrelevant, unable
to protect themselves, let alone their charges, from the salvo of
knife-sharp projectiles flying toward them.

Tactics quickly clarified; it was as if Skorzeny drew energy from
the process of coming to terms with the attack. Over the course
of just moments it took a hardening shape. He and his handpicked
group of commandos would have the responsibility of hurling the
bombs. The Vlasov Russians would handle the soldiers, and most
likely they'd be mowed down in the process. So be it; he had little
sympathy for any Russians, no matter to whom they pledged their
allegiance. All that mattered was that the Russians put up a fight.
He needed them to give his team time to get in and, God willing,

time to get out. They could do that. Especially if they were well trained, if their responsibilities had been drilled into them. Yes, he felt, his conviction building, with the Gammon bombs it could work.

There were two crates of Gammons at Zossen, the expert reported when he returned. He explained that the bombs had been recovered from a cache dropped into Belgium by the RAF for resistance fighters. The Abwehr had stumbled on them a while back. They had been stored away, sitting in the armory until a suitable opportunity arose for the bombs to be put to good use.

Skorzeny asked how many of the devices were packed in a crate.

Twenty-five, he was told.

A total of fifty bombs! Skorzeny rejoiced. That would certainly be sufficient for the Most Dangerous Man in Europe to become the Most Dangerous Man in History.

How soon can the crates be brought to my headquarters at Oranienburg? he demanded.

23

M IKE WAS A CRACK SHOT. Like many boys growing up in Montana, he'd become familiar with guns early on. He'd gone hunting with his dad as soon as he was old enough to carry a rifle, and as a nine-year-old he'd bagged his first deer, a ten-point white-tailed buck. But deer, he knew, did not shoot back. As he sensed the date was approaching for the Big Three meeting, he started making preparations for whatever dangers he might have to face.

In the subbasement of the Treasury building, just a short stroll down Pennsylvania Avenue from the White House, there was a shooting range. It had been built not long before Pearl Harbor, when it seemed increasingly likely that the Secret Service would soon be on a wartime footing, and its agents would need to be battle ready.

It was a small space, just three firing booths, but it had been well thought out, and for once money had been no object. The targets were electronically controlled; at the push of a button they could be set for seven or fifteen yards. The range was soundproof; high-intensity electric lights shielded with protective mesh lit up the subterranean gloom, and a constantly murmuring fan removed the gases from the expelled rounds with great efficiency. To enter the stalls, one passed through two heavy doors that closed with an airtight thud; the shooter was then locked in his own world.

That fall, Mike had started going to the range with some regularity, at least once, often twice, each week. Like every agent, he was armed with a Colt Police Special (twenty-eight dollars had been peremptorily deducted from his paycheck to reimburse the Treasury Department for the cost of the weapon), and its six-round cylinder was chambered with .38-caliber bullets. The gun looked deadly, and in the right hands it was.

Mike had always been able to get his shots clustered around the bull's-eye, but that, he conceded, had been target shooting. It was a hobby enthusiast's talent. He had all the time in the world to fire his six shots, reload, and then carefully sight each new shot as he once more methodically emptied his revolver. But it wouldn't be like that if things turned bad. With the Boss's life on the line, it would require additional, more violent skills.

He went through rapid-fire drills, squeezing the Colt's trigger as fast as he could, reloading in an instant, and then once more blazing away without pause. Speed and accuracy, he lectured himself, were the challenges. Shoot to kill, and shoot fast. He knew that in a real gun battle courage would just as likely determine the outcome as skill. Mike understood that there was no training that would help with that. He'd either find it at the right moment, or live forever with his shame.

Mike grew proficient in these quick-fire exercises, but he soon began considering the limitations of his weapon. A six-shot revolver would stop a deranged assassin dead in his tracks as he rushed hell-bent toward the president. However, if the enemy came for the Boss at the Big Three conference, they'd be well-trained soldiers, and it wasn't too much of a reach to suspect that they'd be coming in a sustained assault, in a battle charge. He needed to be ready for something like that, and his .38-caliber Police Special six-shooter was too puny a weapon. He'd be overwhelmed.

Mike shared his worries with the treasury secretary, and Morgenthau quickly understood the agent's concerns. On his next session at the range, Mike was firing an M1 Thompson submachine gun. It spewed out body-slamming .45 ACP cartridges at a fully automatic, dizzying rate from thirty-round magazines. Soldiers called the M1 the "Trench Sweeper" because it had the power, speed, and accuracy to mow down a trench lined with enemy soldiers. Set it on automatic, pull the trigger, and it was an equalizer against what might've been insurmountable opposition. It took Mike a while to get the hang of it, to shoot precisely where he intended. But he had an athlete's natural skills and a marksman's instincts. In his hands, it was a very dangerous weapon.

Mike knew that if the Nazis attacked, they'd be well armed, too. He was no military man, and so he did not even attempt to guess what sort of firepower they'd unleash. He could not begin to judge who would have the advantage in a battle. And when, in the only way he knew to get some sense of what he might soon be facing, he tried to put a human face on the enemy, all he could imagine was that they were professionals like him, determined to do their job no matter what the risks.

ACROSS THE WORLD IN HIS special operations training camp in Oranienburg, Skorzeny also turned his prebattle thoughts to guns. He had begun to deal with the practicalities of how his teams would be armed for the mission. But when he did, a fresh terror gripped him, and he upbraided himself for not having seen it before. And he knew as any soldier would know that unless he moved quickly to set things right, he'd have little chance of getting out of Long Jump alive.

His own weapon was not the cause for his distress. He'd been heading into tough situations armed with the same manner of gun for years, and it had always served him well. In Holland he'd recovered one of the Sten guns the British had parachuted in, and it had been his weapon of choice ever since. "It could be rubbed in mud but would still fire," he'd say with the conviction of a veteran who'd put it to the test in battle (and depending on who else was around, he'd often add "in contrast to our machine-pistols which even a little dust could upset"). And when some SS ordnance officers, pushed by a proud chauvinism, insisted that the Sten's accuracy was inferior to the German submachine guns, Skorzeny swiftly dismissed their arguments. They were deskmen, not warriors, he'd say pointedly. It did not matter that the gun couldn't hit a distant target. "The Sten gun is a weapon for close quarters," he'd say with the authority of someone who'd clutched its steel grip in his hand as he'd sprayed bullets about a room.

But what had truly won over Skorzeny was that, unlike the Germans' handheld machine guns, the Sten could be equipped with a silencer. "In the event of an unexpected meeting with the enemy, there would be no sound of firing to give it away," he noted. And as he played out the Long Jump mission in his head, he had little doubt that just as there would be a time when the loud boom of the Gammon bomb would be invaluable, there would also be moments when the soft *pfft* of the silenced Sten would be a lifesaver. The Sten, he was confident, would serve him and his assassins well.

The problem, though, was how the fifty or so Vlasov Russians would be armed. Their job would be to hold off the Allied guards long enough for Skorzeny and his Oranienburg team to hurl the Gammon bombs and then escape. Which could work—if the Russians could get into position. And this, too, seemed reasonable enough. After all, the Russians' fundamental operational attribute, the shrewd inspiration behind Schellenberg's decision to bring them on the mission in the first place, was that they could pass for Russian soldiers. They'd march in, and no warning lights would start flashing. But if they were toting British Sten guns, or, for that matter, any German weapon they had acquired since their joining the Wehrmacht, the pretense would be demolished after the first quizzical glance from one of Stalin's military guards.

Skorzeny gave himself an order: Make sure the Russians carried their Soviet army–issued weapons. But in the next moment, he was tearing his own workings to shreds. Armed with the Russian infantryman's regulation five-shot Mosin-Nagant rifle, the weapon they had strapped over their shoulders when they switched sides, the Vlasov recruits could never put up much of a fight against armed-to-the-teeth Allied guards. Skorzeny and his commando unit would have no chance of slipping away while the fifty Russians made a stand to hold off the enemy.

It took him a trip to the Abwehr ordnance depot in Zossen to acquire what he needed. And again his luck held: they had crates of "Daddies." This was what Russian soldiers called the PPSh-41 submachine gun; its three-letter name sounded like *papasha*, and that was close enough to the Russian word for "daddy" for the soldiers' nickname to stick. Yet despite the mild-mannered sobriquet, it was a brutal weapon: it fired metal-piercing Tokarev cartridges at the ferocious rate of one thousand rounds a minute. Skorzeny held one in his hands, considered the reserves of firepower in the thirty-five-round drum magazine, and his confidence started to be restored. Fifty Vlasov Russians armed with this submachine gun should be able to keep the guards busy enough; a regiment could slip away under the cover of the blazing firefight that'd erupt.

Then he tried the submachine gun out on the test range. There was no doubt that it could get the job done; it was a killer's weapon. His new concern, however, was that it wasn't a particularly well-designed gun. Sighting took some practice; it appeared to pull to the left, plus it fired high. Loading the round magazine was difficult even on the range; in combat the task would be, or so it seemed to him in the course of his initial struggles, damn near impossible. Yet after he worked for several hours with an obliging instructor—who wouldn't want to assist the legendary Skorzeny?—he at last got the hang of the weapon. He was even singing its praises. Nevertheless, in the course of his lengthy tutelage, Skorzeny had also come to realize he'd need to bring skilled instructors to Oranienburg to teach the Russians the ins and outs of the cantankerous "Daddy."

Cap in hand, but with his Knight's Cross dangling proudly from his neck, he went to Canaris to request that several Abwehr gunnery instructors be reassigned to his center at Oranienburg. The admiral, although he was well aware of Long Jump, refused. Perhaps he didn't like the arrogant commando. Perhaps he was having second thoughts about the mission; he had already stepped away from his original role, now ceding control of the mission to Schellenberg. Or perhaps he thought that the cavalier transfer of men from his command at a time when Schellenberg was scheming to absorb the Abwehr into the SD would be a tactical mistake. But whatever the reason, Canaris dug in his heels. "Admiral Canaris is certainly the most difficult opponent I have ever had to tackle," Skorzeny would say as their battle raged, and the words were spoken not entirely in jest.

Skorzeny had no choice but to go over Canaris's head to Himmler, and when he did, the admiral capitulated. Ten veteran Abwehr commando trainers were transferred from Lake Quenz to Skorzeny's grand *Schloss* at Oranienburg. They would make sure the Russians would be prepared.

One of the new instructors was Major Rudolf von Holten-Pflug. It had been Holten-Pflug's confident assertion to a student, an unyielding challenge about what fifty men could accomplish, that Schellenberg had overheard months earlier. The echo of those bold words had shaped the spymaster's initial thoughts as at the same time they had also encouraged his strategic ambitions. And before long the reappearance of Holten-Pflug in Operation Long Jump would bring further historic consequences.

BUT WHAT ABOUT SCHELLENBERG? Had he shuffled off to the operational sidelines as Skorzeny took control of the day-to-day planning for Long Jump? While it might have seemed that way if one watched the hours of intense training that the teams at Oranienburg were putting in—long days on the firing range, practice leaps from the parachute jump tower, and hands-on tutorials pounding home the tactical versatilities of a Gammon bomb—behind the scenes

Schellenberg continued his determined pace. His tradecraft, in fact, had never been better.

He had always been a very cautious spy. "In almost every country," he'd acknowledge, "I had a second organization working quite separately from the main one and unknown to the latter. I considered this necessary in order to be able to check and control the information and material received from my regular service."

And true to his operational handwriting, he made the decision to keep a tight rein on Long Jump. For this babysitter's job, as it was called in the trade, he turned to the asset he'd previously shipped off to Tehran to keep a vigilant eye on Operations Franz and Anton. Only Winifred Oberg had never made it to Iran. He'd gotten as far as Turkey and then circumstances, or perhaps it was lassitude, had prevented him from continuing on.

Schellenberg summoned Oberg from Istanbul and gave him his new assignment. And Schellenberg made it clear that while he was willing to grant Oberg a second chance, the agent would not get a third. Failure this time would have very unfortunate repercussions.

Then having waved the stick, he dangled the carrot. Complete this task, do it well, and all will be forgiven. Rewards, advancement—all would be in the offering.

The assignment: Oberg was to go to Oranienburg and keep his eyes and ears open. He was to send a detailed report back to Berkaerstrasse every day about what he heard. And there was more: before the Long Jump force headed off to wherever the mission would take them, Oberg would go in first. He'd lead the way on the ground, an advance man ensuring that all the pieces would be in place when the teams arrived.

Chastised, Oberg reported to Oranienburg, unsuspecting of the tangled path he'd be following, or the many bodies lying at its end.

BUT EVEN AS PREPARATIONS PROCEEDED, as hard men in Washington and Berlin had a sense that events were building, a decision was made that brought the prospects for a meeting of the Big Three to a screeching halt. FDR had lost patience, and Churchill huffily concurred. In their shared anger and frustration, a new, smaller summit was set.

And Schellenberg would learn the details before Mike.

24

A WALK-IN IS THE OUTCAST OF the spy trade, the uninvited guest bearing gifts whom no intelligence officer wants to welcome. The resentment is born out of a myriad of suspicions: Why did he knock on the door, offering his tempting presents, in the first place? Is he seeking money? Is it patriotism? Is it ego, the urge to be front and center on the world stage? Or has his arrival been instigated by the enemy, part of a carefully conceived plot to get a foot inside your house? And then, are his glittering offerings nothing but fool's gold, disinformation dished out by a mischievous adversary? Yet what truly keeps spymasters tossing and turning through the night is the nagging fear that they've made a terrible mistake: they've either taken a double agent into their midst, or they've slammed the door on an intelligence windfall.

This was the unsettled terrain, doubts and suspicions scattered all about, that Schellenberg found himself carefully maneuvering through in the aftermath of his receiving a phone call just moments after sitting down at his office desk on October 28, 1943. The caller was Legationstrat Wagner, Ribbentrop's generally unflappable autocratic aide, only that morning he was bursting with a very uncharacteristic urgency. He asked if he could see the Section 6 head "at once." "On an extremely urgent matter," he added, but that was as far as he'd go toward offering an explanation. The details, he mysteriously persisted, "could not be discussed on the phone."

The story Wagner breathlessly recounted about an hour later was only a preliminary report; the situation was still developing, and the details culled from the initial cable sent by Franz von Papen, the German ambassador in Ankara, Turkey, remained scant. Nevertheless, even at this early stage, Schellenberg grasped with a prescient clarity, the implications were "quite staggering."

A man claiming to be the valet of the British ambassador in Ankara had turned up on the doorstep of Albert Jenke, the German counselor, proposing a deal. In return for 20,000 pounds sterling (about $100,000 in wartime dollars, or more than five times the average annual US income at the time) the walk-in would hand over "photographs of the most secret documents of the British Embassy." And it wasn't just a one-time offer. Regular deliveries of photographed classified material were promised at the price of 15,000 pounds per roll of film. But the clock was ticking. The valet had set a deadline of three days, and he'd made it snidely clear that if he didn't have the cash in his hand by then, well, he knew the address of the Russian embassy.

Ribbentrop, the foreign minister, wanted the spy chief's counsel: Should we play along? Send the money? Or would we be rushing in with our eyes wide shut and our wallets open?

Schellenberg started to give the matter some thought, but he quickly realized there were discouragingly few hard facts for him to consider. Still, he did his best to tally up what he had.

On the one hand, the SD station chief in Ankara who worked under diplomatic cover, Ludwig Moyzisch, was old Abwehr, a capable and trusted spy. He could monitor things on the ground, get a sense of the seller, and certainly make an informed inspection of the film before the money was handed over. The prospect of an experienced professional overseeing the exchange in Turkey brought a measure of reassurance.

Added to this, even if the material proved to be deceptions cooked up by the Allies, this would have some intelligence value, too. Time after time Schellenberg had preached that "it is important to know by what means your enemy tries to mislead you." If the valet's products were counterfeits, then they were also road maps showing the false trails the Allies wanted Germany to go down. The SD's backbeaters could go to work extrapolating what the Allies were trying to protect, and then come away with a better sense of what they were planning.

On the other hand, evaluating the documents would tie up considerable intelligence resources, analysts, and deskmen who could be deployed in other, more fruitful operations. Time, too, would be squandered, and he knew as all the leaders of the Reich had come to know that opportunities were dwindling for Germany. Then there was the cost: 20,000 pounds. "A tremendous sum," Schellenberg complained, especially when there was no guarantee of what it would be buying.

Walking away would be easy, he acknowledged. In his job, he spent most of his time deciding not to get involved, finding the resolve not to chase after phantoms, however seductive. Accepting the offer would take nerve. Or would it be foolishness? he worried.

Photographs of the most secret documents of the British embassy. In the end, he reasoned, that was what it was all about. Either he wanted the product, or not.

Schellenberg decided the offer should be accepted.

The next day, an SD courier boarded a special flight to Ankara. He carried a briefcase crammed with 20,000 British pounds. And whatever misgivings Schellenberg still harbored were assuaged by the fact that the currency was counterfeit, the skillful handiwork of the Operation Bernhard forgers.

THE PRODUCT, SCHELLENBERG REJOICED, "was quite breathtaking." Yet in the weeks that followed, as a steady flow of "highly secret correspondence between the British Embassy in Ankara and the Foreign Office in London" continued to make its way to Section 6, Schellenberg chose not to celebrate. An exuberant Papen had quickly dubbed the valet "Cicero" because his stolen papers spoke so eloquently. Schellenberg, however, lived instead with the throbbing suspicion that when something is too good to be true, it often means that it is not. The valet had delivered precisely what Germany was looking for, and in Schellenberg's cynical world that was reason enough to have second thoughts. With doubts swirling through his mind, he set out to determine if he was being deceived.

He began by trying to get a sense of Elyesa Bazna, as the spy code-named Cicero was known in the overt world. Moyzisch, the case officer in direct contact with Bazna, conceded that the valet "looked like a clown without make-up," a grubby little man from Yugoslavia who had joined a French military unit only to wind up in a penal camp for stealing cars and weapons. But Bazna did indeed now work for Sir Hughe Knatchbull-Hugessen, the old Etonian British ambassador to Turkey who thought it was a hoot to dress his diminutive valet in elaborate embroidered brocade, slippers with upturned toes, a fez with a jaunty tassel, and a ferocious scimitar dangling from the sash around his waist as though he were a character in an *Arabian Nights* tale. Further, the ambassador, Moyzisch confirmed, gave Bazna free rein to roam unrestricted through his sprawling residence above the capital in the lush hills of Cancaya. In fact, such was his convivial relationship with his manservant that Sir Hughe turned an indulgently blind eye when he discovered the valet's affair with his secretary's teenage nanny. If anybody could get away with covertly photographing the ambassador's secret papers, the SD fieldman reported to Schellenberg in Berlin, Bazna fit the bill. He had the access and the guile. And when Moyzisch questioned him, probing for signs that the valet was perpetrating a hoax, Bazna's responses were reassuringly "definite and precise." "A ruthless and very able man," Moyzisch judged, which Schellenberg had to admit were the appropriate qualifications for any spy.

Yet Schellenberg, meticulous, constantly wary, still refused to put aside his suspicions. Instead he struggled on, now trying to get a handle on "Cicero's possible motives." Money, of course, was one, and since he was demanding a fortune, a very convincing one. Yet when Moyzisch, on Schellenberg's insistence, pressed the spy,

Cicero provided an additional reason. He said his father had been shot by an Englishman while hunting in Albania, and he'd hated the English ever since. The account neatly reinforced the valet's decision to run to Germany with his bounty of British secrets. Perhaps too neatly. On a previous occasion Bazna had told Moyzisch that his father had been living in Constantinople during the First World War and had gotten enmeshed in an "unpleasant quarrel" over the spy's sister that had ended with his poor father's being shot. "The discrepancy between these two stories," Schellenberg fretted, "gave rise to some doubts about Cicero's truthfulness."

These concerns were further exacerbated by new questions about Cicero's tradecraft. The way he described his covert workings, he'd grab documents from the upstairs safe while the ambassador rapturously played Beethoven on the grand piano in the downstairs salon during the long afternoons. Or at bedtime when Sir Hughe took his sleeping pill and swiftly fell into a deep slumber, the valet would remain in the bedroom ostensibly to clean and press his master's suit. But the moment he heard the ambassador snoring away, Bazna would grab the keys off the nightstand and open the safe, and then the dispatch box. In Cicero's telling, both the day- and nighttime pilferings had a common operational component: it was a one-man job. He'd photograph the documents with his trusty Leica and, still without any assistance, return them to the safe before the ambassador was any wiser.

Except Schellenberg had noticed something. On the recent rolls of film the SD had developed, two of Cicero's fingers appeared in several of the photographs. Was it possible, Schellenberg wondered, for one person to both hold the documents steady while at the same tense time he worked the camera? He consulted the Section 6 photographic experts, and, after trying to reconstruct Cicero's actions, their verdict was unanimous: it was impossible. Which meant that the spy had an accomplice. But who? And why was he lying about this?

Still, Schellenberg had spent enough time in the company of

secret agents to have come to the conclusion that spies by nature and breeding were a deceitful lot; it was part of what had attracted them to their duplicitous trade in the first place. If Cicero wasn't telling the whole story, well, he reminded himself, what fieldman ever shared everything with his handler? In the end, he decided with a deadly practicality, only one thing mattered.

"The documents spoke for themselves," he said firmly. They were, Schellenberg came to deduce after periods of long and informed concentration, pieces that fit seamlessly into "the general picture of the political situation as I saw it."

He was done vacillating. He no longer had any doubts: the Cicero material was genuine.

IT WAS ONE OF SCHELLENBERG'S precepts, a knowledge acquired through hard experience, that an intelligence service's value was measured by its tangible actions rather than the stash of private treasures locked in its vaults. Therefore, ignoring the personal risks, he boldly went to war with Ribbentrop, who still had frosty reservations about the Cicero material (or perhaps, as Schellenberg would contend, the foreign minister was simply reluctant to support a success that wasn't his). With a focused purposefulness, he moved on to, as he put it, "the utilization of the information." "The seriousness of Germany's position," he stated with an emphatic resolve, "required it."

Driven by this sense of urgency, he attacked on many fronts. Without delay he made sure Hitler and Himmler had summary reports on the Cicero papers. And, further proof of the shrewdness he brought to the internal battles he knew lay ahead, he had the SD experts compile a list of questions that the Führer would undoubtedly ask. This way there'd be no hemming and hawing; he'd have the answers ready. It was a precaution, he had the foresight to realize, that "was of the greatest importance for on it would depend whether the material could be used for decisions of policy."

Yet even as the pages of questions were being prepared, he charged ahead, bold and unrestrained, into other arenas. He asked General Fritz Thiele, chief of the Wehrmacht's wireless security and decoding section, to be so kind as to come to his office "at once." Then he handed over to the general Cicero's photographs of the ambassador's diplomatic communiqués to London before they'd been encoded by the embassy's cipher clerk. Thiele's wranglers, he had little doubt, could compare the plaintexts, as they were known to cryptologists, to the encoded communications the wireless security section had already intercepted. They'd have a tremendous head start in breaking the "unbreakable" British diplomatic code. If this worked, they'd soon be able to read the encrypted cables being sent to and from every British embassy across the globe.

But what had his attention riveted from the start—although he made sure there was nothing in his manner to convey the intensity of his interest to either Moyzisch, Ribbentrop, or Thiele—was a single document in Cicero's original trove. It was a report by Anthony Eden, the British foreign secretary, on the Moscow Conference he attended at the tail end of October with Cordell Hull, the US secretary of state, and Vyacheslav Molotov, the Soviet minister of foreign affairs.

It made clear that the meeting among the Big Three was off.

"There was no possibility of being able to move Stalin," Eden had written with a very undiplomatic firmness.

With that revelation, Schellenberg understood that Operation Long Jump was also no longer a possibility. His anger welled as he considered the dire implications its stillborn death would have for Germany. At the same time, he forced himself to read on.

"It is very awkward waiting around for an answer from Uncle Joe. It is urgent to get dates settled and preparations made," the British prime minister had cabled the American president with an obvious frustration after reading Eden's report.

Roosevelt agreed. He, too, was tired of trying to reach an agreement with the stubborn Russian marshal. In his pique, he decided that the two of them, the elected democratic leaders of the most powerful Allied nations, should meet anyway. He could go to Cairo in November.

"I will meet you in Cairo on the 20th as you suggest," Churchill swiftly agreed.

And just like that, Schellenberg's grand plan was brought back to operational life. The assassination of two of the Allied leaders rather than all three would have to suffice. Still, the deaths of Churchill and Roosevelt, he assured himself, would mean that the Allies' insistence on Germany's unconditional surrender would die its death, too.

With a clarifying sense of the operation, Schellenberg hurried to Oranienburg. He had done it! He had discovered the answers to the two questions that had assailed him for so long, his two perplexing ifs. There is no record of his thoughts as he made the short drive north from Berlin. Nevertheless, it was no doubt apparent to him, the promise of the chase so suddenly revitalized, how variable were the winds of war. One moment all was lost. The next, a British diplomat in Ankara takes a sleeping pill, carelessly leaves his keys on the nightstand, and the course of the war, Germany's very future, could be changed forever. For he now knew where and when the Allied meeting would take place.

He briefed Skorzeny. It was agreed that Long Jump could begin its countdown to launch. The commando teams would be parachuting into Egypt within three weeks.

Then he found Winifred Oberg in the dormitory. When the two men were alone, after taking care that no one would overhear the conversation, Schellenberg confided in his special agent. Prepare to leave for Cairo, he ordered.

25

MIKE STOOD IN THE MIDST of a stand of tall olive trees, protected from the merciless sun and, he hoped, any curious glances as he waited for his contact. He had flown for days—a fitful, intermittent itinerary that had him bouncing in a C-54 from New York to Cuba to Trinidad to Belém, Brazil, to Dakar, and finally to Marrakech, Morocco. Exhausted, he waited not far from the Menara Airport terminal, across from a field of white tents housing platoons of Air Transport Command soldiers, barely hidden from the stream of scurrying airport porters in djellabas, for the meet.

Mike had not liked the plan from the start. For one thing, it was too insecure. In his suit, tie, and fedora he didn't look like a military man, and he certainly couldn't pass as a native. He might as well have had a sign on him announcing "SECRET AGENT." So much for cover. Any enemy watchers staking out the airport must've made him in an instant.

The recognition signals didn't give him much comfort, either. Only a simple visual, and then it was all systems go: proceed. You'll recognize the contact on sight, he was told. Wait till he's alone in the car. The rear door will be unlocked; just hop on in. To Mike's way of looking at things, that was a plan made for disaster. What if he was walking straight into a trap? There was no word code, no emergency signal to abort, for sending a warning if an enemy agent was crouched out of sight in the front seat, waiting for him to sidle into the car before he pounced. And just the thought of the two of them being shoulder to shoulder in the back seat parked out in the open, sitting ducks for a sniper, filled him with a terrible apprehension.

The timing of the rendezvous was more sloppy tradecraft. Mike had traveled halfway around the world for several days, and, to his complete surprise and satisfaction, he had arrived at the prearranged time and place with an hour to spare. Yet his contact would also be coming a long way, all the way from Moscow. To count on their both arriving at the agreed time was too high a leap of faith. Like any good fieldman, Mike always expected something to go wrong—an early snowstorm grounding flights out of Moscow, a faulty landing gear on the plane and damned if the parts weren't readily available, the pilot out of commission from the flu or maybe just hungover from all the vodka. Then if his contact didn't show, how long should he wait? A day? A week? That had not been made clear. Mike was traveling on another mission, too, and it had its own vital demands, its own very precise timetable. He realized he might out of necessity have to choose one mission or the other.

Mike stood in the thin shade, and the next hour passed slowly. There were ages to think; and time to think is always dangerous on an operation.

The cardinal rule in any meet is that the agent in the field sets the terms; he's the one who decides what's safe, what's most practical. He's the one, after all, taking the risk. But Mike's control had written the entire script. He'd said: The man from Moscow will be coming with a message. It might be a single word, perhaps "on," or maybe "off." Or it could be a sentence. It likely won't be much longer. Listen, and that will determine what you need to do next.

Mike had not objected. It had never crossed his mind to share his operational concerns. He had simply said "Yes, sir," and within the week he was at the Menara Airport outside Marrakech in a grove of olive trees as he waited for his contact to arrive from Moscow. After all, how could the case man protest when the controller giving orders was the president of the United States?

It was November 2, 1943—at least a day after Schellenberg had heard the news about the Egyptian summit—when Mike was summoned by the president. Without any of his usual banter, FDR jumped right in. He announced that he was going to Cairo to meet with Churchill. Generalissimo Chiang Kai-shek, the president of the Republic of China, would also be arriving for the conference.

To Mike's eyes, the Boss looked unusually healthy, even youthful. He seemed as excited as any traveler about to head off on an exotic trip.

Since the generalissimo will be coming to Cairo, the president went on, there was no possibility that Stalin would make an appearance. The last thing the marshal needed was for the Japanese emperor to feel Russia was taking sides in the Sino-Japanese War, the president helpfully explained.

Then FDR started on a new tack. He shared a secret, and Mike understood what was behind the Boss's buoyant mood. The president revealed that he remained optimistic about his sitting down for talks with Churchill and Stalin.

It was a piece of intelligence that Schellenberg had not yet intercepted, or even imagined.

FDR explained: "Cordell Hull is in Moscow now. He is trying to make the arrangements for a meeting between Stalin and me."

At the same time, like a veteran spymaster, the president also was careful not to tell the agent he was sending into the field more than the operative needed to know. He did not share that he'd managed to get over his initial pique with Stalin. In the end he'd found the statesman's wisdom that empowered him to shrug off petty, personal annoyances and to focus instead on all that was to be gained. Nor did he reveal that when put to the test, he was a man of great courage; he would not allow his precarious health to be an impediment to the shaping of a postwar world that could create a lasting peace. He did not tell Mike that he had authorized Hull to inform the Soviet marshal that the American president was now willing to meet in Tehran.

FDR simply gave Mike his mission: "The Secretary will be returning home soon, so you had better get over to Africa and meet him on the way back. Whatever he has been able to arrange will be all right with me."

The secretary of state would tell Mike—quite possibly even before the president was informed, FDR acknowledged ruefully—whether or not there would be a meeting of the Big Three. And where it would take place.

If Hull had somehow managed to work things out, Mike didn't have to be told what he'd need to do next. His mind was already looking into the future, already grappling with the still-unknown security challenges. But first he'd need to go to the site Hull had negotiated and get a sense of all the lurking dangers; "take the temperature," as the old service hands would say. Then he would get down to the difficult business of putting together a practical plan that would ensure the safety of the three Allied leaders.

Before he left, the president gave one last solemn instruction: No one must know. No one must know that Mike was meeting with Hull. No one must know what, if anything, the secretary of state had been able to negotiate. And, above all, if Hull had succeeded, no one must know where or when the meeting among the American president, the British prime minister, and the Soviet marshal would take place. The enemy was on high alert, and the course of the war would depend on secrecy being maintained.

IN THE TRADE, THERE IS the maxim that every minute of waiting might just as well be an hour in the overt world. That was the misery that Mike suffered through as he stared toward the spreading fronds of a tall palm tree where Hull's car would, if all went as planned, come to park. Yet in the course of his long, solitary vigil, as he restlessly tossed back and forth all the what-ifs, all that could go wrong, all the many tasks that, depending on the message he received, might soon be required from him, he found one consolation: he liked Hull. There was a quality to the secretary of state, an authenticity and directness, that was rare in most men, and, in Mike's experience, pretty much nonexistent in politicians. Of all the people he had met during his time in the White House, Mike would say without hesitation that "none appealed to me more than the squeaky-voiced, courtly, yet adamant, hillbilly Judge from Tennessee." Only now Mike found himself silently screaming, Where was he? Was he coming?

At last Mike saw a car pull under the palm tree. There was a rotund, white-haired man in the rear. Two GIs sat up front. He saw the man in the back say a few words to the soldiers. They saluted, and then they exited the car, walking off into the terminal.

Mike did not leave his hiding place. He waited until he was certain Hull was alone, that the soldiers weren't returning, that no one else was approaching the car.

He forced himself to walk slowly, as if he were taking a stroll. If any of the enemy watchers had spotted the secretary of state, he knew his caution wouldn't matter. It'd be too late. But he didn't want to give anyone a reason to pay attention to a man racing across the tarmac, to wonder what all the hurry was about, or to stare into the car.

A tug on the handle and the rear door opened, as had been agreed. He climbed in.

Hull was smiling, a man who couldn't wait to deliver his news. "Stalin don't want to do much travelin' of any kind," he said, eager to give Mike a sense of how strenuously he'd had to fight for the Boss in Moscow. "But," he went on triumphantly, "I got him to go as far as Tehran to meet with the president.

"It's Tehran, then," Hull repeated.

SCHELLENBERG HAD SENT AN SD photo technician under diplomatic cover along with boxes of equipment to Ankara, and now a covert photographic lab was up and running in a safe house near the German embassy. Moyzisch would deliver the rolls of film he'd picked up from the valet, and within hours they'd be developed, copies made for the handful of officials in the Reich who were on the Cicero distribution list. A special courier plane would be waiting to fly the product to Berlin. It was a very efficient operation.

It was in that way, sometime in the second week in November 1943, that Schellenberg found out the Big Three would be meeting in Tehran.

"I have just learned that U.J. will come to Tehran," the president had cabled the prime minister on November 11.

"His latest message has clinched the matter, and I think that now there is no question that you and I can meet him there between the twenty-seventh and the thirtieth.

"Thus endeth a very difficult situation, and I think we can be very happy."

Schellenberg received this news and at once all his previous plans for Cairo were discarded. They had been replaced, he recognized, by a new, even more promising situation. There was no longer any need for compromise. There would be three murders. And of all the places in the world—Tehran! He had a network already up and running in the city. He had hunted there before. The enemy who had been advancing from victory to victory, who had been so self-assured that it was drawing up the plans for the final battles of the war, who had been so mired in its absolutism that it was committed to waging a brutal peace, had suddenly taken a disastrous misstep. And with that unwitting mistake, Long Jump was no longer an improbable, far-fetched mission, but a genuine opportunity.

PART III

"A JAUNT INTO PERSIA"

26

THE OPERATIONAL GODS HAD SHINED on Schellenberg. All the pieces had come together as if he had deliberately laid the groundwork, taken one careful step after the other, realizing all along that Operation Long Jump was waiting at the end of the protracted, twisting trail. As if he'd known all along the Big Three would be meeting in Tehran. The reality, of course, was something entirely different. Playing it all back in his mind, he recounted the seemingly unconnected succession of events, the marriage of fore-sight, timing, and luck, that had set the stage for the final act:

Back in the early years of the war, Abwehr and SD agents had gone undercover in Iran, building networks of assets, finding safe houses. Then, despite the Allied invasion, circumventing the in-creased risks, two penetration agents had somehow continued to remain active, one in Tehran, the other in the tribal hill country.

In Operations Franz and Anton, commandos had parachuted into Iran, and in the process established the procedures for aerial-insertion missions, delivered radio transmitters capable of commu-nicating with Berlin to the Qashqai tribal compound and a safe house in Tehran, and presented gifts to Nasr Khan—including a gold pistol—that renewed the chieftain's wavering commitment to the Reich.

Otto Skorzeny, the very tactician who had supervised the train-ing and execution for previous covert missions into Iran, had been chosen by the Führer to direct the assassination of the three Allied heads of state.

And now the Big Three had decided to meet in Tehran.

It was as if unseen forces had been fitting the pieces together, propelling events with the inexorable momentum and inevitability of a Greek drama. It all had worked out to give him an advantage in the field that seemed nothing less than predestined.

Yet even as he enjoyed a sense of confidence, a satisfaction in the rightness of how things had developed, he was also restrained, as any professional would be, by the parts of the plan that remained to be formalized. There were two crucial and, he was forced to concede after much review, still baffling problems that had to be solved.

First, he needed to establish when the assassins would strike. It must be an occasion when all three of the men would be together. It wouldn't suffice to kill just one of the leaders; he hadn't come this far, gotten so close, to settle for that. Therefore, while it would be relatively easy to execute, and it was an attack that promised a good chance of success, he quickly ruled out targeting the official motorcades after they'd arrived in Tehran and were making their separate ways to the three men's accommodations. The hitch was that there was no way of knowing whether they'd arrive at the same time, let alone on the same day. But he had no doubts that in the aftermath of an attack on one of the leaders, the conference would be swiftly canceled, and the security ratcheted up several notches as the two survivors raced out of Iran. He remained convinced it had to be a moment when he could count on all three men feeling duty bound, regardless of their individual schedules, fatigue, or even bad temper, to assemble. One strike—and three simultaneous targets.

As he attempted to solve his own riddle, it became clear that it would be a mistake to launch a head-on attack during a closed-door summit session. Certainly all three would be present. But there'd be no opportunity to infiltrate outsiders into the room where the top-secret discussions would be conducted; the doors would be barred shut, as well as protected by a cordon of troops from three nations. It would be suicide, a direct charge into a fortified position—and it would fail. He needed to find a time when all three would be together for a prescheduled public or semipublic event. A time when there'd be a friendly audience, or perhaps a crowd the commandos could penetrate without attracting attention. A time when even the security apparatus would be feeling at ease, when their degree of watchfulness would be relaxed. A time when they would not be expecting anything. Surprise was his one great weapon, and he needed to determine the best moment to unleash it.

The other problem was how to gain access to his targets. Skorzeny's commandos and the Russians would get the job done, but he had to get them close enough. Once the site of the attack was determined, he'd still need a covert way to get his assassins into the killing field.

Schellenberg did not have the answers to these two interlinked concerns; all his ideas were undermined by too many imponderables. He required more facts, more hard intelligence, before the operational decisions could be made. He set out to get them.

He met Group G, the foreign intelligence division's research department and, doing his best not to divulge his motivation, shared the tip of his problem. The possibility had arisen, he stated with a deliberate tentativeness, that Churchill, Roosevelt, and Stalin would be meeting at the end of November. He ordered his burrowers to go over the files on the three men and find an occasion when they'd be certain to assemble outside the conference room for a joint event. Perhaps to celebrate the anniversary of a prior victory in the war or a national holiday, he suggested. The Group G team knew Schellenberg was playing a coy game; his interest, the specificity of his questions, had to be part of a bigger picture. But they also knew better than to press an SS general. Keeping their suspicions to themselves, they began digging.

He also met with Winifred Oberg, and told his handpicked advance man and operational fixer that his previous assignment had been revised. Forget Cairo, he announced. You'll be going into Tehran within days, and this time you'll parachute; there'll be no opportunity to linger in Istanbul as you did on your last mission, he said pointedly. He ordered Oberg to proceed at once to the Junkers' base in the Crimea. And he also gave him a new mission: In addition to securing safe houses for the team, he wanted Oberg to do a bit of "appraisal," as this manner of mindful surveillance was known. Check out the three embassies—American, British, and Russian—in the city and get a feel for their security measures. Look for weaknesses, chinks in the armor—and bear in mind that after the Big Three arrive the armor will be fortified by a small army of troops. Try to find a way inside—through a side door, or careening down a rooftop, or hidden in a delivery wagon. Anything that will allow Skorzeny and his team to get close to the targets. Close enough so they can't miss. And, Oberg, he warned: Be discreet. If you get caught, or if you simply attract attention, it would be most unfortunate—and not just for the mission, he said with menace.

Finally, he contacted Section C 14, the Iranian desk now headed by the returned hero spy Roman Gamotha. Since Gamotha knew Tehran and had worked its streets, he wanted his advice, too. What did Gamotha know about the British, American, and Russian embassies? Had he ever been inside any of the buildings? Had he any knowledge of their floor plans, their layouts? Could he suggest other locations where official guests, taking a break from their duties, might visit? Perhaps a ceremonial appearance at the shah's palace? A shopping trip to the bazaar? He ordered Gamotha to compile a security report based on his firsthand knowledge of the city. At the same time, he tried to be oblique, as if his concerns were academic, the sort of knowledge spymasters gather all the time. Collateral for the files, he suggested thinly. He was careful not to share the specific details of the mission he was planning. Gamotha, unlike Oberg, was not Long Jump conscious, to use the spy's vernacular. The head of the Iranian desk had not been informed that the Big Three were coming to Tehran. Or that Schellenberg was plotting to kill them.

Still, as Schellenberg worked to discover a solution to the final elements in his plan, he continued in his quiet way to appreciate that things had suddenly moved in his favor. Of all the places for the Allies to have chosen, they had settled on the SD's longtime stomping ground of Iran. The hunter couldn't believe his luck.

LUCK WAS VERY MUCH ON the mind of the hunted, too. Under the cover of night, as well as a cloak of subterfuge, the American president had left the White House at 9:30 p.m. on November 11 and had been driven to the Marine base at Quantico, Virginia. He boarded the *Potomac*, the sleek presidential yacht, ostensibly for a weeklong cruise that would offer him some respite from the grueling demands of the war. But at 9:15 the next morning, with the yacht anchored in the calm waters of Chesapeake Bay, the president was gingerly lifted into a small, colorless gunboat. Moments later, the glistening *Potomac* headed out to deep water, under orders to remain out of sight of the shore for at least a week, and to ignore any radio messages. It was essential to maintain the fiction that the overworked president had taken a long, restorative holiday at sea.

Meanwhile, the gunboat carrying the president plowed through the dark river. It soon approached a steel-gray colossus rising out of the cloying early-morning mist like a primeval sea monster. The USS *Iowa*, the most powerful battleship in the world, nearly as long as the Empire State Building was tall, armed with a formidable battery of huge guns, armored in thick steel, home to 2,700 men, powered by gigantic 212,000-horsepower engines, had been designed to speed through harm's way and annihilate anything that dared to stop it. The tiny gunboat swung around the mighty leviathan's stern and hove to on the starboard side. A gangway was stretched between the two vessels and, not without some anxiety for the Secret Service men, the crippled president was carried across this narrow bridge.

FDR joined the Joint Chiefs, Harry Hopkins, the crusty friend whose advice he counted on, and about one hundred of the military and diplomatic summit staff who were already on board. The plan

was to dash across the Atlantic to North Africa on the indomitable
Iowa, then fly on to Cairo, before making, as FDR had playfully
taken to calling it, "a jaunt into Persia." On each leg of this tense,
secret journey, "the president," the Secret Service had worried in a
classified memo palpably drenched in anxiety, "was running grave
personal risk. . . . If the enemy could learn of his whereabouts, they
would spare no effort to attack by air, submarine, or assassin."

In this world of perpetual threats, the president wanted as much
reassurance as possible. And so that evening at about ten p.m. as the
Iowa finished refueling at Norfolk and made its final preparations
to head out to sea, the president confronted the skipper. Captain
John McCrea, a lawyer who had previously served as FDR's naval
aide before taking command of the newly commissioned battleship,
was someone the president knew well and, a further comfort, liked.
FDR had no concerns about talking frankly.

"John," he suddenly remarked for no apparent reason, "today is
Friday."

The perplexed captain nodded politely.

"You know," FDR continued, "I have a sailor's reluctance to start
out on any sort of project on a Friday."

The president let that sink in, and when he finally spoke his tone
was confiding, yet unapologetic. "This is an important series of
meetings for all of us, and I want them to go over. The decisions
will be important, and I want them to be successful—and Friday is
unlucky."

At five minutes after midnight, the *Iowa* raised anchor and started
its journey across the swift-moving channel that led to the dark,
deep waters of the Atlantic. It was the first minutes of a new day:
Saturday. A life at sea had schooled Captain McCrea in the intractable pull of sailors' superstitions. He also suspected his old friend
would need all the luck he could get as he confronted the many
uncertainties that lay ahead.

———

"I AM BEING SHOWERED WITH every security and every comfort," the president, in high spirits, wrote in a letter as the battleship powered through the waves, heading due east, toward Gibraltar.

The *Iowa* had gone all out for its commander in chief. The entire ship had been scrubbed, cleaned, and made to sparkle. The captain's lugubrious gray-walled quarters, now the president's, had been repainted a cheery blue and lavishly, at least by spartan battleship standards, redecorated. A bathtub suitable for a disabled president had been wedged into the small lavatory. Two portable elevators had been installed. One would raise the wheelchair-bound president from the main deck to his cabin perched on the first superstructure deck. The second would take him from that deck up to the bridge; from there, in case of emergency, he could be wheeled into the oval, armor-plated conning tower, the safest sanctuary on the ship. Six of his attentive Filipino stewards were on board to cater to his every culinary whim (and to ensure against someone's poisoning the president's food or drink). And wicker chairs and smoking stands had been scattered about the top deck, their use restricted to the president's top advisers. A few of the crusty old salts on board moaned that the redecorated *Iowa* had the feel of a cruise ship. But a look across the bow would at once reaffirm the gravity of the voyage: a cordon of three Fletcher-class destroyers, swift ships armed to the teeth with cannons, antiaircraft guns, depth charges, and torpedoes, hovered protectively around the battleship. The growl of the fighter escorts keeping watch in the sky above was constant.

"This will be another Odyssey," the rejuvenated president confided to his diary, full of anticipation of the approaching adventure. "Much further afield and afloat than the hardy Trojans. But," he added with a sudden foreboding, "it will also be full of surprises."

Yet for now, as he wrote in another fulsome entry, "the luck has held—very little sea and wind."

It was to take advantage of this good weather, and to offer the president a diversion from the monotony of the long voyage, that on Sunday, the second full day at sea, Captain McCrea arranged a demonstration of the ferocious power at his command.

At two p.m. the president was wheeled out from his cabin to the port side of the deck, in the forward part of the ship. He sat staring out toward the sea as the wind started to whip, and the crisp ocean spray licked his face. A semicircle of his advisers, including the Joint Chiefs, Harry Hopkins, and a flock of attentive aides, stood deferentially behind him.

On the bridge above, Captain McCrea waited for the president's signal.

Roosevelt had a few last words with the Joint Chiefs. They had been feverishly placing bets among themselves on the Army-Navy game. The president, an old navy man, wanted in on the action. When he was satisfied, he looked up to the bridge and raised his hand in a small gesture that was almost a salute.

On this command, volley after volley of red hydrogen balloons, dozens and dozens of them, were launched. They quickly climbed up and up, silhouetted against the deep blue sky. An eerie anticipatory quiet fell over the ship as the batteries of 20- and 40-millimeter guns began training their weapons, sighting on the high-flying targets. All at once there was a tremendous boom as scores of the big guns opened fire. The noise was ferocious. The entire ship shook in protest, and the observers on deck must have felt as if the entire ocean were preparing to rise up in anger.

Then, like a sharp intake of breath, the guns stopped and a calm settled over the ship. But it was short lived.

"Torpedo on the starboard beam!" a loudspeaker blared with alarm. "Torpedo on the starboard beam!"

The moments that followed were electric, a swirl of action as all on board reacted to the ship's being under attack. Arthur Prettyman, FDR's longtime valet, instinctively began wheeling his helpless charge to the port side as aides closed in around the president, forming a wall of bodies. But the president objected. "Take me over to the starboard rail," he ordered. "I want to watch the torpedo." Prettyman, "shaking all over," he'd say, had no choice but to obey.

At the same time up on the bridge, Captain McCrea had issued the order to bring the ship at full speed to port. The *Iowa* surged violently left, hoping to position itself parallel to the weapon's path. All the captain could hope to do was give the torpedo a smaller profile to target.

The torpedo raced forward, homing in on the ship.

Then it exploded. The battleship shook from the force of the blast. "My God, he's hit us!" Commander Pohl cried out from his battle station in the chart house. He was certain a Nazi U-boat had sneaked through the destroyer cordon and had launched a torpedo to sink the ship carrying the president.

But the commander had been mistaken. The *Iowa* had not been hit. The last-minute evasive actions of the unflappable Captain McCrae had steered the ship out of danger. The torpedo had exploded in the big vessel's churning wake.

And the torpedo had not been fired by a relentless U-boat. It turned out that one of the *Iowa*'s destroyer escorts, the *William D. Porter*, had also been conducting a target drill. The skipper, unaware that the president and the Joint Chiefs were on board, had used the battleship as its point of aim for a mock torpedo attack.

Seven empty torpedo tubes had been fired off at the *Iowa* in rapid succession. When the assistant torpedo director pressed the button for the eighth dummy firing, he heard a sharp explosion. He immediately recognized the sound: an active torpedo had been launched. The tube had not been empty.

In the aftermath of the unnerving incident and his fortuitous escape, FDR, not unlike his adversary in Berlin, felt that his luck was holding. The prospects for the meeting among the Big Three remained heavy with promise. It would not be until later that Mike would fear that the president had dodged a torpedo only to head into a fusillade of bullets.

IN MOSCOW CENTER, THE FIRST Directorate spymasters had no
need for the vagaries of luck. Instead, they relied on the intelligence passed on by the moles they had placed in the enemy's house.
Nikolai Kuznetsov, the trusted double who was posing as a Wehrmacht lieutenant in the Ukraine, had cabled a provocative report
about "something big," an operation spearheaded by no less than
the fabled Skorzeny. And now Roman Gamotha, the SD spy they
had turned, then doubled back, and who'd been rewarded by the
opposition for his daring "escape" from a Russian prison camp with
the Iranian desk, had shared the list of questions his Section 6 boss,
Walter Schellenberg, had posed. It did not take long for Pavel Fitin,
the shrewd head of the First Directorate, to connect the dots.

27

THE RUSSIANS, SOLDIERS AND SPIES, hit the streets of Tehran with a vengeance. Their orders were to round up all the remaining German civilians and Nazi sympathizers in the city. They had not been informed of the reason for the dragnet. They had not yet been told that Marshal Stalin was coming to Tehran, and they certainly would never be privy to the disturbing intelligence that had pushed Moscow Center's murmurs of concern to an operational scream. They were simply given a job, and told to get it done in a hurry.

As FDR made his way across the Atlantic, as Schellenberg struggled to add the final touches to his plan, the Red Army poured into Iran. "New faces began appearing in Tehran," Ernst Merser, the longtime German asset, observed with a cautious apprehension. By the time the buildup was complete, an additional three thousand troops under the harsh command of General Andrei V. Krulev had been deployed. The political commissars of the Near Eastern Area Office had been confident that a massive army presence would be sufficient to keep the troublemakers and dissidents in line. But Krulev believed the only show of force that was truly effective was force itself.

IT WAS A TIME FOR ABSOLUTES. Suspicion was sufficient proof of guilt. And guilt required punishment. The formalities of interrogations, of trials, were irrelevant. Krulev's troops were tough men, and they did things in a savage way.

A truck packed with Soviet soldiers cruised down a wide boulevard in the modernized sector of the city and, as a Belgian diplomat watched, first with curiosity, and then with a surreal horror, a defiant Iranian let out a jeer. "One of the Russians whipped out his revolver and shot the mocking Iranian dead," he recalled. "No more was needed. Henceforth the Russians were feared and no one dared taunt or mock them."

But the absence of provocation did not lessen the Russians' ruthless zeal. Day after day "the great Russian cleanup," as it became known in the city, continued with a methodical efficacy. Hordes of "suspects"—the exact number was never tallied, but several estimates put it at more than fifteen thousand civilians—were marched at rifle point into trucks and driven to the grim Soviet detention camps in the north.

"One after another the influential members of the German colony disappeared without leaving a trace," wrote Alexandr Lukin, a Russian journalist who witnessed the roundups while at the time maintaining a guarded silence. "When the valet of one of them entered the bedroom in the morning," he went on with a stunned incomprehension, "the only remaining evidence of his former employer was a pajama button."

In this way, too, they came without warning for Jakob Kupferstein at his home. "I was taken away with my wife, my mother-in-law, and my two sons," said the German-Jewish émigré owner of a thriving clothing store at a fashionable address on Lalehzar Street. "We were put in a single-story building belonging to the Russian barracks in the town of Meshed. There was room for thirty people at the most, but while I was there some two hundred people were brought in. Those for whom there was no room in the building were taken away every three or four days. I still don't know where."

Kupferstein was put to work sweeping the barracks yard. His two sons were sent to the tailor's shop. He never saw his wife or mother-in-law again.

"They shouted all the time that we were German spies, members of the fifth column. I told them again and again that I was a Jew. But try to explain to a Tartar who doesn't even know Russian what a Jew is."

Seething, his fear, frustration, and anger making him daring, he confronted, he said, "a Ukrainian officer who knew some German." Kupferstein desperately tried to explain that as a Jew he could never be a fifth columnist working for the Reich. The officer swiftly demolished his argument. "If you are both a Jew and a German, you have two good reasons to shut up," he warned.

And the poor Poles! The Russians came after them as much out of habit as for any practical security concern. They had, after all, much practice in treating them disgracefully. Back in 1939, the Soviet Union, then Germany's short-lived ally, had annexed most of eastern Poland after the Reich had made quick work of the Polish army. One and a quarter million Poles were deported and scattered across the vast stretches of the Soviet Union. Many were summarily murdered; the graves in the Katyn Forest alone held 22,000 corpses. Others, about a half-million Poles, were labeled "socially dangerous," members of "anti-Soviet elements." Their fates were the bleak, icy labor camps in Siberia and Kazakhstan, gulags where death seemed to offer the only reprieve.

But in July 1941, Germany invaded the Soviet Union, and yesterday's villains became today's comrades. Then, following Russia's invasion of Iran, the Soviets were happy to ship some of the troublesome Poles to the occupied country, and these survivors, men, women, and children, many of whom who had nearly starved to death in the camps, many suffering from malaria, typhus, fevers, and respiratory diseases, were even happier to leave. One hundred and twenty thousand made their way to Iran, most settling in Tehran.

Now that the Russians were on the warpath in the city, they came after the long-besieged Poles with a sickening inevitability. No Pole in Tehran was safe from the Red Army's roundups. The detention camps in the north, gulags carved out of the desert sands yet as forbidding as those in the arctic barrens, grew crowded with Polish families.

STILL, THE "SUSPECTS" WHO MADE it to the northern camps were the fortunate ones. Those who were picked up by the NKVD, the constantly roving Soviet intelligence forces, were taken to the basement of a two-story sandstone-colored house on Syroos Street. This was a domain controlled by interrogators who had done their apprenticeships in the Lubyanka, the Moscow prison whose thick stone walls were stained with the blood of enemies of the state.

On Syroos Street the interrogators did not ask questions. They did not pretend to listen to any explanations, to pay any mind to the secrets that a naked man chained to a wall promised to reveal in exchange for mercy. Moscow Center had made the mission clear. The sole operational concern was to eliminate all threats to Marshal Stalin. Therefore, according to this cruel logic, anyone who wasn't fighting with the Allies was a potential assassin. Without ceremony or mercy, only a systematic industry, they beat their captives. When the tormentors grew tired of this onslaught, of inflicting pain, they often shot them.

A new station chief had been sent by the First Directorate to ensure that the nearly one hundred or so agents and assets attached to Tehran station would be diligent. His work name was Colonel Andrei Mikhalovits Vertinski (his given name remains locked in the secret vaults of Moscow Center), and by all accounts he was a fearsome boss. He was assisted by an agent with a distinguished, as well as chilling, pedigree. Sergo Beria was the son of Lavrenty Beria, the murderous head of the Soviet security and secret police apparatus ("Our Himmler," Stalin had gloated without a trace of irony), and the son's presence was further affirmation of the impor-tance the center placed on Tehran station's cruel mission—rotten apples, the spymasters had hoped, never fall far from the tree.

The NKVD ranks prowling the city were fleshed out by a below-the-line group who operated independently from the professional Moscow Center–trained hoods. These informal assets went by the ostensibly impressive name of the "Light Cavalry," and the seven members, mostly in their late teens or even younger, liked to say the designation was a tribute to their lithe efficiency, their ability to move unnoticed in the nighttime shadows or through the maze of the bazaar, yet always ready to pounce. The reality was less complimentary. The more established spies at Tehran Station had bestowed the title as a joke: the boys, none of whom owned an automobile or, for that matter, knew how to drive, rode their bicycles as they scurried about the city hunting for German agents.

The leader of the group was a nineteen-year-old would-be secret agent, Gevork Vartanian. His father, a native of Armenia, had been on covert assignment for the NKVD since 1930 in Tehran, working as a shop owner for cover. Vartanian had started out doing the odd bit of watcher's work for his father, but after the Allied invasion, with Iran suddenly teeming with foreign soldiers, he yearned for something more daring. On his own, he recruited six of his friends, the boys fluent in Farsi and Russian, and they offered their services to the Tehran station chief. With an indulgent good humor, Colonel Vertinski took the spirited boys on board, although in a loose, definitely unofficial way. They'd be fine for errands, coffee runs, maybe even late-night patrols, he decided, playing along with the lark.

For now, though, it was the savage diligence of Russia's soldiers and experienced spies that kept Tehran gripped with fear. Persian folktales told stories about malevolent djinns, *shayatins*, who came out at night to steal people's souls. The natives believed those demons had returned.

YET IT WASN'T DJINNS WHO grabbed Franz Mayr, the resourceful SD penetration agent code-named Max. Nor was it the Russians.

The British intelligence forces stumbled onto him, and for Schel-lenberg the timing couldn't have been worse: he'd been counting on the knowledgeable Mayr to help Oberg arrange safe houses for the Long Jump teams.

At the time, the British hadn't been looking specifically for Mayr, although they had heard stories from the American Counter Intel-ligence Corps (CIC) about the German master spy who had been lurking in Tehran for years. A suspected German sympathizer, eager to cut a deal, had led the security forces to the home of Ali Mutti. But Mutti was not alone—he was harboring Werner Rockstroh, one of the Operation Franz parachutists who had gone to ground, as well as a radio set for communicating with Berlin. Joe Spencer, the British intelligence officer running things, shrewdly decided to keep a watch on the apartment. There was no telling who else in the network might show.

That evening a Dr. Qudsi walked in. The dentist saw the Brit-ish soldiers and tried to flee. But he didn't get very far before two soldiers brought him down from behind with a rugby tackle. Un-der questioning, he, too, couldn't wait to trade what he knew for the prospect of leniency; no doubt he had heard about the Russian interrogation methods and assumed their allies would act with a similar brutality if he failed to deliver.

It was the dentist who gave up Mayr. He disclosed that his niece, Lili Sanjari, lived with him and that the young woman was the mistress of the German secret agent. He knew where Mayr was hiding.

When Mayr heard the soldiers pounding up the stairs, all he could think to do was to turn off the lights. Perhaps they would decide no one was home. But the British didn't knock. They burst through the door, guns drawn, and confronted the spy as he stood in an entry hallway. "Are you Franz Mayr?" Joe Spencer demanded. "Yes," he said without hesitation. Minutes later the spy was led off in handcuffs, while two burly soldiers followed, their arms loaded with his secret papers.

THE BRITISH DIDN'T WAIT AROUND for Lili Sanjari to appear; they knew, after all, she was an American asset (although, to their annoyance, her relationship with Mayr had never been revealed by the tight-lipped Americans). But it didn't matter. As she was walking, her arm linked with a girlfriend's on Sabze-Meydan Street, near the main entrance to the Grand Bazaar, the NKVD stopped her. They had thought she might be a Pole. Frightened, yet determined to stay composed, she tried to talk her way out of the arrest. She insisted she was Iranian. They looked at the young woman dressed in her fashionable European clothes with disbelief. So she offhandedly offered that she'd been raised in Germany; perhaps that was the source of their confusion. That's when they decided to take her to the house on Syroos Street.

28

I n Cairo, Mike was once again preparing to head off on a secret mission. He had spent the past forty-eight hours traveling around the city trying to gauge the danger into which the Boss would be heading. From a security professional's perspective, his blunt assessment was that it scared the living daylights out of him.

On his first day, he had embarked from the foot of the Mena district, the air warm and heavy, the flat sunlight illuminating the pyramids rising in the distance, and had been taken for a tour. One of the bright young men employed by Alexander Kirk, the American ambassador to Egypt, was doing the talking, assisted by running commentary from an Army CIC captain.

Setting a leisurely pace under a burning sun, they had crossed manicured lawns shaded by tall palm trees as they made their way to Mena House, where the summit among FDR, Churchill, and Chiang Kai-shek would take place. The hotel had once been a hunting lodge, and with its long verandas, wood screens, and weathered blue-tiled floors, it had a cozy, if slightly tattered, country house ambience. The grandeur was in the view: the pyramids leaped out from almost every window, seemingly close enough to touch. They advanced through the cool hallways, their footsteps echoing on the tiles, and Mike saw where ramps were being installed to accommodate the Boss's wheelchair. An oversize wooden door embossed with a brass filigree in a Coptic design was flung open to reveal a vast, gloomy room, and Mike listened with quiet attention as the young diplomat explained that this was where the formal talks would take place; the great men front and center, the supporting staff gathered on the sidelines, waiting to be called into the game like football players. Armed guards, he assured Mike, would be posted at the door. Mike just nodded, figuring that there was no point in adding that he'd be glued to the president's side, too.

Once they were on the long, shaded veranda, the army captain took over. The green approach to the hotel spread out in front of them like a stage set, and as he talked it became apparent that he was brimming with confidence, certain he'd thought of everything. Guard posts here, antiaircraft batteries there, he said as he pointed about authoritatively. See the sightseeing guides, the camel riders clustered by the pyramids? he asked, gesturing toward the horizon. They'll be shut down. There won't be any native servants in the hotel, either. They've all been given the boot. The president's Filipino mess attendants and military personnel will replace them. And the entire Mena district, he explained, will be cut off tight from the rest of the city. Barbed wire strung along the periphery. No one will be able to come in or out except through a single checkpoint. And that will be staffed by a squad of no-nonsense MPs.

The captain continued, but Mike's imagination was already racing elsewhere. Barbed wire strung along the periphery? When he'd arrived in Cairo, he would say, the memory filling him with nearly the level of distress he'd felt at first sight, "the city was seething with unrest." He'd been driven past the British and French embassies and had witnessed "native heads . . . being bashed in by the hundreds." "Axis agitators," he'd been told, had stoked the riots. Not that it had required much stoking. "For ten dollars," he'd learned to his shuddering dismay, "one could hire a professional agitator who would provide one thousand natives to create a frenzied demonstration for or against anybody. For twenty dollars you could hire two thousand native hecklers." Barbed wire strung along the periphery? his incredulous mind continued to echo. What good would barbed wire do in a city that, he knew, "was filled with Axis spies"? The punishment for murder in Egypt, he'd discovered, was a token sixty-dollar fine. How much would it cost to hire a crowd of rabble-rousers, incite them to charge through the barbed wire barricades, and storm into the conference, guns blazing? Standing on the veranda of Mena House as he stared out across the wide, flat lawn, that vision rose up in Mike's mind's eye with an unnerving reality, and the prospect of miles of barbed wire did nothing at all to calm his fear.

Then he had been driven to the ambassador's villa, where the president would be staying. The diplomat giving the tour had droned on effusively about the house's sublime beauty, about the majesty of the setting, poised on the banks of a tranquil canal with the Great Pyramid and the Sphinx as its neighbors. But once again Mike saw only the potential for disaster. He had read the latest intelligence reports: the German air bases in Crete were chock full of bombers. And with that news, the Sphinx, or for that matter just the canal, was transformed into a beacon guiding the Junkers to their target, unmistakable visual confirmation to the bombardiers that the moment had come to release their payloads.

It was in this mood, sensing danger everywhere he looked, that Mike flew to Tehran. He kept his arrival secret. There was no specific reason for his furtiveness; after touring Cairo and experiencing a world of doubts, all his instincts, however, had told him to tread with care. The British and the Russians were allies, but wartime allies were not, he found himself thinking, the same as friends. They certainly weren't family. And as for family, he did not even inform the American legation (the ranking US diplomat's title was "minister plenipotentiary," but he was usually referred to as ambassador; similarly, the legation's headquarters was commonly known as the American embassy, although it wasn't officially upgraded to embassy status until 1944) of the reason for his trip. Except for Major General Donald H. Connolly, who ran the Persian Gulf Command and a few of his military intelligence officials—the number could be counted on one hand, and he regretted having to make that accommodation—no one knew that he was in Tehran, or the purpose of his visit.

Mike himself wasn't precisely sure what he was looking for in the course of this quick, preliminary trip. He certainly hadn't come to conduct a careful security assessment; there'd be time for that. This trip was, as he'd put it, "to get a feel," for the city, an inkling of the problems he'd be facing soon enough. For one day he would try to play the wide-eyed tourist, the Montana hick who couldn't believe that he was so far from home in such an exotic locale. But, of course, his responsibilities were never out of his thoughts.

When Mike's plane landed at Gale Morghe Airport, the airfield on the outskirts of Tehran now controlled by the Russian army, he was met by a US Army enlisted man. His orders, the soldier explained as they headed to a parked jeep, were to take Mike wherever he wanted to go, and after that snippet of conversation, whether following instructions or simply because it was his nature, he largely kept silent for the rest of the tour.

Mike told him to drive to the American legation, and as they made their way out of the airport Mike couldn't help noticing the huge red star painted in the middle of the airfield or the platoons of armed Russian soldiers moving about the base. And not for the first time Mike had the discomforting thought that allies were not the same as friends, particularly when they were armed.

His tour of the American legation was cursory, and barely even that. It was a grand mansion, which he thought would please the Boss, and it was surrounded by a high wall, which pleased him. The fact that it was outside the city, isolated near the suburbs of Tehran, he decided, was in its favor, too. It'd be easier to surround with a shield of troops, and at the same time anyone who didn't belong would be quickly spotted.

Next he instructed his driver to take him to the British and Russian embassies. He had no intention of making his presence known by entering either compound, and when they drove by he made a point to start a conversation with the enlisted man; that way there'd be less likelihood that the embassy's security forces would suspect the compound was getting the once-over. Yet what he saw in that swift drive-by was sufficient to set off internal alarms. The American legation was nearly four miles away from the two embassies. That meant the Boss would need to drive—how many trips was at this point anyone's guess—to the other embassies for at least some conference sessions and certainly for several official dinners. The prospect of a journey through the twisting, narrow streets of Tehran was at the very top of the list of the many security nightmares Mike could imagine. Even in an American city, Mike had long ago come to the realization that "the President is most vulnerable when passing slowly through a city in a motor cavalcade." The thought of the Boss's having to make a trip by car once, perhaps twice, a day through the city's streets had Mike ready to scream that Tehran was the worst possible choice imaginable for the meeting of the Big Three. But he knew there'd be no point. The decision had been made. His job was to ensure that FDR would be safe.

Still, as he continued on his tour of the city, what he saw gave him renewed doubts, and not just about the Boss. The entire traveling party would be heading into a king-size disaster area. Everyone ran the risk of getting sick. He was rocked by this realization after he watched the locals scooping up their drinking water from the murky, narrow gutter-like canals that ran parallel to the streets— the same fetid water floating with sewage and fecal matter. "Typhus lice abound in great number, and typhoid fever takes a terrific toll of lives," he was quickly informed. But the driver's next words restored at least a small measure of reassurance to Mike's teetering world: the American, British, and Russian embassies were the only buildings in Tehran supplied with fresh, potable running water. "The water," he learned, "was piped from the mountains to the legations."

With one less thing to worry about, Mike flew to Oran to await the arrival of the president.

29

THE PARACHUTIST FLOATED DOWN THROUGH the night sky, making a soft landing at Daryācheh-ye Namak, a dry lake not far from the banks of the Qom River. Mike was not the only operative on a secret mission in Iran. Another agent had arrived to make a clandestine appraisal of Tehran. He, too, wanted to know if the city would be a good place for an assassination.

On a moonless night following the Secret Service agent's departure, Winifred Oberg jumped out of a Junkers's cargo door. His parachute brought him down near the site where the first Sassanian king had fought and won his decisive battle that had succeeded in changing the shape of the ancient world, and Oberg felt that he was heading into a mission that would be even more historic. He gathered up his billowing chute, and a German-speaking Qashqai tribesman offered his greeting; he'd been dispatched by Schulze-Holthus, the stay-behind agent who had picked the drop site in a radio message to Berlin. Then the tribesman shared the bad news.

Franz Mayr, as well as the radio transmitter the Operation Franz team had delivered to the city, were now in British custody, the tribesman announced. It was no longer possible for Oberg to go to ground in the veteran SD agent's Tehran safe house. Oberg listened, all the time silently wondering how he'd deal with these setbacks. He would not be able to rely on Mayr's expertise as he reconnoitered the three embassies. Communicating with Berlin would also be a problem; until he found another agent in the city with a transmitter, he'd need to come up with an alternative plan for reporting to Schellenberg. It was about fifty miles from the drop site to Tehran, a bouncy ride in an old truck, and for the entire journey Oberg couldn't help but have bitter thoughts about how cavalierly Schellenberg had thrown him into the fray, or how impossible his mission now seemed. Sweat dripped from him onto the seat of the truck, but whether it was caused solely by the heat was anyone's guess.

Schulze-Holthus had provided a list of possible hideouts, residences of longtime German assets, and the two men had little choice but to investigate them one at a time. They tried three addresses, and at each one events played out in an identical manner: Oberg waited hunched in the truck, trying to look inconspicuous, while the Qashqai tribesman went off to make contact. There was never any way of telling if the Russians had preceded them, or if the NKVD had a stakeout in place. All they could do was knock on the door and see what happened next. It was like jumping off the roof of a burning building—there was no alternative, but you never knew if you'd survive the leap. Time after time the native returned with more bad news: the asset had been caught in the Russian citywide roundup and summarily marched off. But at least no bruisers had rushed out of the shadows to take them into custody. In the aftermath of each tense attempt, Oberg's antipathy toward Schellenberg sparked anew, and so did his sense of being very much alone in hostile territory.

At the fourth address on the list, however, they found a survivor of the Mayr network who took Oberg in. The fact that this asset didn't have a transmitter seemed like only a small inconvenience, the least of Oberg's problems at a very uncertain time. No agent behind the lines can ever relax, can stop listening for the harrowing sound of the authorities pounding on the door in the middle of the night, but as best he could, an exhausted Oberg settled in to get some sleep.

———

As Oberg moved around the city in the days that followed, he proved to be a very good spy. He had what those in the trade respectfully call "a natural eye"—the ability to see things, to make connections that less astute agents would miss. He did not enter the grounds of any of the embassies, setting himself up instead in static posts—a café, a store, a street corner—that offered good views of the comings and goings in the compounds. He observed merchants making deliveries, the locations of the sentry posts, the number of troops deployed, as well as the timing of the changing of the guards. He scrutinized the walls surrounding the embassies, hunting for side doors or perhaps a hole in the fortification. From a distance he scanned the roofs looking to see how they sloped, if traction would be possible, gauging the distance to the ground, the protective cover offered by a chimney. In the end, all his findings were unsatisfying. He could not find a way in unless Skorzeny was determined to be a martyr—and if that were the last-ditch case, he had every reason to believe the well-positioned and well-armed Allied guards would annihilate the commandos before they made it through the front door.

Then, without thinking about it, he stumbled onto something. It was the very thing Mike had also noticed: the city was a cesspool, the water not just undrinkable but toxic. At first, the significance of this observation hadn't registered; he'd been merely worrying about his own health, his own personal safety. But this concern soon spurred him to take another small step. Where were the embassies getting their water? he wondered. He hadn't noticed any of the water trucks with their distinctive cylindrical vats that routinely appeared at government buildings or the mansions of the rich arriving at any of the embassies' gates. Were the foreign diplomats flying in bottled water? Or simply doing without? But as soon as he tried those answers, he knew that they were improbable, most likely impossible, solutions. There had to be another way.

He asked the merchant in whose apartment he was staying, offering his interest up with a careful nonchalance, as if it were the most natural of questions (which it certainly was for anyone living in Tehran under the constant threat of typhus). In response, he learned for the first time (as Mike had also heard, although in a more abbreviated way) how water made its way to the city—and to the embassies.

THERE IS NO RECORD OF precisely what was said, but there can be little doubt about its substance; subsequent events and statements make that clear. By all accounts the gist of what Oberg heard had its origins in the engineering ingenuity of ancient Persia, a story whose roots stretched back to the time when Scheherazade was spinning tales.

It was three thousand years ago or so, that qanats—as the underground aqueducts came to be called; the word was Arabic for "channel"—were first dug to supply water to villages and farms. The underlying principle was as simple as it was inspired: once an elevated source of water was discovered—say, a mountain stream or a river valley—holes would be dug deep into the ground, and then long, sloping connecting tunnels would be painstakingly excavated to carry the water underneath the desert by the ineluctable power of gravity to where it was needed.

But Oberg learned, just as Mike had, that the ancient idea had paved the way for a modern-day health crisis. The water supply for the bustling metropolis of Tehran had its source in the crystal-clear streams and pure underground springs that flowed in the foothills of the Elburz Mountains just north of the city. Vertical shafts had been dug, and miles of deep, graded tunnels brought the water flowing to the city. But as the qanat systems made their way into Tehran, they reared up, angling to the surface. The water entered into long gutters that had been cut along both sides of the street. People drank the water. And they used the gutters as latrines. In a city crowded with nearly one million inhabitants, the exposed qanat branches became poisonous streams. They carried disease and death. Cholera and typhus bred in the stagnant, fetid pools.

When Major General Donald Connolly assumed command of the American forces in Iran in 1942, he decided to do something about the horrific sanitary conditions—for the Allies, at least. Connolly was an engineer by training, and he'd directed the New Deal construction programs in Los Angeles. He was a man who knew how to get things done.

One of the first projects he embarked on was to ensure that potable water flowed to the Allied embassies. To realize this goal, he shrewdly didn't try to reinvent the qanat system, but rather set about to improve it. And in its direct way, his solution was as simple and as inspired as the ancient Persians'.

In the desert just outside the city limits, his men dug into the existing qanat tunnel that ran with fresh mountain water and created new branches. The diverted streams flowed through newly excavated concrete water tunnels thirty-five feet or more under the desert, continued on underneath the embassy walls, and finally surfaced in chlorinated aboveground aquifers located in isolated sections in the grounds of each embassy.

Pour a glass of water at any of the Allied embassies, and it would be clear. Take a sip, and you'd want to take another. Fresh mountain water flowed constantly through underground tunnels into the embassies.

WITH THE SORT OF OPERATIONAL calmness that envelops any spy when every instinct he has is telling him that at last he's arrived at the heart of his mission, Oberg spent several busy days checking out the merchant's story. Outside the city, in a section of flat desert plain helpfully marked off by a newly constructed wire fence, he found the concrete reinforced vertical shaft that Connolly's engineers had dug. He didn't dare cut a hole in the fence; the last thing he wanted to do was leave a clue that might attract attention. Climbing the fence would be no trouble, but the thought of his being halfway up, totally exposed, with no reasonable explanation to offer for his activity, was too large a risk. What if the site was patrolled at regular intervals by the Allies, or perhaps the Iranian police? He decided to wait until it grew dark, and then he'd make his way over the fence.

With growing impatience, Oberg waited for more than an hour. There was no sign of any patrol. It now seemed clear to him that neither the Allies nor the local authorities had any interest in this empty sector of the desert. If he was wrong, he reasoned, it was just as likely they'd catch him at night as during the day. Besides, there was nowhere to hide out there. And the heat was broiling. The safest place to be would be in the tunnel, out of sight. It'd certainly be the coolest.

The metal fence was electrified, or at least that was his terrified thought after he first grasped it with his hands. But then he realized the metal was burning from the sun; the next time, he told himself, he'd bring gloves to protect his hands. He made his way over the top and jumped down to the ground. The system had been designed to ensure that the water could be frequently tested, and therefore when he attempted to lift the large metal rectangular cover that protected the entrance to the vertical shaft, it came off easily, like the lid on a box. He saw the ladder that led down into the tunnel, and he started his descent.

His second mistake, he quickly realized, was that he hadn't brought a flashlight. He could hear the water below, but he couldn't see it. If he fell, he had no idea how far he'd drop before he hit the ground. He tread carefully on each leg of the ladder. It took him a while, but the coolness of this subterranean world was a welcome relief. Finally, he was standing in water that rose just below his knees; and he made another note to himself: Next time, wear boots. He found a match in his pocket and lit it. He walked forward, sloshing about in the eerie half-darkness until the stream began to branch off. The ground beneath his feet was reassuringly solid; probably concrete, he judged. He thought about following this new tunnel, but then he saw in the shadows that there were two additional branches. Which, he told himself, made perfect sense: one leading to each of the embassy compounds.

Rather than follow any of them, he made a spontaneous decision. He'd return the next day with a flashlight, gloves, and proper shoes; there was little advantage in continuing when he couldn't see what lay ahead. He headed back toward the ladder, and as he retraced his steps he made it a point to notice that the concrete tunnel was wide enough to accommodate three men walking shoulder to shoulder. Or, for that matter, three commandos.

Over the course of the ensuing week, days filled with great apprehension yet at the same time a building sense of triumph, Oberg completed his reconnaissance. He walked each of the underground branches, and they were, for all tactical purposes at least, mirror images of one another: a river about two miles long or so of cool, fast-moving, knee-deep water that emptied into a raised aquifer. The aboveground vats were similar to those used for pressing grapes, only much larger, and he had a few rough moments trying to imagine commandos swimming across them, pulling themselves over the rims, only to emerge soaking wet on the embassy grounds. Then he retraced his last steps and, focusing new attention on the route, discovered that before the water funneled into the vats, the engineers had conveniently placed ladders identical to the one he'd climbed down to enter the tunnel. Sitting at the top of the ladders were metal lids, again similar to the one he'd lifted to make his descent. He thought about climbing out and exploring the grounds of the embassy, but then decided that the risk outweighed any possible reward. If he were spotted, that would put an end to Skorzeny and his men using this route to arrive undetected at the killing zone. The Allies would weld the lids on tight and station armed guards along the tunnels for good measure. Instead, he simply inspected each lid to see if it was secured. None of them were; it took only a little muscle to raise each one a very discreet, yet still satisfying, inch or so.

Leaving the tunnel for the final time, Oberg made his way back to the safe house. He now forced himself to confront the problem he'd been avoiding since his first day in Tehran: How would he inform Schellenberg? If he was unable to let Schellenberg know what he'd discovered, then Skorzeny wouldn't be able to put the water tunnels to operational use. And the clock was ticking. The Big Three's visit to Tehran would be in the last week of November—less than two weeks away.

The only idea he could come up with was to make a mad dash to Turkey. He'd ask the Qashqai tribesmen to help find a back door that'd get him past the Russian lines in the north. Then he'd make contact with Moyzisch in Ankara. The SD agent would undoubtedly have a way of reaching Schellenberg. But, Oberg asked himself with a new despair, how long would it take him to sneak out of Iran? And there was no guarantee he'd even reach the border before the Russians grabbed him; like everyone in Section 6, he'd heard what had happened to the ill-fated Gamotha when the spy had tried traveling pretty much the same escape route out of Iran. But it was the only plan he could think of, and so he decided he'd ask the Iranian asset with whom he was staying to reach out to the Qashqai. He needed to get to Turkey as soon as possible.

Yet no sooner had Oberg started to explain what he needed to his host than he realized: there was another way. Schulze-Holthus had a radio; the Abwehr agent had selected the landing site by the Qom River, sent the coordinates to Berlin, and arranged for the tribesman to meet him and then guide him to Tehran. He could use his transmitter.

IT TOOK TWO DAYS' TRAVEL across baking desert and steep, twisting mountain roads before his accommodating Iranian host, apparently eager to be participating in genuine spy work for the Reich, led him into the Qashqai camp. Schulze-Holthus was summoned, and with his customary professionalism, he offered his assistance. A lengthy encoded cable, marked for Schellenberg's eyes only, was transmitted to the SD radio headquarters at Wannsee.

Oberg returned to the safe house in Tehran in high spirits. He'd come to a strange, foreign city and had, against all reasonable expectations, managed to find a way that would allow Skorzeny and his men to get close to the Big Three. Close enough to kill them.

He had finished a celebratory glass of arrak, and was preparing to pour another, when the door burst open. It was the NKVD. They didn't ask any questions, not even his name. He was ordered to raise his hands high as at the same moment a rifle was shoved into the small of his back.

30

THE RESCUE OF LILI SANJARI, Franz Mayr's recklessly disloyal lover, from the NKVD prison was, the participants joked, a joint Swiss-Iranian operation, the first one of the war. And humor aside, it was certainly unique. It was also a suicide mission.

The idea originated with Ernst Merser, the short, tubby Swiss man-about-town who was the linchpin of Mayr's network, and that made it even more improbable. He was a spy who plied his covert trade at society dinner tables or in the barrooms of clubs, making smart conversation and enjoying his wine as he picked up intelligence morsels. He was not a tough guy, not the sort of muscle who'd lower his shoulder, charge through the door, and, fists clenched, deal with whatever was waiting on the other side. Holding a door politely open for a glamorous woman—that was more his style.

So why was this gentleman spy so intent on rescuing Lili at all costs from the house on Syroos Street? One explanation—and this was the one Merser gave at the time and therefore arguably the least likely—was that he was a gentleman, and therefore he owed it to his handler, Mayr, as well as to Lili to rescue her from the clutches of the NKVD. The brutality the Russians doled out in the grim basement of their headquarters was no secret; the NKVD, in fact, had calculatingly helped spread the gruesome stories, since fear, they had learned firsthand back in Moscow, was often a more effective weapon than force. Another explanation was that Merser, like many others in the city, was smitten with the dark-haired, doe-eyed, fun-loving Lili. With Mayr locked up tight in a British jail for the rest of the war, perhaps he thought he'd have the field to himself, and Lili, needing a protector, would succumb to his charms. But the reason that made the most sense at the time—and a lifetime later continues to be persuasive—was that Merser was scared. If Lili talked, if she gave away the names of the members of Mayr's network to the Russians, it wouldn't be long before the NKVD came crashing through the door of his grand villa on Kakh Street. And it'd be his turn to be manacled to the wall in the basement of the Russian spy headquarters, pleading for his life.

Whatever his motivation, Merser's first operational step cannot be faulted. He knew his own limitations and therefore reached out for Misbah Ebtehaj, the burly Pahlevani wrestler whose own loose network of hard men and hustlers had routinely rolled up their sleeves to take care of Mayr's dirty work.

Ebtehaj was everything that the Swiss spy was not—thuggish, vicious, and decidedly not a gentleman. When Merser revealed what he wanted to do, the wrestler said it was impossible. And with that, the negotiations began.

Merser offered Ebtehaj 1,000 British pounds for his help, a considerable sum.

"If you want innocent people to be sacrificed," the wrestler shot back, "turn to someone else." Merser had misjudged him, he insisted.

Two thousand pounds, the Swiss countered. He had been to the bazaar many times. He knew how this would play out. It was simply a question of the seller's sensing he'd been offered the highest price he had any chance of receiving.

Ebtehaj growled that a rescue would be hopeless, certain to fail. It wasn't just his own skin he'd be risking, but also the lives of his friends. How could he do that in good conscience?

Three thousand pounds. This is my last offer, Merser announced, his resolve as emphatic as if an auctioneer had slammed down a gavel.

"Then let's discuss the details," agreed Ebtehaj equably.

IT WAS A DIVERSIONARY ATTACK, a false flag operation, although not a very sophisticated one. What did give it some credibility, however, was that one of Ebtehaj's crew, a Russian-speaking hustler who had been doubling up, doing odd jobs for the NKVD, had a number to call at Syroos Street. And he knew the word code for declaring there was an all-hands-on-deck emergency.

"My brother is severely wounded," he announced after the phone at the Russian headquarters was finally answered at two thirty in the morning.

"Is there a doctor at hand?"

"There is no doctor and he is bleeding badly."

"All right, you can talk," said the Russian, satisfied that the catechism had been correctly delivered.

The caller shared a tantalizing story: A group of Iranian and German agents were gathered in a house at the corner of Firooz and Makhous Streets. They were armed, plotting some manner of fifth columnist sabotage attack. He wasn't sure of the exact number of men, but he estimated there were at least thirty, perhaps more. And they were there now. Within hours, sometime before dawn, they'd be heading out on their mission.

It was a message that Merser knew would mobilize the Russians into taking immediate action. However, the key part of the message—and this was Ebtehaj's inspired contribution—was that the corner of Firooz and Makhous Streets was on the western side of Tehran. And Syroos Street was in the eastern sector. Nearly the entire length of the sprawling city lay between the two distant addresses.

When the NKVD squad led by Colonel Vertinski attacked the building, hammering at the door, pistol and submachine gun fire erupted from an upstairs window. The Russians quickly retreated, regrouping out of the range of fire. Then they charged again.

This time they broke into the house. But all they found were two

Mann pistols, two submachine guns, and a scattering of papers written in German—all props that had been placed according to Ebtehaj's careful script. As for the shooters, they had escaped through an underground passage that opened up on to Jamshidieh Street.

While Vertinski and his men scoured the neighborhood in the predawn darkness looking for the fifth columnists, Merser, Ebtehaj, and seven of his street thugs approached the house on Syroos Street. They had watched as the large force of Russians hurried off to the other side of the city, but they had no idea how many men remained inside, or what weapons they had. Or—and this was the large fear thumping away in Merser's secret heart—how soon the main group of Russians would return.

The wrestler's plan was to smash a window above the street, and climb through. Once he was inside, he'd overpower anyone who tried to stop him as he made his way to unlock the front door.

Brave, but also foolish, Merser said. They hear the sound of breaking glass, they'll grab their weapons. They hear a knock on the door, they'll answer it. They'll think it's just some of their men coming back. Instinctively, the Swiss spy appreciated the tactical value of surprise in any attack.

One of the wrestler's men was chosen to approach the door and knock. There was no response.

This time he pounded on the door as if he were beating on a drum. An angry voice called out in Russian. He responded in Farsi, and it didn't require much acting for him to sound scared, or for his voice to be loud and agitated.

A Russian guard eventually opened the door. By now the Iranian was caught up in his role, shouting vociferously in a language the Russian couldn't understand, and pointing up the street as if to explain.

When the curious Russian walked outside to see what the commotion was about, he was hit from behind with a lead pipe. His unconscious body was dragged off into the darkness. And the men waited.

They didn't need to wait too long before two more Russians came to search for their missing comrade. The Iranian once again began shouting, gesticulating. As they rushed up the block, heading toward where he was pointing with much animation, they were ambushed. The two inert bodies were bound and left next to their friend's. Then with Ebtehaj leading the way, the crew walked through the unlocked door.

There were four Russians inside, all asleep. Shaken awake, they stared groggy-eyed at an armed mob. They didn't even attempt to put up a fight.

Merser found Lili in the basement. She lay unconscious on a straw mattress. He talked to her softly in German, trying to bring her back to life. When she tried to speak, no comprehensible words came to her lips. She uttered only a soft moaning sound. But she was alive. Elated, Merser ordered one of the Iranians to lift her up and carry her in his arms. Gently, he urged.

The wrestler, meanwhile, was freeing all the other prisoners. He did not want the Russians to realize that Lili had been the focus of the attack. If the NKVD went looking for revenge, Lili would never be safe.

Merser headed to the door. All the previous fears that had shaken him during the course of the long, eventful night were beginning to recede. In their place was a mounting exhilaration. He had broken into an NKVD headquarters, he had found Lili, and he'd rescued her. It would not be long before he was home—if his luck held.

Then he heard a low voice calling to him in German. He looked, and the man was standing by the doorway, waiting for him. Close enough to touch him. Merser had not expected to find any Germans in the NKVD prison, and at once all his previous fears rose up anew. He looked for the wrestler in case he needed help, but Ebtehaj was nowhere in sight. So Merser stood his ground, taking care not to make a sudden movement, knowing that there was no preemptive blow he could strike. He looked at the German-speaking man and at once decided he was a soldier; he had a martial bearing, and an unnerving confidence. But was he really a Russian, pretending to be German? All Merser knew for certain was that the stranger looked like the sort of man who could easily snap his neck.

"Are you German?" the stranger asked.

Merser didn't answer. He needed time to think. The stranger broke the silence by explaining that he'd heard him talking to the girl downstairs in German. He had overheard the conversation because he had been in the basement, too. Another prisoner.

"And you?" Merser challenged, his sense of control beginning to return. "Who are you?"

"Sturmbannführer Oberg," he announced, clicking his heels as he snapped to attention. "I had been in Iran for some time before I was arrested. I need help and a hiding place. May I count on you?"

Merser hesitated. He had a decision to make and he knew he had to reach it quickly. The Russians could return at any moment.

"Come with us," he decided.

IN THE VILLA ON KAKH STREET, a doctor examined Lili. There were bluish circles around her eyes and long, inflamed welts criss-crossed her rib cage, but there was no permanent damage, he diagnosed. Nothing was broken. He gave her medication for the pain, and then administered a sedative to help her get some rest. In another bedroom of the large house, Oberg did not need any medication to help him sleep. He slept for nearly an entire day. It was time that allowed Merser to reconsider his impetuousness. And as he contemplated his spontaneous gesture of hospitality, his suspicions grew—as did his apprehension.

Who had he brought into his house? Merser asked himself. What did he really know about Oberg? He said he was a German major, but that did not necessarily mean he was one. What if he were a double agent; after all, he had found him in the NKVD headquarters. Perhaps he was part of an Allied plan to infiltrate the SD assets who remained at large in Tehran. The more he thought about it,

236 ·   Howard Blum

the more Merser grew convinced that it would be prudent to dis-
associate himself from Oberg as expediently as possible. He did not
want to put himself in a position in which he'd be manipulated by
an Allied scheme. Or, a sudden vision of the basement at Syroos
Street taking hold of his thoughts, become a target of the NKVD's
wrath. He had foolishly put himself in a very precarious situation.
He needed answers.

With characteristic courtesy, Merser waited until the famished
Oberg had finished a big meal before confronting him. "If you can
prove your identity satisfactorily," he began, "my house is at your
disposal. If not, I shall continue to help you, but it would be better
if you looked elsewhere for shelter."

Oberg listened mutely. He was concealing the greatest secret of
the war. The last thing he wanted to do was to go out on the streets
where he might be once again arrested. From the moment the Russians had come for him, Oberg had started working out what he
would tell them, what he would give up to keep them away from
the secret that lay at the bottom of his mission to Tehran. He knew
that under torture every man breaks. But he'd been determined to
buy Schellenberg and Skorzeny as much time as he could before
he revealed Long Jump, time that would allow the commandos
to arrive in the city and make their deadly way through the water
tunnels. It'd been only luck that the Russians hadn't paid much
attention to him on Syroos Street; they'd been busy tormenting
others. But he knew they would've gotten around to him before
too long; just as he knew he would have eventually divulged the
colossal secret he had buried deep under all his layers of resistance.
He very much wanted to remain hidden in the comfort and safety
of the house on Kakh Street. He knew how vulnerable Long Jump
would be if he was captured.

"I could mention a dozen people who could vouch for me," he
began at last, trying not to sound too desperate. "And not unimportant people, either. However, this can only be done if and when

you find an opportunity to contact Berlin and get a reply . . ." he said, his voice tailing off in despair.

"That will take exactly thirty minutes," Merser said flatly.

Suddenly Oberg grew excited. Was his good fortune even greater than he'd previously imagined? Not only had he been rescued from the Russians but he'd been brought to a house with a radio transmitter? He remembered how he'd been ready to embark on a dangerous journey to Turkey just so he could communicate with Schellenberg. As it was, he'd needed to travel for days, to the Qash-qai camp in the mountains. "You have a transmitter?" he nearly shouted.

Merser was still on guard. He knew that if he admitted that he had one of the radios the Franz team had delivered months earlier, he could be giving a double agent the evidence that would be used in his own death warrant.

"Please, name the person in Berlin who can give the required information about you," replied Merser, as if he had not heard the question.

Oberg gave the name of SS general Walter Schellenberg. "Is that satisfactory?" he asked.

Minutes later the Swiss spy was in his attic sending a message to the Abwehr in Berlin: "In the course of a raid on the Russian intelligence headquarters, my local agents liberated a man who alleges he is Sturmbannführer Winifred Oberg and quotes Schellenberg as reference. At the moment Oberg is in my house and asks for my help. I am waiting for instructions."

What had he set in motion? Merser wondered as he waited for an answer. What would happen in Berlin? Would the Abwehr contact Schellenberg? Would he need to wait a day, maybe two, before they responded? Longer? Would they reply at all? No doubt the general was a busy man and would not appreciate having his name bandied about by some major or, an even direr possibility, an impostor. Merser could not help but fret that he had acted rashly in sending the transmission. Would the Abwehr respond by questioning his credulity, his fitness for intelligence work?

The reply came later that same day. Merser read it, then went downstairs to Oberg's room. He did not say a word. He just put the text of the message on the nightstand next to the bed where Oberg had stretched out.

Oberg sat up and started to read in a firm, clear voice:

"The person mentioned should be given every assistance and vouchsafed contact with us in this way. Cooperation with him and others will become necessary in an action of primary importance."

I am at your service, Herr Sturmbannführer, Merser announced.

THREE DAYS LATER, MERSER ARRANGED for three of Ebtehaj's men to pick up Oberg in front of the house on Kakh Street. They had procured a military truck as well as the papers that would get the vehicle swiftly waved through any Iranian police checkpoint—as long as a substantial wad of cash was handed over, too.

On Oberg's instructions, they drove out to the dry lake near Qom, the site where he had parachuted into Iran. It did not take them long to locate the dark, coffin-shaped metal containers that had been dropped by parachute the previous night. They were heavy, and it took two men to lift each one and load it into the truck.

Oberg waited until the containers were stored in the cellar on Kakh Street in an orderly line. Then he opened them, one after another.

They were filled with weapons and ammunition. Sten guns. Russian submachine guns. And Gammon bombs. Enough firepower to kill Roosevelt, Churchill, and Stalin. And the men who would die trying to protect them.

31

MIKE WAS AWAKENED AT MIDNIGHT by the ringing telephone, realizing at once that a call in the middle of the night never brought good news. And since he was being pulled from his sleep as he lay in Oran, Algeria, with the president scheduled to arrive in three days, he knew that the insistent ring was screaming a three-alarm disaster.

The caller was Colonel Frank McCarthy, the aide to the scholarly army chief of staff, General George Marshall, and he was in an unfettered state. His words rattled out quickly, like the rapid pounding of typewriter keys, and, more cause for dismay, the tone was heavy with doom and gloom. Mike's presence was immediately needed at General Eisenhower's headquarters in Algiers, he as good as groaned.

The precipitate summons alone would have been sufficient to fill Mike's imagination with notions of all sorts of tragedies that might have befallen the Boss as he traveled across the wartime Atlantic. But when McCarthy steadfastly refused to share any details, Mike proceeded to fill in the blanks with the worst possible of visions. The most the colonel would offer was a small explanation for his guardedness. There was no telling who might be listening to their phone conversation, he said ominously. And he repeated: You need to come to Algiers immediately. Then he slammed down the phone.

Now fully awake, Mike looked out the window. A storm was raging in Oran. Cresting waves bounced the fishing boats anchored in the port harbor high above the turbulent sea before they came crashing down. The spires of Fort Santa Cruz reached up into a dark night sky electrified with jarring slashes of lightning. Torrents of slate-gray rain pelted the entire city. And Algiers was four hundred miles away.

Flying was impossible on a night like this. The only way to get there would be to drive. So Mike roused Secret Service agent George Durno, and together they set out on the perilous journey. The roads in North Africa were a trek in any weather, but that night the asphalt was slick with rain, and those proved to be the most accommodating stretches; too often they found themselves plowing through bogs of mud or navigating bumper-high flood-waters. Visibility was a joke; all they could do was pray that no one else would be reckless enough to be driving on a night like this. The one small godsend in the entire tense, totally miserable trip was that Mike's mind was fixed on the road, his concentration focused on the immediate problems and perils. He had little time to dwell on what might have happened to the president, whether he was alive or dead.

With the new day breaking and the storm nearly played out, they arrived in Algiers. Mike was totally spent; it was as if all his internal resources had been drained away in the course of the harrowing ride. Yet Mike didn't hesitate. He went straight off to find McCarthy. He needed to know what had happened to the president. It was all that mattered.

The Boss was fine, as things turned out. Churchill was the problem.

Mike learned that the prime minister wanted to change the site of the first conference from Cairo to Malta. His reason? As best a testy, exhausted Mike could understand, there was no compelling logic to the last-minute request. It was merely, Mike grumbled, "one of the Prime Minister's fits of whimsy or something." But a decision had to be made whether to give in to Churchill's mood.

Eisenhower and Marshall, with the self-protective astuteness of natural politicians, wanted not only Mike's assessment of the two sites, but also him to be the one to inform the president. And by putting the decision on his broad shoulders, Mike couldn't help but feel they were making a tacit point: it would be his head on the chopping block if anything happened to the president in either location.

Which was fine with him. At this cranky point, after having been pulled from sleep, frightened out of his wits by the colonel's cryptic message, and beaten down by the agonizing all-night drive, Mike had no trouble speaking his mind. He quickly sent a message to the *Iowa* relaying the prime minister's change of heart, but also taking care to add pointedly that he'd carry out the original instructions he'd received unless he heard to the contrary directly from the president.

He didn't have to wait very long for a reply, and it came, as he'd requested, straight from FDR: "No change in my plans as to Cairo. Repeat no change in my plans as to Cairo. Hull told me he talked to you."

It was with a small sense of satisfaction that Mike watched as a terse message was sent to Churchill at sea: the prime minister would be expected in Cairo. Then, his torturous night finally over, Mike went off to find a bed where he could lie down and catch up on his sleep before he was awakened by the next crisis.

HE MANAGED TO RETURN TO Oran before it reared up: the Germans had a new weapon. The Nazi glide torpedo—officially the Henschel Hs 293—was a fast-moving guided missile that had been zeroing in on Allied ships with a calamitous accuracy. Dropped from a bomber, the torpedo would crash into the sea with its rocket engines churning at the incredible speed of 750 feet a second, its sensors homing in, until it smashed into a ship's hull with 650 pounds of high explosives. It had already sunk so many British ships that the Royal Navy had suspended anti-U-boat patrols in the Bay of Biscay (and in six days an Hs 293 would sink a troop transport; over one thousand soldiers would perish). Tomorrow the *Iowa* carrying the president and the Joint Chiefs would be heading through the Strait of Gibraltar—a contained hunting ground. As soon as this intelligence was shared with Mike, the phrase "shooting fish in a barrel" began reverberating through his mind.

A decision was made, and a flash message was sent to the skipper of the *Iowa*: Be prepared to change course to the alternate port of Dakar. Only within the hour there was new intel: A flotilla of German subs was now racing to Dakar. This news threw Mike into a quandary. "Dakar meant subs," he mused forlornly. "Oran meant glide torpedoes." Either, he had little doubt, could get the job done. And just as distressing, he now concluded, "it looked very much as if someone knew something." The Nazis had responded to all his moves with an unerring accuracy, and the conference hadn't even begun. He doubted it was simply luck that was informing their decisions. He did not like the way this was shaping up at all.

But Admiral Henry Hewitt, the naval commander in the region, was not a man to back away from a fight. He had successfully helmed the US task force during the invasion of North Africa, and he felt the best choice was to "bull the *Iowa*" through the Strait of Gibraltar under the cover of darkness. At the same time, his forces hit the area hard. One sub was sunk by a US plane, and a squadron of fierce destroyers had the other enemy ships on the run. The *Iowa* plowed its clandestine way undisturbed through the pitch-black passageway.

Suddenly, the huge battleship was bathed in a bright light. From the Spanish shore, a battery of powerful searchlights had been trained on the ship, trapping it in a harsh white halo. The distinctive superstructure was perfectly silhouetted against the night. The *Iowa*, dramatically illuminated, was a sitting target, nearly impossible for the enemy to miss.

It was never determined who gave the reckless order to shine the bright lights on the ship as it made its way through the strait. And fortunately there was no need to convene a court of inquiry. At daybreak the *Iowa* anchored without incident near Oran.

Mike bounded on board at eight a.m. He wasn't sure what to expect, but he was cheered to find the Boss looking so chipper after the long sea voyage. As for his agents who had made the ocean journey with the president, that was another matter. Mike found that "they were in a worse nervous condition than I ever was." When they told him about the torpedo that had nearly hit the ship, his own stomach dipped as violently as if he'd been there, too.

He lifted the crippled president in his strong arms and with great care began to lower the commander in chief gently into a seat on the *Iowa*'s whaleboat. At that moment, cradling the president's limp weight, Mike found it impossible not to think about the man's vulnerability.

As the motorized craft made its way without ceremony in the bright morning light to the Mers el-Kébir boat landing, Mike was glad to be back at the Boss's side. It was November 20. In two days they would be in Cairo, and before the next week was over they'd arrive in Tehran. It was a dangerous world, and in wartime anything could happen. Uncertainty was the dialectic that shaped each new day. Yet Mike looked down at the fragile, disabled man who was his friend and uttered a silent vow: He'd get the Boss back home safe and sound.

SCHELLENBERG, AS IT HAPPENED, was also contemplating the calendar as he searched for his own bit of certainty. He wanted to believe that one day this month held the specific clue he needed. It would be the answer to the two remaining questions that continued to hover over Long Jump: Precisely when and where in Tehran should the assassination take place?

He had ordered the Group G researchers to compile a list of occasions in the month ahead—November 1943—when the Allied leaders would conceivably gather together to celebrate. Only now that he had the memo in his hand, he wondered if he'd been too hopeful. How would he be able to determine the answer, isolate the one moment when no matter what else in which the three Allied leaders were involved, no matter the state of their own variable moods or their entrenched personal antagonisms, no matter how divisive the summit debates proved to be, they would all put everything else aside and get together in Tehran outside the conference room? The burrowers had done their research, but his process would be entirely subjective. He would need to be guided by his instincts. Facts were one thing, but he was looking for something much more human. He was not a sentimental man, but he would need to think like one. All he could do was hope that he had a sense of the men he was hunting.

It was a short list, and, with so much at stake, he spent a good deal of time considering each of the items. Yet since it was by necessity a recitation of Allied victories—what else would they be celebrating, after all?—it was a particularly grim voyage back through recent history.

With a Teutonic orderliness, the memo had been arranged chronologically, and therefore the first event he considered was the anniversary of the victory at El Alamein a year earlier on November 11, 1942. The Big Three, he acknowledged, would not be convening in Tehran until later in the month, but it was indisputably a significant Allied victory. It had put an end to Germany's ambitions in Egypt, in the entire Middle East for that sad matter. And it had ensured that the Nazis would never get control of the Iranian oil fields. Perhaps that alone made it an event that would be appropriately commemorated with an official dinner in Tehran, he told himself. But in the next low moment, he conceded that even if they did decide to celebrate their rout at El Alamein, that knowledge hadn't taken him any closer to discovering a specific day or place for the celebration in Tehran.

He continued down the list, mentally crossing off one after another of the possibilities until he saw something that made him come to a sudden halt. Now he was intrigued, and he began to play with this piece of intelligence, trying to fit it into the puzzle he'd created. If Churchill, FDR, and Stalin were looking to celebrate a regional victory, he asked himself, wouldn't the Allied invasion of North Africa fit the bill more precisely? November 16, 1942, was the date cited by the Group G burrowers. That was when the shooting had officially stopped. It was the first American-British joint operation, and it had been a resounding success. Of course, there were no Russian forces involved, but he suspected even crusty Stalin would find it was worthy of an appreciative toast: it was the first step toward the now inevitable Allied invasion of Europe, toward the opening of the second front that would take the pressure off the besieged Red Army. Yes, he started to feel, there very well might be a dinner in its honor. But like a fisherman who tosses his hard-won catch back into the sea, he knew in the end that the date was not quite right. On November 16 the Big Three would still not have arrived in Cairo.

In fact, he further remonstrated, if Stalin wanted to commemorate a military victory, he would hardly be content with a battle in which the Russians didn't do the fighting. Especially when there was one that fit into the time frame. A year earlier, on November 23, his forces had completed the encirclement of the German Sixth Army at Stalingrad. Schellenberg could imagine the Soviet marshal pouring rivers of vodka and shoveling mountains of caviar for his fellow Allies at an anniversary dinner at the Russian embassy. But as he held the thought, he ultimately found it unsatisfactory. Would the dogmatic Churchill, bristling with all his antipathy for the Bolsheviks, really want to attend a dinner honoring the Red Army? he asked himself. Once the question was raised, the answer became apparent.

He played with his problem. And as he did, Schellenberg grew convinced he'd been approaching things from the wrong direction. It wouldn't be a military event that would coax them to drop everything and go off and celebrate. Each of the men was too jingoistic, too proud to cheer another country's soldiers. The occasion would be something less charged with political or martial connections, something more benign.

With his mind traveling down this new avenue of possibilities, he scoured the list again and saw that the American holiday of Thanksgiving fell on November 26. Yes, he thought, that would very likely be an occasion when Roosevelt would host a dinner at the American embassy. But would Stalin have ideological concerns about attending a dinner, a feast, celebrated by American capitalists? And there was no guarantee, if the intelligence reports Cicero had been sending were accurate, that the Big Three would have arrived in Tehran by that date.

But Schellenberg felt assured that at last he was plowing the right terrain. He returned to the list and paid close attention to national holidays, wedding anniversaries, birthdays.

Then he found it.

It was the one event they'd all be certain to celebrate, when they'd all convene regardless of national politics or personal feuds. It was the one occasion when they'd have no concerns about putting aside their differences for an evening and acting like allies. He was certain he had the date he needed.

He also knew where the celebration would take place. It was the only location that made sense. That would be appropriate.

At last Schellenberg possessed the time and place for the murders of Roosevelt, Churchill, and Stalin. With a vision of the impending battle shining in his eyes, he went off to inform Skorzeny. The moment had come to send the teams of assassins into Iran.

32

FROM THE START OF FDR's journey across North Africa, it had been Mike who'd been gripped by the single-minded fear that the Nazis would target the president's plane. When the "Sacred Cow" had taken off from La Sénia Airport outside Oran for the three-and-a-half-hour flight to Tunis two days earlier, Mike had helped the president settle into his seat, and not for the first time a grisly image had lodged in his mind: the crippled president laying helplessly in the shattered plane's debris. And there would've been nothing he could have done, Mike knew, to have prevented such a catastrophe—except to have stopped the Boss from getting on the plane in the first place. He had tried to deflate the enormous tension pressing down on him with a morbid joke: "Any Luftwaffe pilot who knocked off that plane would have very little trouble getting himself a weekend pass to Berlin." But he quickly realized it was a statement that cut with more truth than humor.

Mike had not been alone in his assessments of the risk. On the day the president had arrived in Oran, Henry Stimson, the usually temperate secretary of war, had sent off a cable boldly warning of the danger that surrounded the upcoming flight to Egypt. He wanted the trip called off:

"If I were an Air Force Commander having control of between 90 and 100 JU 88 bombers and had received the press reports as to a specifically described target of unique importance within easy range of my advanced airports . . . I should stake every plane on the chance of winning such a prize."

But his ominous prediction had gone ignored, just as Mike's apprehension had remained stubbornly bottled up. And once the first leg of the journey, the flight to Tunis, had touched down without incident, all these anxieties had been somewhat shoved aside by last-minute preparations for the Cairo and Tehran Conferences, as well as some sightseeing.

Still, it was impossible to escape the war. Its monstrous presence hovered everywhere. The president spent two nights in Carthage, in a luxurious bone-white villa that, Mike, swelling with a patriotic pride, crowed "only a few months before . . . had been the home of the crack Nazi general, Rommel." (While much later, deep in another sort of mood, he would make the historical connection between Rome's vengeful destruction of Carthage and the genesis of the Nazi plot into which he had been heading.) And there had been battlefield tours, with no less an authority than General Eisenhower providing vivid running commentary to the commander in chief, as Mike trailed closely behind in a separate jeep. They drove by the fire-singed carcasses of burned-out American and German tanks, past minefields that remained seeded with buried terrors, and gazing up toward the steep summit of Hill 609, they tried to put themselves in the boots of the dogged American GIs who had found the raw courage to fight their way to the top under a nearly constant torrent of artillery and small arms fire. Yet what Mike found most affecting—"Poignant," he'd say—was a sight he'd happened to observe when a large, steady, purposeful drone of airplane engines caused him to crane his neck reflexively to the sky. He looked up and saw at least fifty medium bombers returning from a mission on the other side of the Mediterranean. They were several groups and they were all flying in neat Vs, only the formations were not complete. Each empty space, Mike knew, meant "they had left companions on the other side." It was a sight, chilling and empathetic, that left Mike with a renewed understanding of the importance of what the Boss hoped to accomplish in the week ahead, as at the same time it served as a distinct reminder of the genuine danger the president would be exposed to as he ventured closer to enemy territory.

Mike knew he needed to work on clamping down his emotions. He tried telling himself he was seeing things out of proportion.

Then on the morning of the flight to Cairo, Mike's recurring nightmare suddenly became real for the officers and air traffic controllers at the North African flight command headquarters. The president's plane vanished from the radar screens. For two hours it was missing. The big C-54 had been scheduled to arrive in Cairo at eight a.m., but repeated attempts to contact the pilot, Major Otis Bryan, were futile. Fighter escorts that had planned to rendezvous in the first light of dawn with the plane as it approached Cairo from the south were now flying a search mission, scanning the desert for smoldering wreckage. And the irony was that it was all Mike's fault.

Yet while Mike was to blame, in his defense the case could be made that he'd been following the commander in chief's orders. The "Sacred Cow" had taken off for Cairo in the furtive darkness of a North African night from El Aouina field outside Tunis. As a further precaution, radio silence had been ordered; rather than risk alerting an eavesdropping enemy to the identity of the passengers on the flight, the pilot had been instructed neither to transmit nor receive any messages. The huge plane had reached cruising level when Mike was summoned to the president's cabin, the Boss already strapped in, ready for sleep. The president wore the bulky, chemically treated socks that he'd received as a going-away present for the trip; after a tablespoon of water had been added, they were as comforting as a heating pad.

"We've traveled this far, we should fly up the Nile and over the pyramids," the president announced, grinning like a happy child at the prospect. "Tell the captain to change the route," he ordered. Mike should awaken him as soon as they got close. He didn't want to miss a thing, he said with excitement.

Mike relayed the orders to Major Bryan, and at once the navigator got to work plotting the new itinerary. At that moment Mike considered breaking radio silence, informing the Allied Air Command in Cairo that the president's plane would be delayed, but he swiftly rejected the idea. What if the Luftwaffe was monitoring the late-night airwaves? He'd be providing them with the coordinates they'd need to attack. It would create one hell of a panic, he imagined, when the president's plane didn't arrive on schedule, but there'd be no permanent damage (except for Mike's standing with the generals). But, Mike firmly reminded himself, there was only one man to whom he had to answer, and he outranked them all.

Mike never slept on planes; he felt that with the president so defenseless, he needed to be on alert in case there was a sudden call to action. He was awake, therefore, at seven a.m. when the aircraft started up the Nile toward the southernmost pyramid. He hurried to rouse FDR.

The Boss stared out the window and was thrilled. As a boy, he'd been captivated by his studies of the ancients at the Groton School and had won prizes for his knowledge. Now the past was becoming real for him in a way that he'd never imagined as a youth. He sent word to the pilot that the plane was to continue circling until he ordered otherwise. Around and around it went, as FDR, transfixed, continued to look out the window at the monuments, their bleached, weathered stones caught in the harsh glow of the day's early sun. "Man's desire to be remembered is colossal," the president said to Mike as he looked with pensive wonder at the Great Pyramid.

The president's plane landed in Cairo two hours later than anticipated—and without the protection of the fighter escort that had been sent to shepherd it in. As Mike had predicted, "our unreportable sight-seeing jaunt set the Cairo air headquarters on its ear . . . you could hear the brass sizzling all over headquarters."

But by ten that morning—November 22—they were at the sumptuous canal-front villa of US ambassador Kirk, the residence set in a cool, verdant oasis, now the president's home for his stay in Egypt. The first session of the conference would not start till after lunch. Mike had hoped he'd be able to catch up on the sleep he'd missed on the plane, but the same terrors that kept him awake through the night assaulted him during the day. He found himself anxiously contemplating the prospect that man's colossal desire to be remembered applied with equal measure to pharaohs, presidents, prime ministers, dictators—and Nazi assassins.

ON THE VERY DAY THAT Mike flew to Cairo, Skorzeny and his commando teams had taken to the air, too, heading east into a city steeped in death.

The send-off from the *Schloss* at Oranienburg had little ceremony; the gravity of the mission had been sufficient. Yet despite all that was at stake, despite the audaciousness of their ambitions, it was a time of high confidence. Schellenberg had huddled with Skorzeny and Holten-Pflug, who'd serve as the famous commando's adjunct on the ground in Iran, and together the three had worked out the final operational details. They were convinced they had conceived a plan that would enable the teams to beat the security screen the Allies would erect around the Big Three. The tactical advantages were all theirs.

The enemy would not be expecting men in Russian uniforms. However, in the event they grew suspicious, the assault teams could pass any test. They were in every way what they appeared to be: genuine Russian soldiers. Except, of course, for one defining, yet imperceptible detail—they had switched their allegiance to Germany.

Security forces would be everywhere in Tehran—but the water tunnels would, as always, remain unguarded. The tunnels would lead the teams undetected into the killing zone, just as effectively as the gliders had covertly delivered Skorzeny's men to the Italian mountaintop to rescue Mussolini.

At close quarters, the Russian submachine guns and the British

Sten guns on full auto would purr like sewing machines, spewing out twenty rounds in under three seconds, savagely cutting down the three targets and their cordons of protectors—that is, if the explosions from the Gammon bombs hurled across the enclosed space hadn't already annihilated the enemy.

And there was no longer any doubt about the specific time for the attack, or where it should take place. Schellenberg had worked it out, and when he'd ran his findings by Skorzeny and Holten-Pflug, both of the commandos agreed that it was not a hypothetical deduction, but something definitive. It was the key to open the final lock, and now that it had been turned, the door was wide open. They could walk right in, with little to stop them. They would take their targets completely by surprise. Nothing had been left to chance.

With the strategy finally settled, the tactical battle order had fallen into place with a concomitant and reassuring swiftness. There would be two teams of Russians, each consisting of eighteen of the fiercest Vlasov renegades as well as a native Iranian translator recruited from the ranks of the Brandenburger Interpreters Training Unit.

The North Team, as it became informally known, would lead the way. They'd parachute into the flat plain outside Qazvīn, the city once the capital of the ancient Persian Empire and now part of the Soviet occupied zone. They'd be met by Qashqai tribesmen and loaded into trucks for the one-hundred-mile or so trip to Tehran. It would be a long journey, but the judgment had been made that Russian soldiers traveling from the Soviet zone would not attract attention. And if the Vlasov soldiers were stopped by a Soviet patrol, they'd have no trouble talking their way through any difficulties. In the city, they'd go to ground in safe houses until the signal came to rendezvous at the entrance to the water tunnel. There had been some discussion over whether it was wise to lie low in the city, or if it made better sense to bivouac in the desert closer to the tunnel site. Schellenberg insisted that the rambling city of Tehran offered more protection than the open desert. Skorzeny, though, suddenly had new doubts. Bristling with an operational caution, he proposed another schedule: wait until the last minute to infiltrate the teams into Iran; that way, they could proceed directly to the water tunnel. But Schellenberg, for once growing angry, overruled this. As soon as the conference started, he explained in a testy rebuke, the Allies would be on high alert for enemy aircraft. Success depended on the teams being in Iran before the entire country was shut down tight. When he put it that way, both Skorzeny and Holten-Pflug acknowledged that he was correct: they should go in immediately, and make their way to the Tehran safe houses.

Hans Ortel, the experienced SS executioner handpicked by Schellenberg to work with the Russian recruits, would command the South Team. They would parachute into the dry lake site outside Qom where the Franz teams had landed. They, too, would be met by the tribesmen and taken to the safe houses that Oberg, assisted by Merser, had spent the past week inspecting and whose locations had already been passed on to Section 6.

Holten-Pflug would be jumping from a separate plane, but he would also come down in the Qom landing zone on the same night as the Ortel group. His team would consist of four Oranienburg commandos and a native-born Iranian, Gorechi, who had come to Berlin three years earlier to fight for the Reich. None of the members of this unit would be wearing Russian uniforms; it was a disguise that was an anathema to men who had lost friends fighting in the East. And Holten-Pflug, like Skorzeny, wanted the victims to know in the last moments before their death that they were staring into the guns of German soldiers.

Skorzeny and his five-man team would wait behind, ready to make the tactical adjustments necessary if any unforeseen problems arose once the teams were settled in Tehran. Ortel had been in-structed to radio when the situation had clarified. If there were no unexpected fires to put out, he'd relay the go signal, and Skorzeny would head out at once.

Now the teams were airborne to Simferopol in the Crimea. It was a city the Nazis had captured in November 1941 and then quickly drenched in blood. The Einsatzgruppe D squads had dispersed methodically through the old Tatar neighborhoods and mercilessly rounded up Jews, Russians, and Gypsies. When the executions were over, the lifeless bodies of more than twenty-two thousand civilians had been crammed into a vast, deep pit. In the aftermath of this massacre, neighborhoods throughout the city had become ghost towns, the empty streets and homes steeped in the unnerving, heavy stillness of the graveyard.

The team's flight to the Simferopol airport was uneventful. They made their way to long, gray barracks where they would receive the signal to board the Junkers transports that would fly them into Iran. This last period of waiting was difficult, but they were men whose emotions were constrained by iron bands of discipline. Their spirits did not falter. Everything had been considered. From now on there would be no shrinking back, no reason for hesitation. They were certain Long Jump would not fail. Holten-Pflug had already settled on the scale by which he would be measured, the reward he'd claim. He boasted he'd soon be "the next Skorzeny," his soldier's renown forever a part of the glorious history of the Fatherland.

"*Man's desire to be remembered is colossal,*" the president had warned.

IN ALL THE FEVERISH PREPARATIONS for Long Jump, there was a small incident that had gone unnoticed at the time. A routine request had been made to Section 6's Iranian desk to provide Schellenberg with daily weather reports for the cities of Qazvīn and Qom for the week beginning November 22.

Roman Gamotha, the deskman in charge, dutifully prepared the information and regularly passed it on to the SS general. He had no knowledge of what sort of operation Schellenberg was mounting, but it apparently involved aerial insertions into Iran. As for the details, he'd let his bosses at Moscow Center figure that out.

33

THEY COULD BARELY BREATHE. Their hearts were racing. They kept checking the oxygen levels, only to realize it wouldn't be long until the tanks were empty. The Vlasov Russians had begun to fear they'd lose consciousness before the jumpmaster, Luftwaffe staff sergeant Paulus, announced that they were over the drop site. It was not an auspicious start to Operation Long Jump.

The problem was the altitude. The special operations pilot, Captain Karl-Edmund Gartenfeld, was an old hand, an SD specialist in long-range covert aerial insertions, who'd received the Knight's Cross after he'd delivered the Franz and Anton parachutists to Iran. It had been a smooth flight, the biting cold that seeped into the poorly insulated cabin more a cause for grousing than a real concern, as the speedy Ju-290 had risen above the Simferopol steppes and headed south across the Black Sea toward Iran. But as the plane approached neutral Turkey, Captain Gartenfeld pulled back the stick, and the plane's four powerful BMW engines lifted it high into the dark sky, above the clouds and hopefully out of the sight of radar. Then he crossed into Iran, and the walls of formidable mountains as well as the possibility of lurking Soviet fighter patrols made him take the aircraft even higher, climbing up to nearly 18,000 feet.

At that altitude experienced parachutists would not have had any troubles. They knew the drill: sit quietly; no unnecessary gestures or conversation; don't move about the cabin. Maintain control, and the oxygen in the tanks would be sufficient. But the Vlasov Russians hadn't had much training. Sergeant Paulus had guided them

through only a single practice jump from the tower at Oranienburg; Skorzeny's rationale was that repetition would only increase
the odds of one of the Russians breaking his leg, and he needed
every one of them. And, an unforgivable oversight, there'd been no
instruction at all in the necessity for rationing the intake of oxygen
once they were airborne.

As the Ju-290 climbed rapidly, bone-rattling icy blasts penetrated the cabin, the increased air pressure slammed down on their
chests like anvils, and the anxious men reacted by gorging on
more and more oxygen. They'd boarded the plane with the solemn knowledge that they were heading off on a mission behind
enemy lines that would change the course of history. They also
understood that many of them—perhaps all, the most practical had
already conceded—would not return. They had been resigned to
their fates. In the world of a soldier, there was always the awareness
that a moment's calm can be ruptured by an unseen bullet. But they
had not been prepared for this, for the gasping for breath, for the
light-headedness, for the utter collapse of their mission before it had
even gotten underway. Tension built in this vacuum. When the first
Russian slumped inertly forward, panic would take hold.

Then, just when it seemed like it would never happen, a yellow
interior light was illuminated, and the plane began its descent. The
jump level was set at 330 feet, and breathing was no longer difficult.
The men struggled to their feet, shook off any lingering disorienta-
tion, hooked their D-bags containing their chutes to the static line,
and made their way single file to the rear drop door.

A sickle moon hung in the sky. There wasn't much wind, always
a blessing for a jump. And below, just beyond the city of Qazvīn, a
flat, dark plain stretched across the pitch-black desert. Then as the
plane flew closer to the drop site, a semicircle of headlights suddenly
lit up the terrain in an unnatural glow. This was the signal the
jumpmaster had been hoping to receive: the Qashqai welcoming
committee and their trucks were in place.

The interior light turned green. Go! Go! Sergeant Paulus shouted.

One rapidly after another, the Russians jumped into the blackness of the night. Within a quick thirteen seconds all the parachutists had exited. Captain Gartenfeld started his ascent, climbing back above the radar, eager to head back to the safety of the Crimean base. His mission was accomplished.

The parachutists felt a sharp yet reassuring jolt as their canopies opened. They were floating calmly, propelled by only a thin wind. When they looked down, they could see the elongated, opaque shadows the trucks' headlights cast across the flat plain.

The descent continued, and the men standing by the trucks became discernible, something more than gray stick figures.

Then it must have happened. There undoubtedly was a terrifying moment of realization as they processed what they were seeing: the men flanking the trucks were not native tribesmen. They were wearing khaki uniforms like theirs, the identical red shoulder boards, the identical peaked hats.

At once the desert stillness was shattered. Flashes of light jumped up into the sky. Trapped in the beam of the headlights, unable to maneuver, defenseless, their faces imploring, the parachutists were illuminated targets as they fell to earth. The stream of bullets from the Soviet troops ripped them apart as if they were rag dolls. Three of the Vlasov recruits had the good fortune to land wide of the drop zone, and with the brutal sound of the massacre in their ears they ran for their lives, heading toward the mountain foothills. By the following afternoon, the Russian troops would track them down. None of the captives survived their questioning, which was precisely as the interrogators had intended. They died without having a chance to unravel the web of treachery that had betrayed them.

MIKE, TOO, HAD BEGUN HIS day worrying about the problems caused by the high-altitude flight to Tehran. Actually, it had been Admiral Ross McIntire, FDR's attentive physician and confidant, who had first raised the issue, insisting that the rigors of flying at an altitude necessary to clear the imposing Iranian mountain ranges would be too much of a strain for the president as well as his middle-aged advisers (just as it had nearly been for the young, fit Vlasov soldiers). But it was Mike who had been ordered to go without delay to Tehran and investigate an alternate route into the city.

He did not mind. In three days the Big Three would be in Tehran. It was high time, he knew, that he conducted a full-blown security assessment. And this go-round he had no intention of slinking about in the shadows. He'd make his presence known, as at the same time he took the measure of the allies he'd be working with. Or, as he was beginning to suspect, against.

Earlier that morning the president had filled him in: the intrigues had already started. First the Russian first assistant commissar for foreign affairs, the unctuously polite A. Y. Vyshinsky, had come calling at a bright-and-early ten a.m. to extend Marshal Stalin's invitation to stay at the Russian embassy in Tehran. This was quickly followed by a cable announcing that Prime Minister Churchill was offering the president the hospitality of the British embassy. The ostensible reason for both invitations was convenience: the American legation was on the periphery of the city, while the two embassies were in a walled, parklike compound nearly shoulder to shoulder to one another. Rather than having to embark on a tense motorcade through twisting streets, the president would be wheeled past gurgling fountains, reflecting pools, and green lawns to attend the conference sessions. But Mike suspected something else was afoot. He had little doubt the president was on to it, too.

The lamp on FDR's desk in the Oval Office concealed a microphone. Back in 1939, fuming that unscrupulous (or so the president had subjectively seen it) reporters had twisted his words, a device employing motion picture sound recording technology was installed in a room directly below the Oval Office. At the flick of a switch hidden inside his desk drawer, the president could activate the mike. During his campaign for a third term, he made good use

of the device, recording press conferences and private conversations. Then, for reasons he never explained (or at least not to Mike),
he'd stopped flicking the switch in his desk drawer. But FDR also
was well aware that the Soviets shared a penchant for bugging, too.
A microphone had been discovered embedded in the wall directly
above the desk of the US ambassador in the Moscow embassy. Mike
couldn't help suspecting that there were ulterior motives, and none
benignly generous, similarly embedded in the allied invitations to
the president. The president, too, was not inclined to be a house-
guest. He "wished to be more independent than a guest could hope
to be," he told Mike, the words bristling with a tacit reproach.

At eleven thirty that morning, Mike, with two of his burly
agents in tow, flew off to Tehran. Major Bryan, the president's pilot,
told him he could fly the entire way under six thousand feet. That
altitude wouldn't put a strain on anyone's heart in the well-insulated
Sacred Cow. Admiral Mac (as the inner circle called FDR's convivial physician) was just being a worrywart, the confident airman
insisted. Show me, replied Mike.

Major Bryan did. In the course of the entire trip, the altimeter
needle never crossed six thousand.

WHAT HAD IT TAKEN TO put the White House on wartime footing? Mike recalled glumly as he toured the American legation.
Machine gun nests and artillery installations. Fluoroscopes and a
"talking fence." A rooftop antiaircraft battery. Prowling Secret Service men with communication microphones on their lapels. The
transformation had taken months. And this had been in Washington, DC. Yet even after all the precautions had been put in place,
he had never felt at ease, had never felt totally confident. His mind
would not rest, and he often found himself staring into visions of
potential disasters. As at the same time he relived an old one: a knife
hurled at the president's chest and he standing yards away, helpless

to intervene. Now in Tehran that disconcerting image gripped him once again. In a city he was certain was "crawling with foreign agents," how could he ensure the Boss's safety?

He had no choice but to go to work. He posted snipers on the legation's roof. Doubled the guard around the surrounding wall. Ordered the MPs to set up checkpoints along a cordon stretching around the legation. He inspected the grounds, making sure soldiers would be strategically positioned as sentinels. He made certain the ramps would be in place for the Boss's wheelchair, and he inspected the presidential bedroom, checking that all the windows were locked and the curtains could be tightly drawn to prevent a sniper from sighting his target. He toured the kitchen, where the president's own Filipino mess staff would be running the show, and he ordered that no Iranians should be employed as kitchen workers or as domestics while the Boss was in residence; GIs would take up the slack. And when he was told there was running water in the legation's faucets and that it was eminently drinkable, he said he wasn't taking chances. He had already requisitioned bottled water to follow the president to Tehran. At least, Mike reassured himself, the city's water was one less problem over which he'd need to fret.

He drove the four miles to the British embassy and was given a tour of the dining and conference rooms. He could only hope the English would have sufficient guards in place, but after what he'd observed when Churchill was in Washington, he had little confidence. All he could do to bolster his sagging spirits was to remind himself that he'd never be far from the Boss's side. The British were very proud of the surrounding grounds, a verdant, carefully planted park inspired by a stately English home. All Mike could see was a jungle where enemy agents could hide.

It was just a short walk across this park to the Russian embassy. A long, very imperial flight of stone steps led up to a lofty, colonnaded portico and the front door. The immense building had the gilded look of a Tsarist palace rather than the residence of a proletarian Bolshevik official.

As Mike was being given a not-very-forthcoming tour—his hosts, he'd complain, "suspicious," "grim," and "frank beyond the point of rudeness"—a Russian officer approached. Mike had met him earlier that day at Gale Morghe Airport, and he had introduced himself as General Dmitry Arkadiev. Mike knew he was NKVD and thought of him as "my opposite number" in Tehran. The forty-three-year-old Russian general was an intelligence officer, but his post was not as exalted as Mike had presumed. He headed the NKVD department of transportation; Lavrenty Beria, the NKVD spymaster who had sneaked into the city to help make preparations for the summit, and Andrei Vertinski, the Tehran station chief, preferred to stay in the shadows rather than expose themselves to the scrutiny of an American Secret Service officer. But regardless of his place in the Soviet intelligence hierarchy, Arkadiev delivered an unnerving report.

German parachutists had dropped into the Russian sector outside Tehran the previous day, he announced, referring to the North Team of Vlasov Russians who had landed near Qazvīn. He said that a few were still at large, hiding in the mountains, which at the time was true. He did not add that the majority of the commandos had been shot even before they'd touched the ground. Or that Russian troops had had prior knowledge of their insertion, and had been lying in wait, poised for the ambush.

The Russian said it was not a significant enemy operation. He was informing Mike about the parachutists more out of a fraternal politeness than any real concern. He believed it had been a Nazi mission to sabotage the railroad that delivered the American Lend-Lease supplies to Russia. How could it have been anything more? The Germans did not even know about the Tehran Conference. There had been many other attacks on the Trans-Iranian Railway by the enemy, he helpfully pointed out.

Perhaps, Mike agreed succinctly. He was not about to share what was on his mind with a Russian intelligence officer. But at that moment all his old anxieties were rekindled, illnesses that had risen up from their dormancy to strike him down. "This was bad news," Mike told himself. "In a few days Roosevelt, Churchill, and Stalin would be in Tehran." He found himself wondering if everything that he had been calling fear was really vigilance. Or intuition.

After leaving the embassy, he flew on to Basra on the Persian Gulf. He had no choice. If Admiral McIntire continued to insist that the flight to Tehran was a heart attack in the making, he needed to get a sense of what sort of alternative a trip by train from Basra would be. Nothing he saw left him heartened. The tracks running to Tehran climbed at some points to a heart-pounding eight thousand feet while at the same perilous time they wound willy-nilly around narrow mountain crests. Native tribesmen often raided the trains, and many dead and wounded American MPs were testimony to their ferocity. And when Mike inspected the shah's personal train, the four private cars that had been proposed to be FDR's accommodations for the two-day trip, he found gold-plated fittings on the doors, mahogany-paneled cabins, a dinner service fashioned out of solid gold, and, he suspected, a rampant breeding ground for typhus lice. "The train was certainly the finest typhus-laden piece of traveling equipment in the world," he judged mercilessly.

Having done his duty in Basra, he flew back to Cairo. He'd tell the Boss and Admiral Mac what he'd seen, offer his recommendation, and the final decision would be up to them. With that resolved, he pushed aside any further thoughts on how the president would get to Tehran. Instead, he spent the return flight pondering what might be in store for the Boss once he arrived in the city.

The German paratroopers, he knew, "could have been dropped for one of two reasons": either to "sabotage the railroad" or to "assassinate the Allied leaders." Either their mission had failed, and that was that, or more paratroopers would be coming to kill the president. By the time the C-54 landed in Cairo, Mike's mind was set. He couldn't rely solely on the Russians or the British; one was restrained by its political agenda, the other by its institutional complacencies. No longer trying to rein in his memories, he knew with every ounce of his being that he was not about to stand by idly once again as knives were thrown at the president. A battle plan hardened in his thoughts.

YET EVEN AS MIKE PREPARED to rush into battle, two Ju-290s, one carrying Ortel and his Vlasov troops, the other Holten-Pflug and his commandos, had flown off from Simferopol, heading across the night sky south to Iran.

In Berlin, Schellenberg could only wonder why the North Team had not sent a signal to confirm they'd landed. Perhaps their transmitter had been damaged during the jump. Soon, though, they'd be in place in Tehran. He was confident that once they reached the city, they'd locate a radio and send a report.

34

I T WAS TIME TO REEL Lili Sanjari in. The operational decision had been Mike's, and it had been shouted out in red-hot anger. Usually reserved, normally taking great care to project a professional demeanor, Mike had snapped. At that uncontrolled moment all his frustrations, as well as all his growing intimations of what lay ahead in Tehran, had bubbled over.

He'd returned from Basra on high alert, yet also as a man holding a handful of different theories at once, and giving each one its due before he found himself knocking it down. Part of him wanted to believe the Russian general had been correct, that the insertion of Nazi parachutists into Iran the previous night had been just another operation aimed at disrupting the Lend-Lease supply trains. But even as he tried to accept that explanation, he reasoned that the timing of their arrival on the outskirts of Tehran just days before the conference was too serendipitous. Then again, there are of course coincidences, he conceded. Yet was it so preposterous to assume the German intelligence services had gotten wind of the meeting, that they knew the dates when the Big Three would be in the city? Once he analyzed it like that, he knew he couldn't cavalierly shrug it off. He had to get to the bottom of things, to ferret out the crucial intelligence. Still, how could he? He was, he liked to say only partly in jest, "an Irish cop with more muscle than brains." And he was a long way from home. He had no experience in the exotic streets and bazaars of Tehran, no grasp of the spy networks the Germans had in place. This was not his turf. Yet he'd better learn what he could, and fast. It was a chase that, he acknowledged, would be hampered by his needing to be by the president's side. Nevertheless, he still had resources, not least a team of more than a dozen Secret Service agents, men he'd picked, men he'd trained. From this swirl of thoughts, doubts, and emotions, a resolution emerged: He'd follow his instincts. He'd not be put off course by either the passivity or rationalizations of others. He knew he could not simply wait for the enemy to strike. This time it would not be enough to put his body in front of the bullet.

In that mood of mounting alarm, Mike bullied his way into a meeting with Binks Penrose, the Cairo-based head of the Near Eastern desk of the OSS, the fledgling American spy service. Perhaps the spooks, he believed, would be able to give him a more complete picture of what the Nazis had going on in Iran. However, the tweedy Penrose, a former professor at the American University of Beirut with an undergraduate degree in chemistry and a doctorate in philosophy, was not very enthusiastic about talking shop with a hulking Secret Service man—even if the matter involved the potential assassination of the president. His tone was brisk, as if to say, We secret agents have more important matters to pry into than to consort with lowly bodyguards. The best Penrose could do—and he was being very accommodating, he insisted unconvincingly—was to put Mike in touch with an army Counter-Intelligence Corps (CIC) officer in General Connolly's Persian Gulf Command. Sabotage of the Trans-Iranian Railway was their bailiwick. And sabotage, he had no doubt, had been the German parachutists' sole objective. Nothing more, Penrose declared, flat and definitive.

A secure phone was found and Mike, his temper starting to boil from the runaround he was getting, was soon having a conversation with a CIC man in Tehran. The army officer had none of Penrose's haughty guardedness. He was only too glad to help, he said. He was proud of what his unit, working with the British, had accomplished.

He began his story as if it were a spy novel: Posing as an army

266 ·   Howard Blum

transport clerk, one of his men had also been spending his nights playing in a dance band. At the dance hall, he'd met a pretty, young Iranian woman, Lili Sanjari, known to have contacts in Tehran's German community. It wasn't long before they were spending their afternoons entwined in each other's arms. Their pillow talk had led to the arrest of Franz Mayr, a canny long-term Nazi penetration agent, several of his local assets, a German parachutist sent in on a sabotage mission who had gone to ground in the city, and the recovery of a cache of secret Nazi documents as well as a radio transmitter.

Mike listened patiently, but all the time his iron quiet was growing dangerous. Why was this the first time he was hearing all this? Why had it taken intelligence from a Russian—a Russian!—to start him walking down what he only now understood was a well-trodden trail? Didn't these spies realize the urgency? The president would be in Tehran in two days. Didn't they appreciate that we were all on the same side, fighting the same war?

Mike knew better than to explode. Instead, playing the plodding Secret Service man, affecting a deadly casualness, he asked whether he could send a couple of his men to talk to the woman. Perhaps they'd be able to wring some more intelligence out of the girl. Something that had been previously overlooked. There was always the possibility she might know people who were still communicating with Berlin.

The CIC officer took his time before answering. When he did, his tone was sheepish, all his previous swagger gone. The thing is, he said, we cut her loose. Haven't paid much attention to her since then. Didn't seem any point. Not sure we even know where Lili is.

That was when Mike had heard enough. You let her go? he challenged incredulously. Haven't paid much attention? Hadn't it occurred to you that she might have some idea what the Germans are up to in Tehran? If the Nazis have any surprises in store for the president? Bring her in! he ordered in a voice welled over with frustration, loud enough, the story would be told later, that people rushed into the office certain a bomb had been detonated, which in its way had been the case.

That same day, Robert Merrick, the musical CIC undercover agent, was told to find his onetime lover Lili Sanjari and arrest her.

Like many a fieldman out on his own, rather than blindly obeying an order, Merrick improvised. He was playing it long, he'd later contend. But whether it was a matter of tradecraft or simply lust, the pair wound up in a borrowed bedroom. In the confiding serenity that followed their lovemaking, Merrick found out everything— the address of the house she was staying in on Kakh Street, as well as the identities of her two roommates, one a German asset, and the other a heel-clicking German major on a secret mission. After they dressed, Merrick arrested her.

The CIC swarmed into the villa on Kakh Street. Not a shot was fired. Merser surrendered with an elegant bow. Oberg denied that he was a German major, insisted it was a misunderstanding. Then the canisters loaded with weapons were found in the basement, and since there was no way he could explain that, he stopped talking.

This was the report Mike received in a call from Tehran just minutes after the raid, and nothing in it did anything to douse the fire of concern burning inside him. He was told the CIC's interrogators would get Merser and the German major to talk; it was only a matter of time. But time was something he didn't have. The president would be leaving for Tehran in less than twenty-four hours. The cruel thought occurred to him that it might have been more productive if his new friend, the genial Russian general Arkadiev, had picked up the two Nazi agents rather than his own countrymen. At least the NKVD wouldn't be so squeamish, he imagined. They'd have no trouble getting the prisoners to confess to everything they knew, and then some.

As his anger and frustration subsided, he began to think things through. And a plan took shape.

But first Mike needed to talk to the president and Admiral McIntire. He laid out what he had learned over the past day the way a jury foreman might when reading a verdict—firm and to the point. The train from Basra to Tehran, he said, was a rolling plague site; it was loaded with typhus lice. Major Bryan, he went on, had flown the entire route while he'd been on board without ever once taking the plane above six thousand feet. His recommendation, then, was "to fly direct from Cairo to Tehran."

"Okay," the admiral agreed without putting up a fight. And the president seconded the decision.

Encouraged, beginning to feel that at least one problem had been solved, Mike left the president. He returned to the secure phone to launch his next offensive. He put in a call to General Arkadiev of the NKVD.

The general was not available, he was curtly informed by a Russian who spoke surprisingly good English. It will be necessary for him to call you back.

As soon as possible, Mike said. It's urgent. I'll wait by the phone.

It was an uneasy wait. Mike knew he was the supplicant, but he also recognized it'd be unwise to act like one. Although his opinion had been shaped by only a few brief meetings, he suspected the Russians would never respond to weakness. Therefore, he would not make a request. Rather, he'd tell the general what he intended to do, and then see if it raised any hackles. There'd be plenty of time to play the tough guy; or, for that matter, to beg. He realized that as soon as he'd made the call, there was no longer any possibility of retreat; he'd already crossed a border.

When the phone in front of him rang, Mike launched right in. I'd like to assign some of my team to work with you and your men. If additional parachutists are sighted, if there are more arrests, I want my people present. I want my men on the front lines with yours. We're fighting the war together in Europe. I want us to wage it together in Tehran, too.

Mike deliberately left unsaid what else he was thinking: without an accurate appraisal of the Nazi activity in the city, he was operationally blind. He needed to know what was happening in Tehran outside the sealed doors of the conference rooms. His post was by the president, but the presence of his men on the front lines, prowling the city side by side with the Russians, would, he desperately hoped, keep him prepared for whatever might be coming.

He waited for the general to respond. In his mind, he had already determined that he would not be put off. He had resolved to press his case very forcefully.

Have them report to me, the general said finally, his tone more resigned than enthusiastic.

With that settled, Mike hurried to Ambassador Kirk's residence. The president was hosting a Thanksgiving dinner. Churchill and his daughter Sarah, FDR's son Elliott, Harry Hopkins and his son Robert, and a few others from the presidential staff sat down for turkey, cranberry sauce, and pumpkin pie that had traveled over on the *Iowa*. The president, propped up in his chair, did all the carving. "A jolly evening," recalled Churchill, "among the most agreeable features of the halt at Cairo."

It might have been less jolly. Schellenberg had considered launching his attack in the midst of Roosevelt's Thanksgiving dinner. He'd rejected the idea because the timing might prove premature. There was no guarantee that all the targets would be present.

The next day, though, November 27, the Big Three would be in Tehran.

IT WAS THE SAME NIGHT, and the flat landing zone just east of Qom was lit by trucks' headlights. In contrast to the endless darkness of the surrounding plain, it might as well have glowed. The South Team, sixteen Vlasov Russians led by SS Sturmbannführer Hans Ulrich von Ortel, floated down silently through the night sky. As they scanned the ground below, the presence of the trucks, of the surrounding circle of tribesmen, left them reassured. The parachutists brought their legs together, firm but not rigid, heels touching, the way they'd been taught at Oranienburg, and prepared for their landings. They descended, getting closer, closer. Then they landed.

This time there were no Russians waiting, no shots fired at helpless parachutists. Had Gamotha failed to inform his spy bosses of the second landing site? Or had the mistake been Moscow Center's, their garbling of his transmission? For that matter, it could have been that the Russian troops remained busy pounding through the foothills up north, determined to make sure there were no survivors of the previous night's insertion hiding in the rocky terrain. The questions have never been satisfactorily answered.

Ortel and his men quickly rolled up their chutes and, with the help of the Qashqai tribesmen, began putting their equipment in the trucks. There were fewer vehicles than had been anticipated, but the natives had also brought camels. They'd have to do, and besides, the animals would be good cover.

The trucks were efficiently loaded, and the men were on board, but Ortel wavered. It was essential that they arrive in the city, at the safe house, before dawn. The darkness and the empty streets offered crucial protection. But the plan had been to wait for Holten-Pflug and his team. Their plane had been on the Simferopol runway right behind the first Ju-290. They, too, were scheduled to jump out over Qom. They, too, would make their way into Tehran led by the Qashqai. What had happened to them? Ortel wondered.

It was conceivable their plane had suffered engine trouble and had been forced to return to the Crimea. He also knew it could have been shot out of the sky by enemy fighters. Then again, it was also likely that it'd flown off course, and the commandos had jumped far from the designated landing zone. And there was always the possibility that if he found the patience to wait a little longer, he'd look up to see chutes dotting the night sky, the team drifting down.

The SS major had no idea whether Holten-Pflug was alive or dead, if he was already making his way to Qom or if he was hopelessly lost in the desert. Ortel soon grew certain he couldn't wait any longer without jeopardizing the safety of his men. He gave the command, and like an advancing army, the ragtag caravan of battered trucks and wheezing camels started its journey across the desert sands, toward the heart of the sleeping city, and the challenge of their historic mission.

35

THE NKVD's NIGHT PATROLS IN wartime Tehran were long, dreary duty. Nothing ever happened. It was the hours before dawn, though, life lived in the half-light of a new day, that brought their own unique tedium: the realization that another tour had passed uneventfully, yet it was still not over. It was a time when it was easy to grow lax, to feel there had been no sign of peril and there never would be. Lookouts started pining for their beds.

The Light Cavalry, however, were formed from a different mold. They were all young men, none older than twenty, and their ties to the Soviet intelligence service were not just loose, but officially nonexistent: they were unpaid volunteers whose work was tolerated with amused smiles by the professionals at the Tehran station. Yet they were gung ho, secret agents in the making. They'd come of age at a time when Mother Russia was fighting for her life against an evil and vicious enemy. The fact that they were far from the battlefields only encouraged their zeal. They wanted to do their share, to contribute as best they could for the cause they believed in. Under the earnest leadership of nineteen-year-old Gevork Vartanian, they took every assignment, no matter how trivial, as a call to action. When they hit the streets with clockwork regularity at eight each evening, it was as if a bugle had blown "Charge," and from then on the pace barely slowed. The Light Cavalry kept at it till seven each morning, cycling through the city, vigilant, conscientious pickets on patrol.

Their orders were vague. This was not because Andrei Vertinski, the NKVD station chief (or *rezident*, in Moscow Center's spy speak) was dismissing the young men with small regard, but more that he simply had no specific idea of what they should be looking for. Other than an obvious calamity, one of Rommel's Panzer tanks bulldozing its way into the bazaar, for example, he had little concrete guidance to offer; and from his expert's perspective, there was no advantage to be gained by conjecture. So he told the boys to use their judgment. Poke around, look for anything that doesn't seem right, and then sound the alarm. We'll take care of the rest, he said with a rock-hard confidence.

It was before dawn on November 27, the sun rising over the mountains and breaking through the darkness, that young Vartanian, as watchful as when he'd started his patrol, saw something that caught his eye. He had no inkling that it was anything untoward, but with nothing better to fill his time he pedaled closer to get a better look. But not too close. He knew better than that; after long practice, he'd mastered the art of street watching, a discipline in which naturalness rules.

His first thought was that the caravan seemed . . . odd. Trucks full of Russian soldiers, nothing out of the ordinary there. But why were tribesmen at the wheel? He couldn't imagine a Soviet commander allowing natives to chauffeur Red Army soldiers. Then there were the camels loaded down with crates. That was what had caught his eye in the first place. It wasn't just that camels were prohibited by the shah from entering the city. It struck him as, again, odd that the animals had been recruited for a military caravan. The Soviet motor pool out by the airfield had battalions of trucks parked in orderly rows. Why bother with camels? And with that question, he noticed something he chided himself for not having previously spotted: there were no military markings on the vehicles; the red stars were absent from the bumpers.

All of which, he realized, could mean nothing. He could think of a dozen, no, two dozen reasons why the army would be setting out in unmarked trucks, putting natives at the wheel, and recruiting camels for transport. But none of the explanations he hurried to process made any sense. The entire circumstances left him perplexed. He pedaled off in haste to round up the rest of his crew.

Tehran is a good city for surveillance. A maze of side streets and alleyways offer the watcher protection, natural static posts that allow him to lay back behind his prey, out of sight, while still keeping the target in close range. And when the watchers are on bicycles, not only do they have the benefit of perfect cover—who pays attention to kids on their bikes?—but they also have the invaluable asset of mobility. In the twisting city streets, a cyclist is not likely to be outraced by a truck, or, for that matter, a camel. The Light Cavalry kept discreet pace with the caravan.

Still, the South Team led the boys on quite a chase. They drove down a broad avenue, then made a succession of sharp lefts and rights into side streets. For a moment, it looked like the caravan would be heading straight to Syroos Street, the NKVD headquarters, and Vartanian had the unsettling notion that he'd inadvertently barged into an ongoing intelligence operation and there'd be hell to pay. But the trucks avoided the street and continued on through the city. At just before seven a.m., on a narrow road parallel to the western boundary of the bazaar, the trucks came to a halt. Down the block, cautiously peering around the corner of a stubby, sandstone-shaded building, the boys watched with great attention as the soldiers unloaded the trucks and disappeared into what appeared to be a rug warehouse. If they still harbored any doubts that they had stumbled onto something that was all wrong, those disappeared when they saw the tribesmen drive off in the trucks, the mounted camels following closely behind.

With the resolute determination of an officer mobilizing his troops, young Vartanian began barking out orders. Two of the boys were dispatched to keep an eye on the rear of the building in case there was a back door that offered a chance for escape. Another shimmied up to an adjacent roof; it offered a view into the warehouse's top floor. The rest would stay in place, sheltered, but eyes glued to the front door. Anyone left, they were to follow; and, he warned, they'd better not be seen. In the meantime, he'd pedal over as fast as he could to Syroos Street and share with the NKVD his certain knowledge of what the Light Cavalry had discovered: German operatives, disguised as Russian soldiers, had sneaked into Tehran.

THE LOUDEST NOISE WAS OFTEN not the boom that demolished the door, but the muffled, deliberately secretive sounds that preceded it: footsteps creaking on the stairs; whispers too faint to decipher; the click releasing the rifle's safety. In the taut silence, small noises were enhanced.

This was what Hans von Ortel heard. This was what alerted him. In the first shock of recognition, did he peer furtively out the window for confirmation of all his worst fears? Did he spot NKVD agents, some with rifles on their shoulders, some already taking aim, fanned out along the street? Did he rouse the Vlasov Russians, tell them to prepare for a firefight?

All that is known with authority is that when the pack of Russians came charging in, Ortel was at his transmitter. He was reporting to Berlin, giving the word code he'd been instructed to use in the direst of emergencies. Abort! Abort! Mission Canceled! he signaled.

Then the shooting started. The NKVD regulars along with Russian troops led the way into the room, and in the back of the pack, Vartanian, stoking up his courage, was a shocked witness to all that happened. He watched as one, then a second of the men disguised as Red Army soldiers raised their submachine guns and at that same instant were slammed backward by an unerring burst of gunfire. He saw the others throw down their weapons and raise their hands high in quick, meek surrender. In that same long moment, his eyes darting wildly about, he glimpsed the man at the radio shouting frantically into the microphone even as bullets riddled the transmitter and there was no longer any point. When it was over, Vartanian was up close, staring, as the anxious prisoners, faces as pale as invalids, were marched out, loaded into genuine Red Army trucks, to be taken to the house on Syroos Street.

In the course of their detention, he came to hear, they told the entire story of Operation Long Jump, and how it had come to its sudden end when the soldier at the transmitter had sent his desperate message. The boy never learned what happened to the prisoners. No one did. They just vanished, like so many others who had been led at gunpoint to the bloodstained Syroos Street basement.

THE JU-290 WAS ON THE Simferopol runway, ready for the commandos to board, when Skorzeny received the news: Ortel had sent the signal to abort the mission. He was already aware that no transmissions had so far been received at the Wannsee radio center from either the North Team or Holten-Pflug and his men. He'd been sorting through the operational implications of this silence for the entire afternoon. All his experience in the field reminded him that there were many logical reasons why the teams had failed to communicate. They could've gone to ground in the city, and security required a radio blackout. Perhaps they'd landed far from the drop zones and were trudging through the desert, their transmitters damaged in the jump. That and a dozen other scenarios were reasonable, nonalarming explanations for the teams' quiet. But in the aftermath of Ortel's stunning message, he could no longer have any doubts. There was no need to rely on instincts, or on theories. With a soldier's dispassionate battle sense, he understood what had happened. The men were dead. Or they were prisoners, staring death in the face and wishing it would come swiftly.

But what should he do? The question—no, Skorzeny quickly realized, the challenge—remained. The plane was on the runway. He could board with his hard men and still attempt to fulfill the mission. If he succeeded, his legacy would be assured. Hadn't he faced impossible odds in the past and yet prevailed? Courage and bold-ness were a soldier's virtues. Recklessness went hand in hand with victory. He was the Most Dangerous Man in Europe. He could outsmart them all.

Or could he? There was, Skorzeny firmly believed, honor in a soldier's death. But there was little honor, and certainly no fame, to be won walking stupidly into a trap. By now the captured men would have talked, their resistance broken by torture. The Allies would know he was coming, and they'd be waiting. He would not have a chance. He and his men would be slaughtered. Or worse: captured and put on taunting display, fools mocked by the world for their incompetence.

Skorzeny told the men to head to the plane. When they were on board, he approached the pilot. Change of plans, he ordered. Take us back to Berlin. As the plane headed west over gray clumps of forests and weary, war-ravaged towns, Skorzeny began to put Long Jump out of his mind. He was already turning the page, imagining the next fresh adventure, the triumph that would guarantee his legend.

IN IRAN, STURMBANNFÜHRER RUDOLF VON Holten-Pflug sat by the warming campfire, growing increasingly concerned as he waited for his recon man to return. He had sent Gorechi, the native translator who'd parachuted into Iran with his team, to Tehran to get a sense of things. At the time, after the disaster of the drop, after the failure to rendezvous with Ortel, all his military instincts had told him it was a sensible plan. That was what a good field officer did. He reacted to tactical reversals. Yet he'd expected Gorechi to have returned by now, and Holten-Pflug found himself wondering if he had made a mistake. Had Gorechi been captured? Would he lead the enemy to his camp? The surrounding desert was quiet, only the buzz of small night sounds. But he knew it offered no safety. Peril felt as if it were closing in.

But what else could he have done? There had been one setback after another. The pilot had dropped them wildly off course, at least thirty miles from the dry lake landing site outside Qom. Then it was the radio; either it'd been broken when they came in hard on rough ground, or it had been defective when they'd flown off from Simferopol. They couldn't get it to transmit. And when they'd finally trudged their way to the designated drop zone, the sun was coming up bright and strong and there was no sign of Ortel or the trucks. Holten-Pflug had the location of the safe house in Tehran, a rug warehouse. But would he and his men be able to make the journey in daylight without being detected? They'd be on foot, and, one more reason for caution, they were not wearing intimidating Russian uniforms like the Vlasovs. In their native clothes, haphazard outfits put together by Section F, the SD technical staff, they looked like locals. That could mean trouble. Without the hulking Vlasovs to scare off the Iranian police, there was always the risk they'd be stopped at one of the checkpoints guarding the entrance to the city. The authorities start asking questions, what would they do? It seemed more practical to send Gorechi, who had lived in Tehran before the war, to the safe house. With luck, he'd be able to get his hands on a truck. Then they could drive into the city under the cover of darkness, Gorechi handling things if they were stopped by a patrol. In the meantime, Gorechi would get Ortel to send a message back to Berlin confirming their arrival; he imagined Schellenberg and Skorzeny pacing about, waiting for a report. But Gorechi had not returned, and Holten-Pflug was faced with improvising another fallback plan with only rickety options to choose from.

Nevertheless, the resilient major tried to come to terms with his situation. He was thinking it all through when Gorechi, soundless as a ghost, plunked himself down by the fire. The report he delivered was worse than anything Holten-Pflug had imagined.

The translator had made his way into the city without attracting any attention. Then, rather than barge into the warehouse, he hesitated. With shrewd caution, he took a table at a nearby café. A previous life spent in the city had taught him that this would be the best place to gather intelligence. The tables were filled with animated patrons, many of them recounting the chilling events that had unfolded just down the block. Heavily armed Russians had stormed the rug warehouse. There had been enough gunfire, or so the rapidly inflating accounts suggested, to have laid siege to the entire city. But in the end, only a dozen or so subdued, frightened soldiers, outfitted in Russian uniforms, had been marched out. The uniforms, it was explained with a knowing authority, were disguises. The prisoners were in fact German saboteurs. When Gorechi heard all this, he finished his coffee in a gulp, and without even glancing at the warehouse, headed back to the makeshift camp in the desert.

Holten-Pflug now took stock. He realized Long Jump was blown. Ortel and the Vlasovs would have surely divulged all they knew. But what did they know? They could reveal the existence of the North Team and the location of the safe house where they were hiding. He could assume those men had been rounded up, too. Clearly the mission was no longer a secret. The Allies had been warned that commandos were planning to assassinate Roosevelt, Churchill, and Stalin. The element of surprise was gone.

Or was it? he asked himself, even after he'd just written off the possibility. He still had advantages. Yes, it was a certainty that under torture the South Team had revealed that they had been scheduled to rendezvous with his six-man squad. But they wouldn't have been able to disclose his whereabouts, because they didn't know. No one knew, not even Berlin. And that was not all about which the captured men had no idea. The key elements of the plan had been shared only among Schellenberg, Skorzeny, and himself. At the time, this operational security had seemed necessary because the Vlasovs might have withdrawn if they had learned precisely what they were heading into, and how their lives would be sacrificed in the firefight. But in the light of all that had happened, this secrecy now seemed inspired. The interrogators would never be able to learn the day of the attack, or how it would be launched. Surprise was still very possible. The Allies would hear there were six commandos on the loose in Iran, but they'd still need to stop them. And he had a crate of Gammon bombs, as well as automatic weapons and rounds of ammunition.

Of course, the dangers had grown. Now that the Allies knew an assassination was planned, the protection of the Big Three would be ramped up. In the end, however, only one question mattered: Could his team penetrate the security screen? He reviewed the plan that had been worked out in Oranienburg, and he decided it was foolproof. It would still work. It would get his men staring into the faces of the Big Three.

That was all that mattered. He did not concern himself with the question of whether six men could complete a mission that had been planned for fifty. As long as there was the possibility, it was a soldier's duty to persist. And what if he succeeded? His name would live on forever in the histories of the Fatherland.

Holten-Pflug told his men to prepare to move out. They were heading into Tehran.

Man's desire to be remembered is colossal.

36

WINSTON CHURCHILL WAS SCARED. His car was stuck in traffic, wedged in, unable to move forward or back. At the same time, the crowd had surrounded the immobile vehicle, surging closer and closer. Seated in the rear, he had nowhere to hide. He'd be impossible to miss. He might as well have had a bull's-eye pinned to his back. "There was no kind of defense at all against two or three determined men with pistols or a bomb," he worried. One minute after another ticked away as he wondered if the next moment was destined to be his last. The prime minister had just arrived in Tehran, and he feared he might be assassinated before he reached the safety of the British embassy.

His concerns about security had started growing as soon as his plane from Cairo had landed at Gale Morghe Airport at around eleven on the morning of November 27. Churchill had hoped to tiptoe unnoticed into the city, which had seemed the logical way to arrive for a conference that didn't officially exist, that his press office continued to deny was about to take place. He was also not dismissive of the dangers of war or the ruthlessness of the enemy. He had no doubts that Hitler would rejoice at his death or that the Nazis remained on the hunt for opportunities to strike; the memory of Flight 777, the plane shot out of the sky by the Luftwaffe in an ill-conceived attempt at his murder, was all the proof he required. He also recognized, as well as embraced, the responsibilities of command. For all those sobering reasons, he had wanted to arrive without fanfare in Tehran.

But moments after he'd gotten off the plane, there had been a small welcoming ceremony hosted by the British ambassador, which the prime minister had endured with a testy, willful blankness. Yet that proved to be just a minor annoyance when compared with the fiasco he was caught up in as soon as his car pulled out of the airfield. The road was lined with glowering Iranian cavalrymen sitting high on their mounts, each rider decked out in brightly colored comic opera uniforms. The pageantry continued for a full three miles, and all a fuming Churchill could think was that the gaudy display was an announcement "to any evil people that somebody of consequence was coming" as well as at the same time highlighting the route. Worse, the dandified guards, he appraised with a withering glance, "could provide no protection at all." The police car leading the way was no help at all, either; it perversely "gave warning of our approach." In his agonized mind, the car's flashing lights might as well have been a signal to any gunman to hoist his rifle and take aim.

His apprehension crossed over to a sickening fear when his car turned into the block leading to the embassy compound and it was forced to a sudden halt. A roadblock erected outside the perimeter of the British compound had brought traffic to a standstill—with the prime minister's car stuck in the midst of a line of vehicles without any chance of maneuvering. It was the perfect moment for an assassination. With the crowd closing in, his sense of jeopardy growing more and more acute, all the prime minister could do was attempt to find solace in a mournful irony. "If it had been planned out beforehand to run the greatest risks, and have neither the security of a quiet surprise arrival nor an effective escort," he piquantly brooded, "the problem could not have been solved more perfectly."

Then the line of cars started to move, and Churchill's vehicle passed through the checkpoint. It continued slowly on until it was behind the high walls of the British compound. Protected by a staunch cordon of armed troops, Churchill at last felt safe. In the embassy he no longer had to fear an attack from "two or three de-termined men with pistols or a bomb."

MIKE WAS NOT CAVALIER, nor was he an innocent. He had taken great care not to expose the president to any of the risks into which the British had led their prime minister. The Boss's C-54, after a small delay caused by a lingering fog that had stubbornly refused to lift, headed out of Cairo West Airport at just after seven on the morning of November 27. The pilot "kept his word," as Mike, who put great stock in promises, put it, and never climbed above a heart-friendly six thousand feet for the entire trip. When they landed in Tehran at 3:00 p.m. on the dot, there was no ceremony, only a brisk and efficient ride in a car with bulletproof windows through empty streets to the American legation. Mike was very satisfied with how it had all worked out, particularly since he'd planned it just that way.

Equally pleasing, Mike, after settling the president in his room, received word that General Dmitry Arkadiev was downstairs, want-ing to speak. For Mike, this was further confirmation that the collaboration he'd had initiated was receiving serious attention. Starting that day, a half-dozen of his men would be working hand in hand with the NKVD, but he was grateful the general had also politely come by to welcome him to Tehran.

A look at the general's grim face, his damp jowls and his blank, hangman's eyes, and Mike at once understood he'd misjudged the purpose of Arkadiev's visit.

The Nazis have dropped thirty-eight parachutists around Tehran over the past few days, the general announced gravely. He paused dramatically before going on in the same low voice to state that they'd all been captured by his men.

Mike breathed a silent sigh of relief. When he finally felt able to speak, he blurted out the first thought that came into his mind.

"Are you sure it was thirty-eight?" he asked, immediately realizing it was an inane question.

"Very sure," said the Russian. "We examined the men we caught most thoroughly."

Mike held Arkadiev's stare, thinking "the way he said it made me happy I had not been present when the Nazis were questioned." Nevertheless, it was also difficult to be too judgmental. The threat had been removed. The president was safe.

Then the general said that in the course of the interrogation, the prisoners had revealed that his men had not captured all the Nazi parachutists. Six heavily armed commandos were still on the loose. He had no idea where they were, or when they might strike.

And all at once Mike's blood ran cold.

PART IV

SIX DAYS

37

THE RUSSIAN GENERAL'S REPORT LEFT Mike stunned and angry. You do your job always knowing it could happen; so when your worst fear comes true, why should you still feel blindsided? But Mike did. He waited a long time before speaking. Yet all the time he was aware: Yes, this was how it was in Pennsylvania, the knife flying through the air straight toward the president. Now it was happening again: the Boss was a target. Only this time there were six assassins.

Nevertheless, Mike was too much of a professional to betray his complicated emotions; and, in truth, he also was not entirely prepared to reveal anything to the NKVD man that was not essential to their collaboration. He ushered the general into a downstairs room in the legation where they could speak without being overheard. They sat opposite one another, as if they were two old acquaintances, nothing in their manner to suggest the gravity of what was at stake, while the Russian did all the talking. Mike listened, while at the same time intently exploring his own thoughts.

Arkadiev had none of Mike's fears. His analysis of the situation in Tehran was both confident and encouraging. The threat to the Big Three had been eradicated, he baldly proclaimed. After the Russian forces had rounded up the thirty-eight Nazi commandos, the operation had come to an end. Not that the Germans could ever have succeeded—the security garrison surrounding the three leaders was impenetrable. As for the six men who remained at large, they'd be running for their lives. With the other teams in custody, they had to realize the mission was over. Six men against three thousand troops? They'd have understood they wouldn't have a chance. Besides, the Allies had been alerted. There was no longer any opportunity for surprise. At this moment, the general assured Mike, the six commandos were scrambling to make their way out of Iran and into Turkey. The Russian troops in the north had been put on alert. The border patrols would intercept them. It wouldn't be long before he received word that the six Nazis were in custody, he guaranteed.

Mike paid close attention to everything the Russian said. He wanted to believe that the general was correct, that the Boss was out of danger. By all the laws of the game, it would seem a disaster had been averted. All that remained was to tie up the loose ends, to apprehend the six Nazis as they attempted to cross into Turkey. But Mike, the longtime student of assassinations, had spent his professional career trying to understand killers. And all he had learned told him that the plot was far from over.

Now it was Mike's turn to speak. If everything he believed was true, he'd need the general's help in the days ahead. He began, therefore, by acknowledging the debt owed to the Russian forces. The time he'd spent in the company of politicians had taught him that flattery could be a very effective weapon. Also, his gratitude had the added weight of truth. Mike shuddered to think what might have been if the thirty-eight Nazi commandos had not been detected, if they had successfully infiltrated into Tehran.

With that heartfelt courtesy delivered, he moved on to make his case. At the same time he took care not to be confrontational; in a chauvinistic shouting match with the Russian general, there'd be no winners. This conversation was his summit conference, and, like the following day's talks among the Big Three, so much hung in the balance.

It is conceivable, Mike began equably, that you are right, according to summaries of the conversation. At this moment the six men are making their way to Turkey. That is certainly one possibility. But I don't think it's the most likely. Let me explain.

In the course of your interrogations, you discovered a carefully designed operation. The preparations had gone on for some time. The men had been handpicked. There was extensive weapons training. Safe houses had been arranged. Correct?

The general warily agreed.

So Mike plowed on. Then it can be assumed that these six came to Tehran with a very specific plot in mind. A mission they had been trained to execute.

Now the general stepped in with some force. But the men we apprehended had no knowledge of the operational specifics, he corrected. They didn't know when the attack would take place. Or where. They would've been informed in Tehran. Only the signal to abort had been sent to Berlin. Mission over. No one else would be coming.

Then the general hesitated. There was something in his manner that suggested to Mike he was under some restraint. Perhaps he was unwilling to reveal what else had been discovered during the prisoners' interrogation. (It's a matter of record, for example, that he never mentioned Skorzeny's involvement in the mission.) Whatever Arkadiev had on his mind, though, was not shared. He kept his counsel.

All Mike had to bolster his argument was what the Russian had previously disclosed. He would use it as best he could.

He said: We have to assume the six men at large were handpicked like all the others had been for this mission. Men chosen because they were experienced commandos. Correct?

The Russian nodded.

And no doubt they were well armed when they parachuted into Iran. Like the others.

Another small, confirming nod.

But at the same time they're not like the others, he continued.

They're different. For one thing, they didn't enter the country with the men you detained. They were a separate unit. And I suspect they weren't disguised in Russian uniforms, or else your men would've found them by now. You have informed your troops to be wary of men trying to infiltrate their ranks. Right?

The Russian's guardedness had returned. Then, grudgingly, Arkadiev acknowledged that the troops had been so informed.

So who are these six men? Mike asked rhetorically. They are similar to the ones you apprehended—handpicked, carefully trained veterans. But they're also not like them. They're not disguised as Russians. That would suggest, I believe, they were going to play a different role in the plot. I think they were the command team. Therefore, we have to assume they came to Iran fully informed of the entire plot.

What I'm saying is—they came to Iran with a carefully formulated plan to slip past all the security. A way they consider foolproof. A way to get at the Big Three.

The Russian started to speak, but Mike cut him off.

The fact that we haven't caught them proves something else, he went on. These are six very resourceful men. They don't panic. They're patient. All my instincts are telling me—

At last the Russian seemed irritated. Instincts? he as much as challenged. According to one report of the conversation, he made it clear he did not want to explore any arena as nebulous as the American's feelings.

But Mike ignored the barb. He refused to be diverted. Too much was at stake.

These are not the sort of men who are going to run, he continued. They have a mission. They're not going to give up. They're going to execute their assignment. They have the means: they're heavily armed. And they have the opportunity: an ingenious plan designed in Berlin. I believe they're hiding out in Tehran—waiting for the moment to attack.

After Mike had laid it out like that, even if the general didn't agree, he was not prepared to say Mike was wrong. As Mike would later explain, "If anything happened to the President of the United States, we in the Secret Service would be deeply embarrassed, but the Russian Secret Service men would be dead by nightfall."

It was agreed that new security measures would go into effect. The number of guards surrounding the embassies would be increased. There would be no deliveries of any kind to the buildings; all trucks summarily turned away before they could enter the compounds. Snipers were to be posted day and night on the embassies' rooftops with orders to open fire immediately at the first indication of any attempt to breach the surrounding wall. Additional roadblocks would be erected to prevent people from entering or leaving the city.

And—their best shot as Mike saw things—a house-to-house search of the city would begin at once. He'd at last be on the offensive. He'd find the killers before they attacked. Before everything depended on his putting his body in front of the Boss. Before it all came down to his taking the bullet. Mike's agents would accompany the Russian forces as they went door to door throughout Tehran. They would ask the British to help, too. In a city the size of Tehran, it would be, Mike admitted, "a real headache." But there was no other way to find where the commandos were hiding.

But even as the new security precautions went into effect, even as the men started knocking on one door after another, these actions offered only small balms to Mike's apprehension. He continued to believe that "half a dozen fanatics with the courage to jump from airplanes could probably figure out some way to get a shot in." "And," he also suspected, "it was logical to assume that, with the Nazi 'chutists shooting, one shot would be plenty."

Unless Mike could stop them.

THAT NIGHT, BERLIN WAS IN FLAMES. The RAF's bombers had intensified their nocturnal attacks on the city when the Cairo

Conference had started and had kept at it as the Big Three arrived in Tehran. Each unforgiving night there was the wail of the sirens, the sputtering dirge of the antiaircraft batteries, and then, inevitably, the thick, powerful growl of the enemy bombers, as many as 750 planes in a dense swarm filling the dark sky for miles. A tense anticipation—until the moment when the bombs rained down, pounding, destroying, annihilating centuries of history. In the morning the firestorms would continue burning, spreading a dangerous mayhem across the city.

Sir Arthur Travers Harris, the head of the RAF Bomber Command, had no regrets. "They sowed the wind, and now they are going to reap the whirlwind," he promised.

Schellenberg, who lived on edge through the nightly thunder, who in the light of each new day saw the smoldering piles of ash and rubble, had no doubt that an even more tumultuous whirlwind would soon be unleashed. The vindictive nightly attacks were, he predicted, only a prelude to the extraordinary retribution in store for Germany when the Allies won their unconditional surrender.

Unless something could be done.

In this tumult of fears and regrets, his thoughts turned to Long Jump. In a matter of days his ambitious plan had come tumbling down, one disaster after another until it had been broken apart like the city all around him. Ortel's desperate radio message made it clear the South Team had been captured; by now they'd have paid for their daring with their lives. The North Team had never even managed to radio confirmation that they'd arrived in Iran. They had a transmitter; the only explanation for their silence was that they were dead. Same, too, for Oberg. He'd suddenly gone off air and hadn't acknowledged any of Wannsee's priority flashes requesting—pleading would be more accurate, he suspected—an immediate reply. And Skorzeny? He'd simply walked away from the wreckage, always the great survivor.

Nevertheless, Schellenberg tried to convince himself that there remained a reason to be hopeful. He wanted to believe that there was still the possibility, however unlikely, that Holten-Pflug and his team had managed to escape the Allies' dragnet. That they were alive and kicking under the rubble. Was it, after all, so improbable that they'd discovered Ortel had been blown? That they never had an opportunity to send a signal from his set? That would explain their silence. When he looked at it all that way, it required only a reasonable leap of faith to believe that Holten-Pflug, the implacable aristocrat, and his team were still operational. That they had gone to ground with the plan locked in their minds. That they were at this moment in Tehran waiting for the prearranged moment to attack.

Encouraged, lifted out of his mood of morose resignation, a sudden memory rose up in his thoughts. There he was at the Lake Quenz commando school listening as the imperious instructor, bursting with confidence, unwavering in his conviction, lectured a student. "Fifty men!" vowed Sturmbannführer Rudolf von Holten-Pflug. "That's all I need. Fifty men who are able and willing. Men who have the courage and the know-how to worm their way into the right places. One small bullet from one small revolver can do more damage than a whole regiment of artillery."

Holten-Pflug did not have his fifty men. But he had courage and know-how. Yes, Schellenberg wanted to believe, if anyone could still succeed, it would be Holten-Pflug.

IN THE STILLNESS OF THE Tehran night, the man who had once promised he could change history with fifty men was lying low. He felt threatened, his sense of desperation mounting. Gorechi, the native interpreter, had found an abandoned mud hut on the periphery of the city. It was barely standing, but Holten-Pflug agreed it would have to do.

He'd arranged for the men to sleep in shifts; that way there'd be someone always on guard, and the team had hunkered down for the night. But Holten-Pflug couldn't sleep. His mind was a ferment of questions and anxieties. He suspected that if they stayed in place, they'd be discovered in the morning. There were too many huts nearby, all apparently crowded with inhabitants. They would need to leave before daybreak. But where would they go? The journey across the surprisingly cold city to this temporary refuge had been made in a constant state of looming peril. He had suspected danger around every corner, peering out at him from every window. The awareness that he was leading his team through hostile territory patrolled by enemy soldiers had kept him keyed to every stray sound. He had to take stock. The increasing likelihood that they'd be caught before they could strike forced him to consider changing the plan. What if they tried storming one of the embassies tomorrow? But even as he threw out the idea, he could not muster up any false hopes. He knew how that sort of wild attack would end. They'd all be dead before they had gotten off a shot. His only chance of success, he reasoned, lay in his following the operation as it had been worked out in Oranienburg. He needed to keep to the timetable Schellenberg had set. And that meant waiting. But where could they hide in the meantime?

His thoughts were interrupted by the sound of a truck pulling close to the hut. At his hushed command, the others were instantly on their feet, their weapons leveled. They were prepared to make a last stand.

In to the hut walked Gorechi. Following him was a bear of a man, broad and bearded. The nighttime shadows obscured his face except for a halo of dark, curly hair and glowing, dangerous eyes.

Earlier, Holten-Pflug had sent Gorechi out into the city; Iran was still the interpreter's other life, he could move about undetected. His instructions had been to find a place where they could stay until it was time to launch their attack. Gorechi, therefore, had made the rounds, appearing at the homes of the men he had known years ago in the Melliyun movement, the native pro-Nazi party. He had asked if he and some friends could hide for a few days. He did not reveal it was a group of German soldiers who were seeking refuge, but it would not have been a leap for anyone to have presumed as much. After all, the Russians had already started going house to house, looking for foreigners. Everyone refused.

Then he went to the home of Misbah Ebtehaj, the Pahlevani wrestler. This was the native who had been one of Franz Mayr's longtime assets, the same man Ernst Merser had recruited for the bold rescue of Lili Sanjari. And, like the two spies before him, Gorechi bought the wrestler's cooperation. He offered him 1,000 pounds and the promise of a job. After the Nazis won the war, the authorities in Berlin would make sure Ebtehaj was appointed Tehran's chief of police. The British pounds were counterfeit and the prospect of the Reich ever deciding municipal appointments in Iran was ludicrous, but the wrestler either didn't suspect that anyone would dare to fool him, or he figured that at any odds it was a gamble worth taking. Whatever his reasoning, he agreed to help.

Ebtehaj would not, however, let the men stay in his house. He had a wife and four daughters; he did not think it would be appropriate to have six unknown men in close proximity. And he had heard about the house searches; it wouldn't be long before the Russians would be knocking on his door. But, always enterprising, he had a better idea. He knew somewhere that would be secure, the perfect safe haven.

When he shared his suggestion with Gorechi, the translator agreed. It would be the last place the Russians, or for that matter any of the foreigners, would think to look.

The commandos piled into the wrestler's truck. The night was still dark, and they tried to believe it offered them a chance to make their escape unnoticed. The drive across the city, though, kept them on high alert. The streets were empty, and Holten-Pflug couldn't decide if that was a blessing or a curse. He feared the truck roaring down the vacant streets would attract attention from enemy patrols. He kept telling Ebtehaj to drive slowly, but the wrestler pretended he didn't understand. They finally arrived without incident at an address on Farahzadi Street.

Holten-Pflug stared at a strange, unfamiliar building. It had a round base and high walls that tapered at a steep angle as they rose, climbing to a roof that seemed as sharp as the point of a spear. At first he thought it might be a mosque, but then the wrestler explained.

The major considered. Yes, he decided, no one would think to look for us here. He sensed that things had finally turned in his favor. He had found the perfect hideout, the perfect place to lie up until it was time.

He ordered his men to grab the equipment and hurry inside.

AND AS THE CLOCKS IN the city struck midnight, the phones rang in the American and British embassies in Tehran. The caller was Vyacheslav Molotov, the Soviet foreign commissar. He needed to speak with Averell Harriman and Sir Archibald Clark Kerr, the American and British ambassadors to the Soviet Union. Both men had already gone to sleep, determined to get a good night's rest. The first session of the Tehran Conference would begin in the morning. But Molotov insisted they must be awakened. He had to see them right away.

With the new day still enveloped in darkness, the two ambassadors, now wide awake with alarm, rushed to the Russian embassy.

It was November 28.

38

A T THE DECIDEDLY UNDIPLOMATIC HOUR of nine a.m., Ambassador Harriman knocked on the door of the president's bedroom in the American legation. He needed to report on the emergency meeting to which he'd been summoned from his warm bed in the middle of the night by the Soviet foreign minister. He had received a warning. And a threat.

The warning, as relayed by Harriman, was succinct: "The risk of assassination of Mr. Churchill and Marshal Stalin while coming to visit President Roosevelt was very real."

And the threat was no less ominous: "We would be responsible for any injury that Marshal Stalin might suffer in driving through the town to consult with President Roosevelt." And by "injury," Harriman explained helpfully, in case the president had missed the point, Molotov meant "assassination."

The foreign minister, however, had not just thrown thunderbolts. Without so much as a smirk of vindication, he'd also offered a suggestion—which happened to be identical to one he'd previously made. He reiterated the Soviet invitation for the president to stay in their embassy. Only now, the rationale for the move was no longer for convenience's sake; with Nazi assassins on the loose, it was a necessary precaution. "It would bring the three Heads of State," said Harriman, relaying the Russian's logic, "so close together that there would be no need for any of them to drive about town."

On that morning of the first full day in Tehran, the British swiftly chimed in, too. They made it clear to the president that they were also anxious. Churchill, of course, had been jumpy from the moment he'd arrived in the city, brooding about "determined men with pistols or a bomb." Then Molotov had informed Ambassador Kerr that the prime minister's fears were not just sensible but could be prophetic. "Soviet Secret Intelligence," as Churchill would recall the disconcerting news he'd received, "had uncovered a plot to kill one or more of the Big Three." Churchill now had all the confirmation he needed to realize that he hadn't been seeing things out of proportion: the threat was very real. And it wasn't only his life that was in jeopardy, he knew, but the entire future of the war. Was it too much to say that the three of them, all in the later acts of their lives, had been given a mission to hold the world together at a perilous moment in history? What would happen, he wondered with dread, if the Nazis succeeded in murdering the three Allied leaders in Tehran?

Goaded on by that dire vision, by the fact that all his inchoate suspicions had been given a terrifying life, the prime minister made it clear to Roosevelt where he stood. "I strongly supported Molotov," Churchill would declare, "in his appeals to the president to move forthwith inside the Soviet Embassy, which was three or four times as big as the others, and stood in extensive ground, now ringed by Soviet troops and police."

Pressured by both his allies, FDR turned to Mike, the man in charge of his security, for advice. And Mike was only too glad to give it. For on the morning of his second day in Tehran, he had awakened to the dismaying notion that he was little more than a mystified spectator unable to bring a halt to the crisis building all around him. He'd arrived in this nightmare of a city only to have been swiftly confronted with the news that six Nazi commandos had managed to parachute into Iran. Then with the passing of each new hour the initial intelligence had turned more despairing: the six men could not be found. A house-to-house search had been initiated, and so far it had not turned up any sign of the assassins.

It was as if they had vanished not just from the city, but from the planet. They must have help; someone must be hiding them, he surmised. But who—a single contact? A network? Locals? Embedded German agents? His inability to locate the six men despite all the extraordinary efforts that were being taken coupled with the fact that the assassins had not launched an immediate attack only served to reinforce the creeping horror that he now accepted as truth: the killers were waiting, patiently biding their time for the single moment that had been carefully predetermined in Berlin, a time when they'd be able to slip past the Allies' security and strike.

So when the question was posed, Mike did not hesitate to tell the president what he thought: he was "in complete agreement" with a move into the heart of the city. At this tense moment, any act that would reduce the risks, he was convinced, was worth taking. Eliminating the need for the Boss to travel through the streets of Tehran as he drove back and forth from meetings at the other embassies was at the very least a prudent start. Dozens of other worries continued to assault him, but for now Mike found a degree of reassurance in putting one potential catastrophe to rest.

"Do you care which embassy I move to?" FDR asked.

"Not much difference, sir," said Mike. All that mattered was putting the Boss behind the high, protective walls of the joint compound.

"All right," announced the president. "It's the Russian, then. When do we move?"

It was not until that moment that Mike realized he had, as he put it with a professional's cool understatement, "a problem." How would he manage to get the president to the Russian embassy? "It would have been a tough enough job normally, but with six Nazi paratroopers around somewhere," he sensibly expected the journey would be a lot riskier. "I had no stomach for sending him through the crowded streets of Tehran," Mike confided. But he had no choice.

He went to work devising a plan.

THE BUILDING WHERE THE WRESTLER had taken the commandos was a *zurkhaneh*. It was the gymnasium where Ebtehaj trained, and the name was meant to convey the demanding mix of mind and body discipline required of Pahlevani athletes; the word meant "house of strength."

In the initial predawn hours after Holten-Pflug, bone weary, a man on the run in a strange city, had settled in, it was as if he, too, had tapped into a revitalizing flow of inner strength. At last he felt safe. The entrance door was deliberately cut low, forcing one to bow as was required when entering a holy place; which, the Nazi major assessed, would also make it impossible for a platoon of soldiers to come charging in without warning. The pit where the athletes trained—called a *gowd*, he would learn—was lined with a layered composite of weeds, dried straw, coal ash, and clay that, he discovered, was as comfortable as the mattress in his apartment in Berlin; his men, who had been looking over their shoulders since they had landed in Iran, were at last able to grab some much-needed sleep stretched out across this cushion. And, putting a damper on his greatest concern, he felt confident that the Allied patrols would never bother poking their noses into an Iranian sports club; they'd be too busy investigating more obvious hideouts. Cheered by his excitement that Long Jump was back on track, he had found his house of strength. He pushed aside any lingering apprehensions. His resolve intensified. His confidence in the mission's success was restored.

But an assassin never lives for too long on a steady plane. As the hours of waiting ticked away, as the attack drew closer, doubts were invariably rekindled. That was what Holten-Pflug tried telling himself as his previously quieted concerns once again erupted. Yet despite all his efforts at self-persuasion, Holten-Pflug couldn't help but think he'd made a crucial operational mistake in coming to the *zurkhaneh*. No less demoralizing, he admonished himself, it was a situation he should have anticipated.

For in the very hours when across the city Mike was struggling to come up with a scheme for the dash to the Russian embassy, Holten-Pflug's own safety was increasingly being put in jeopardy. His men were no longer alone. Athletes kept coming to the gymnasium. The mat was crowded with beefy men swinging Indian clubs, grappling with one another, a deer-skinned drum all the while pounding out an accompanying cadence with a portentous rhythm. The athletes stared at the six commandos, never daring to approach. But Holten-Pflug was certain nonetheless that his once cherished hideout was no longer secure. It was the oldest maxim of the game: a secret stops being a secret once it has been shared.

Ebtehaj tried to calm the major's fears. Each *zurkhaneh*, he explained, had its own political affiliation. This one was aligned with the Melliyun movement, the pro-Nazi party. The athletes lauded Hitler Shah as Iran's savior. They celebrated the Reich's soldiers as heroes. They could be trusted not to talk about the visitors to their club.

Besides, he continued earnestly, Pahlevani athletes adhere to a strict moral code, their lives guided by firm principles of honor and duty. They would never betray their guests. But it was the wrestler's concluding argument that struck Holten-Pflug as the most convincing: There's nowhere else to go, he said definitively. The Allies are combing the city. You leave here, you'll be caught, he guaranteed.

Holten-Pflug did not trust any Iranian, especially one whose allegiance had been bought with 1,000 pounds and the ridiculous promise of the police chief's job. He would have had no compunction about taking his knife and driving it with one swift lunge into the wrestler's broad chest, aiming right above the left rib and twisting the razor-sharp blade up into the heart. That would have been a fitting payment for leaving his team exposed to this public scrutiny. But then where would they go? In two days he would make history.

He just needed to wait until then. He just needed to adhere to the plan. In the meantime, all he could do was hope no one would dare betray him. We'll stay, he told the wrestler.

He told his men to stay alert. Be on guard, he ordered. Keep your weapons in your hands at all times, loaded and ready to fire. And he shared with them the promise he had sworn in his own secret heart: In two days we will make history. They listened, and it was as if the words reverberated through their thoughts, another insistent drumbeat setting the cadence as they waited until they could claim the destiny that would be theirs.

IN DESPERATION, MIKE HAD LINED the entire route to the Russian embassy with soldiers. He made sure the armed men stood shoulder to shoulder. An assassin would have a difficult time bullying his way through to get off a round at the president's car. If, however, a well-trained German sniper was crouched furtively on a rooftop or peering through a window, the odds of his getting off a kill shot, Mike conceded, were damn good. And the chances of preventing it were pretty close to nonexistent. But at three that afternoon Mike, resigned, ordered the presidential cavalcade to pull out of the American legation.

Two jeeps filled with armed, attentive soldiers led the way. Two more, similarly loaded for war, had the rear. The soldiers' eyes darted about, scanning the rooftops, gazing into the crowd, looking for a gun. In the middle of the motorcade was the president's limousine. He sat in the rear seat, a smile fixed on his face, a hand raised to acknowledge the cheers of the locals.

Only the man in the back seat of the president's car was not the president. It was Secret Service agent Bob Holmes.

The moment the cavalcade had pulled out, Mike had bundled the president into a dusty army sedan. Keep your head down, sir, he ordered, and FDR, enjoying the adventure, obeyed. With only a single jeep leading the way, the two vehicles raced at a mad speed through Tehran's side streets. The president was being wheeled into his suite of rooms at the Russian embassy while Bob Holmes continued to wave to the crowd assembled along the official route. The agent would have had enjoyed the charade, he said, if he hadn't been worried all the while about a bullet suddenly crashing through the window and lodging in his skull.

LATER THAT NIGHT, MIKE WAS standing watch at a dinner the president was hosting for Churchill and Stalin. For the first time since he'd arrived in Tehran he was feeling pretty good about things, thinking that maybe he had the situation under control. After all, he'd succeeded in getting the Boss to the safety of the Russian embassy without incident. He was "happy to see our own Filipino boys working on our own food in our own kitchen." "You get that way in the Secret Service after a while," he explained without embarrassment. And the inveterate drinker that he was, he couldn't help but be both amused and a bit awed as he observed his old friend Churchill throughout the festivities. "His Britannic Majesty's First Minister could easily drink toast for toast with any given battalion of Russians," he noticed with admiration. But then Mike's short-lived calm was shattered.

As the party was breaking up and the president was being wheeled to his bedroom, an American CIC officer approached. You remember the German spy who had been picked up when we raided the house where Lili Sanjari had been living? he asked. He's started talking. And you need to hear what he's saying. Now!

39

TWO SEEMINGLY UNRELATED EVENTS HAPPENED in the aftermath of Mike's troubling late-night conference with the military intelligence officials. Both had their operational roots in the story Sturmbannführer Winifred Oberg, the handler Schellenberg had dispatched to Tehran to set the stage for Long Jump, had finally decided, after some persuasion, to share. And these actions, Mike knew with a gratifying sense of exoneration, might never have occurred if he hadn't blown his top and demanded that the CIC spymasters haul in Lili Sanjari. It was, after all, the capricious woman spy who had promptly provided the intelligence that had led to Oberg's arrest.

The first act was the immediate deployment of a platoon of soldiers to guard the entrance to the water tunnel that General Connolly's engineers had dug in the desert outside the city. After Oberg had been informed that thirty-eight parachutists had been apprehended, he'd realized that the entire mission had died its death. Then, more impetus to confess, he was pointedly reminded that spies were executed in wartime. So with nothing to save but his own skin (he never suspected six men were still at large), he went to work saving it. He cooperated, recounting with a fieldman's pride how he'd methodically gone about discovering a way into the embassies' grounds. But no matter how intently he'd been first badgered, then bluntly threatened, he couldn't provide any of the operation's working details. He couldn't answer the large questions his inquisitors repeatedly boomed at him. He couldn't reveal which embassy would be the site of the attack. Or when it would occur. He just didn't know.

Oberg's ignorance was one more tribute to Schellenberg's steady tradecraft. From the start of Long Jump, the Section 6 head had been determined to keep the planning compartmentalized, sharing with the participants only as much as they needed to know to get their jobs done. In that secure way, the Vlasov Russians had never been told how they'd be specifically deployed when the attack occurred. And after Oberg had completed his invaluable reconnaissance, he, too, had been cut out of the loop. Oberg was never made aware of the final plan that Schellenberg had laboriously stitched together, because there'd been no necessity for him to know. Once Oberg had settled the men into the safe houses, his job would've been done.

But even with these gaps, what the CIC had shaken out of Oberg was sufficiently disconcerting. No sooner had Oberg recounted how he had scouted the water tunnels than truckloads of combat-ready GIs were put in place to guard the entrance. They quickly dug in, and were prepared to repel, if it came to that, a Wehrmacht battalion. Six men, Mike felt certain, wouldn't stand a chance. They'd be mowed down before they got to the wire fence.

At the same time, though, Oberg's ingenuity had left Mike's confidence shaken once again. The German operative had managed to find a way into the embassy compound that could have succeeded in putting the assassins on the Boss's doorstep. The spy had skillfully uncovered a danger that Mike, despite all his meticulous surveillance and planning, had never noticed. What other secret knowledge, he wondered with a fresh chill of terror, could the six men at large be harboring? What sort of inventive plan had they shaped? And, he continually reminded himself, he had no idea when they would strike. Mike racked his mind, but he remained unable to find any clue that definitively pointed toward the moment that had been selected for the attack. After hearing the gist of Oberg's confession, Mike had new respect for his adversary. And hand in hand with that appreciation, he saw with a new clarity that it was crucial that the six commandos be found as soon as possible, or else it might be too late.

The second event that took place, then, was also a direct result of Oberg's information and, concurrently, the agitated state in which Mike as a result now found himself. After patrols had knocked on doors throughout the city, had stridden into every alleyway, poked into every café, even searched the back rooms of the bazaar, they had still not found a trace of the six assassins. Now this growing frustration had been further exacerbated by a new, startling understanding of the threat. As a result, a joint Allied decree was issued: a $20,000 reward would be paid for any information leading to the arrest of six German parachutists at large in the city.

The bazaar was quickly jumping with the news, the incredible opportunity passed on from stall to stall. A fortune could be earned by anyone fortunate enough to know where six Nazis were hiding.

HOLTEN-PFLUG KNEW NONE OF THIS. He had no idea that Oberg, the handler to whom he'd been instructed to report, had revealed the plan to march through the water tunnel. And he was also ignorant of the colossal price that had been placed on his head.

He remained locked in the narrow, reconciled world of a soldier heading off on a mission from which he knew he very likely would not return. At the same tangled time, he remained energized by the approaching prospect of his immortality. He would accomplish a deed that would set him apart from other, lesser men. He would change the course of the war. His name would live forever. Those were achievements, he believed with all his warrior's heart, that were worth dying for.

He told his men to stay steady, to keep their focus. In twenty-four hours they would move out of the hideout. Tomorrow they would make history.

IN BERLIN, SCHELLENBERG HAD RECEIVED a new report from Cicero. He took up the file not knowing, as was always the case with the shipments from Turkey, what to expect. He started reading and quickly realized this delivery was pure gold. The product was nearly real-time intelligence detailing the workings of the Cairo Conference, which had concluded less than a week earlier. With startling detail the pages described Roosevelt's promise to Chiang Kai-shek to return Manchuria to China after the defeat of the Japanese.

Schellenberg pondered the immense gift Roosevelt was cavalierly bestowing on the Chinese for their support, and his thoughts, not for the first time, grimly returned to what the Allies would take from Germany when the war was concluded. In his despair he found himself wanting to believe, although he knew it was contrary to reason, to all acceptable logic, that Holten-Pflug and his men had somehow managed to remain at large. That they were still operational. And he knew: either the team would strike the next day, or the victors in their moment of triumph would shatter the Reich into pieces.

WHILE SCHELLENBERG GRAPPLED WITH HIS worst fears, they grew closer to being explicitly confirmed that evening in Tehran. The occasion was the splendid banquet Stalin hosted. As the evening progressed, the marshal rose to his feet to offer a toast. The strength of the German army, he began, depended on about fifty thousand officers and technicians. Raising his glass of vodka high, he calmly proposed that at the end of the war, they be shot "as fast as we capture them, all of them."

Churchill was aghast. Rising from his chair, the prime minister solemnly stated that "the British Parliament and public will never tolerate mass executions."

"Fifty thousand must be shot," Stalin repeated, undeterred.

The prime minister's face colored with a crimson rage. "I would rather," he said, each word precisely articulated in the perfect calm of a resigned anger, "be taken out into the garden here and now and be shot myself than sully my own and my country's honor by such infamy."

Then Roosevelt intervened. He suggested a compromise. Rather than executing fifty thousand, he proposed, "we should settle on a smaller number." "Shall we say 49,500?" the president asked.

Was FDR trying to defuse the situation with a preposterous joke? At that unsteady moment, it was difficult to decipher his motive. But then the president's son Elliott, rose and gave a snarling, hard-edged speech saying that he agreed with Marshal Stalin's proposal, and he was sure the US Army would support it, too.

That was too much for Churchill. He jumped up and stormed out of the banquet hall, disappearing into an adjacent room. The space was dark and empty, but he didn't seem to notice. He was still trying to make sense of all that had been said when two hands clamped on his shoulders. He turned to see Stalin, with Molotov at his side. Both men were grinning broadly. They insisted, as Churchill would describe the conversation, "that they were only playing and that nothing of a serious character had entered their heads."

Churchill was not convinced. And Schellenberg wouldn't have been, either.

LATER THAT NIGHT, AFTER HE'D made sure the Boss was settled in and that an armed guard was posted outside the bedroom door, Mike returned to his own bedroom. He was dead tired, and he looked forward to getting a good night's sleep. But for some reason, he found himself studying the schedule of events for the next day, November 30. Perhaps he just wanted to get a head start on the challenges the day would bring. He began going down the precisely enumerated list the presidential staff had put together, and when he turned to the second page he read something that made him come to a sudden halt. He played with the possibility for a moment, and then he was sure: he now knew when the assassins planned to strike.

With all thoughts of sleep abruptly abandoned, he hurried from the room to alert his men.

40

TUESDAY, NOVEMBER 30, 1943, the day of Winston Churchill's sixty-ninth birthday, began as another cold morning in Tehran. Holten-Pflug rose, as was his soldier's habit, with the first light. Whatever else the momentous day would bring, he knew it would be his last in the *zurkhaneh*. The days of waiting were over. The team would strike that night. Six men would accomplish what had been planned for fifty. They would make their way through the water tunnel to the British embassy and then, when the enemy least expected, as they were squawking their smug, fulsome, self-congratulatory party toasts, gorging on champagne and birthday cake, his men would storm in and kill Roosevelt, Churchill, and Stalin. He went to prepare the others.

Did Holten-Pflug give a small speech to encourage his team, offer a few ardent words to celebrate the approaching climax of their mission? If he did, no record exists. But it would not have been in his nature to have been subdued at this moment. He would have set out the credo that Schellenberg had overheard at the Lake Quenz commando center: How capable men, men with courage and skill, could accomplish great things. How "one small bullet from one small revolver can do more damage than a whole regiment of artillery." And he would have concluded with a sincere promise of the laurels that would crown their heads when the mission was over: their names would live forever in history.

There certainly was a weapons check. The men, encouraged by Skorzeny's example, had Sten guns equipped with silencers, and the order was passed to make sure they'd be carrying sufficient spare magazines. Once they entered the embassy compound, even with the initial advantage of surprise, they could expect a firefight. They needed to be prepared to shoot their way in, and then shoot their way out. In addition to the submachine guns, the team was armed with Walther PPK pistols, and, like Holten-Pflug, they wore combat knives strapped to their calves.

The crate of Gammon bombs was pried open, and two were distributed to each man. During the quiet, ruminative time spent in the sports club, Holten-Pflug had decided that the bombs, not submachine gun fire, would form the primary thrust of the attack. The Gammons would compensate for the lack of manpower. In an enclosed space, the damage would be catastrophic; as effective as if they were fifty commandos, he had reasoned. And with Skorzeny out of the picture, Holten-Pflug had drawn up a new battle plan: He would hurl the first bomb. That would be the signal for the others to follow. He instructed the men to set the fuses for immediate detonation. They would escape in the chaos, or they would die trying.

Gorechi was ordered to get Ebtehaj's truck. Holten-Pflug remained confident the native translator would not attract attention moving through the streets. When he returned, the men would quickly be loaded into the enclosed back of the vehicle, and Gorechi would drive to the water tunnel's entrance just outside the city. That would give them sufficient time to make the long, sloshing trek through the stream flowing along the concrete-encased waterway. If all went according to schedule, they would emerge in the embassy grounds after the birthday celebration was already well underway. They'd head in the darkness across the garden, past the reflecting pool, to the dining room patio doors. They'd arrive just when the champagne corks were popping, as the festivities were in full swing—at the moment they'd be least expected.

It was only after Gorechi had left that Holten-Pflug told the four remaining commandos there was a change to the plan.

———

WHEN MIKE HAD FIRST SETTLED the Boss into the six-room suite at the Russian embassy, the sight of all the servants had made him uneasy. "Everywhere you went," he'd gripe, "you would see a brute of a man in a lackey's white coat busily polishing immaculate glass or dustless furniture. As their arms swung to dust or polish, the clear, cold outline of a Luger automatic could be seen on every hip. They were NKVD boys, of course."

But today he took comfort in their lurking presence. In fact, he hoped there would be more of the menacing "brutes" on display that night. He had already alerted Arkadiev of his suspicions.

It had taken him too long, he chided himself, but nevertheless he had finally figured out the Nazis' plan. The previous night when he'd read the president's schedule, everything had fallen into place with a definitive certainty. He had found the single conclusive fact that proved the theory he'd been shouting. He had been insisting the commandos had been biding their time, their attack on hold until all was in place. And at last he had identified the final element in their patient strategy. All along they had been waiting for tonight, for the party celebrating Winston Churchill's birthday. The Nazis had recognized that it would be the one evening when they could count on the Big Three, no matter what else was happening, to be present. How could Stalin or Roosevelt turn down Churchill's invitation to raise a glass to commemorate such a milestone? Politics, national ambitions, the tempers of three oversize personalities—all would be shoved aside for one evening. In keeping with the jolly occasion, it would be a respite from all the bickering and hard-fought negotiations. A festive evening when even the security would be relaxed. It was the blueprint that had been drawn in Berlin, and he felt foolish that it had taken him so long to have recognized it. If the Russians had not eliminated the bulk of the commando force, if Oberg had not disclosed the scheme to use the water tunnel to enter unnoticed into the embassy compound, it would've succeeded. Fifty commandos would have burst in on Churchill's birthday party. He contemplated what might have been, and the vision in his mind was something terrible.

But could it still work? Could six determined men manage to find a way into the birthday party that evening? Despite all the Allied efforts, despite all the combined resources of three mighty nations, the Nazi team had managed to slip through the net that had been thrown over the city. These were not ordinary men; it would be a mistake, Mike reminded himself once again, to underestimate them. Until they were caught or dead, their mission would not be over. In his overwrought imagination Mike saw only catastrophe, the Boss slumped in his wheelchair, his body riddled with bullets.

He walked the short distance to the British embassy and did a tour of the kitchen, hoping his instincts might lead him to identify a chef who didn't belong, a waiter paying only scant attention to his tasks. When nothing caught his eye, he went into the large dining room. A long table had been set with crystal and heavy silver for more than thirty guests. At each place was a menu handwritten in a free-flowing, artistic cursive. It was difficult for Mike to decipher the words, and when he could he still had a problem; it was in French. What was *"Dinde farcie garni"* he wondered? No doubt the Boss would know. Perhaps that was standard fare, too, at the president's Hyde Park mansion.

His eyes scanned the room and went to the pair of french doors in the rear that led to a patio. Outside he could see the garden and a small, rectangular ornamental pool. When he jiggled the handle, the door opened easily. It hadn't been locked. He turned around and looked toward the dining table. Directly opposite him was the place card for Prime Minister Churchill, and flanking it on one side was President Roosevelt's name; on the other was Marshal Stalin's. The three men would be seated in a neat row only a couple of yards or so away from an unlocked door that opened into the embassy garden. Mike stood seething, trying to restrain his rage, trying to control his impulse to race across to the table and send all the fancy china, all the well-polished candelabrum flying, to take any action necessary, however drastic, that would put an end to this party before it even started. But he controlled this impulse. All he could do, a cop with more muscle than brains, as he liked to say, was stay near the Boss, be ready for anything, and pray from the depths of his Irish heart that they would get through the dangers lurking in this endless night.

HOLTEN-PFLUG TOLD HIS MEN THE new plan. He wanted them to put on their German uniforms. There was no longer any tactical reason for disguise. And honor required this gesture: a proclamation. It was important that when they emerged in the embassy garden, when they burst into the birthday celebration, they would be clearly identified to the world, to history, as soldiers of the Third Reich. He wanted to make sure that as he hurled the Gammon bomb across the dining room that the last astonished thought Roosevelt, Churchill, and Stalin would have in the moment before their certain deaths was this: German soldiers had hunted them down to the ends of the earth.

The men agreed. They put down their weapons and found their uniforms in their rucksacks. They were busy stripping off their Iranian outfits, in various stages of undress, as a group of wrestlers quickly converged into the ring. There were sixteen husky men, and some held iron bars, while others brandished Indian clubs.

Holten-Pflug realized what was happening. He lunged for his Sten gun.

He was not quick enough. An Indian club crashed down on his head, and he collapsed unconscious to the mat.

When he woke up, he was bound. And so were his four men.

Two intimidating wrestlers clutching heavy iron bars stood guard. The others had gone off to the house on Syroos Street to tell the Russians they had captured the Nazi commandos. They would demand the reward.

THROUGHOUT THE DINNER, MIKE KEPT his eye on the pair of french doors. Two guards now flanked the doorway like bookends, but that was not sufficient to ease his fears. In his mind, he kept seeing the doors fly open and a wave of bullets slamming the three great men back into their seats, slumped and helpless. With each new twinge of his imagination, he instinctively moved closer to the president.

The three men seated shoulder to shoulder at the table, as Churchill would say, "together controlled practically all the naval and three-quarters of all the air forces in the world, and could direct armies of nearly twenty million men, engaged in the most terrible of wars that had yet occurred in human history." Yet Mike could not put aside the horrifying expectation that at any moment six commandos would find a way to snuff out their lives. He feared all his vigilance would prove insufficient, overwhelmed by a bold and fanatic enemy.

But in the end it was just a happy party. The recitation of many good-natured toasts; an immense cake with sixty-nine glowing candles; a spirited communal rendition of "Happy Birthday to You"; and the only thing Mike observed out of the ordinary, he'd say, was the prime minister "dancing a gay and abandoned hornpipe."

It was two a.m. when the last guests started leaving, and Mike was finally feeling that he had escaped unscathed from all the wild thoughts and premonitions that had menaced him throughout the past twenty-four hours. He was also encouraged by the fact that tomorrow—no, it was already tomorrow, December 1—they would be leaving this madhouse of a city, flying back to the relative security of Cairo. He had no knowledge of where the six Nazi commandos were, but once the plane had taken off and was flying over the mountains of Iran, their fate was immaterial. They would no longer be a threat.

He was enjoying this prospect when one of the president's aides approached. Mike, he said, a small change in the itinerary. The president has agreed to Churchill's request that the meetings continue on for another two days. We won't be leaving till December 3.

AT SYROOS STREET, THERE WAS a problem. The NKVD station chief, his adjunct, and nearly the entire force of agents had been summoned to the embassy to guard Marshal Stalin during that night's birthday dinner for the British prime minister. There was no one who could release the payment of the reward. Just tell us where the six Nazis are hiding, we'll pick them up, the duty officer offered helpfully.

No money, no information, was the firm reply from the Iranians. We'll wait. The Nazis aren't going anywhere.

HOLTEN-PFLUG COULD NOT BELIEVE IT was going to end this way, he and his men trussed like chickens for the roasting as they waited for the Russians to claim their prize. So much for his place in history. Ignominy would be his legacy. The totality of his failure filled him with shame. His dedication had been flung back in his face. His faith had been betrayed, and worse, he knew, he had not even fired a shot.

Minutes later two shots rang out in rapid succession, the noise thundering in the enclosed gymnasium. One of the guards fell face-first onto the mat. Then the other slammed forward, too. They both had been shot in the back. Gorechi had entered the gym, taken one look at his comrades with their arms tied behind their backs, and without a word, shot one Iranian guard, then the other. The Walther PPK was still level in his hand, ready in case a third guard emerged.

Hurry, Holten-Pflug ordered, untie me! We must get out of here. The Russians could be here at any moment.

The six men and their weapons were in the truck, racing away from the sports club, before Holten-Pflug was fully able to come to terms with all that had happened. His instinct was to rage at the duplicity of the wrestlers, but he knew this wasn't the time. He focused his thoughts and promptly came to the grim conclusion that it was no longer possible to proceed with the original operation. By the time they emerged in the embassy grounds, the party would have concluded. How would they locate their targets? He had no idea of the upstairs layouts of the buildings. He needed, he understood, to rethink and then redeploy. They were on the loose, they had the Gammon bombs. An attack was still very possible. But first they needed somewhere safe to spend the night, somewhere he could think it all through.

I've an idea, said Gorechi finally.

41

GORECHI DROVE THE COMMANDOS TO a police station.

It had been a nerve-racking journey across the city. Holten-Pflug kept looking about apprehensively, watching for any sign that Russian soldiers had arrived at the sports club and then picked up their trail. The men gripped their Sten guns, fingers tightened on the trigger guard, ready to open fire at the first indication that the enemy was in pursuit. Their watchers' eyes searched through the moonlit shadows.

The sudden collapse of their original plan, their ignominious capture by a crew of greedy, muscle-bound Iranians, had left the team primed for another chance. They had experienced a feeble defeat, but miraculously they'd rebounded, emerging still armed, still dangerous, still committed to the murder of the Big Three. They had the will. Their targets were still in Tehran. They would regroup and devise an alternative strategy. They would redeem themselves.

When Gorechi, then, said he knew a place where they could be safely sequestered for a night, Holten-Pflug listened with attention, as well as gratitude. Hungry for acclaim, he would not allow a tawdry betrayal to deprive him of his opportunity to make history. The Iranian explained that Sadraq Movaqqar was an old friend from their youthful days as torchbearers marching in strident pro-Nazi Melliyun demonstrations. He suspected Movaqqar, an ardent admirer of Hitler Shah, would take them in, especially if he was paid for the risk. There was, however, one minor caution he felt obligated to share: Movaqqar was Lieutenant Movaqqar, the night duty officer of the police commissariat on Albassi Street.

At once Holten-Pflug was on guard. All his suspicions, all his raw resentment at having been betrayed by a motley group of Iranians, reared up. But he managed to find perspective. A mission in enemy territory was a succession of incredible hazards, one perilous gamble after another. At this late hour in the operation with all his previous plans in disarray he had no choice but to grasp any hand that was offered—as long as he remained attentive, as long as he was prepared to shoot his way out if things turned. And he found tacit encouragement in his unshakable faith in his ultimate success. He agreed to go to the police station.

Once there, a deal was quickly reached. For 5,000 pounds to the lieutenant, and an additional thousand to each of the two men on duty, the six commandos could spend the night in the vacant jail cells. The price was irrelevant; the money that he paid out, Holten-Pflug silently smirked, was counterfeit. Yet he could not help but fear that his newfound savior's allegiance was equally false. Nevertheless, he'd run out of alternatives. He steadied himself with a silent pledge of resolve: This time he wouldn't be taken without a fight. He ordered his men to sleep in shifts, weapons ready. If the lieutenant and his cohorts tried something, well, this go-round they'd be the ones in for a surprise. Still, it was disconcerting to be in a jail cell, even if the door remained unlocked. He was not a nervous man by nature, but that did not mean he was free of worries.

The night passed without incident. And in the seclusion of his cell, Holten-Pflug worked out the beginnings of a plan. It was a compromised, admittedly flawed strategy, but he'd convinced himself it still could succeed. His men would need some information for the scheme to take fuller form, but he suspected the practical police lieutenant would be able to provide what was required; that is, as long as he was sufficiently compensated.

It was just after dawn when Movaqqar entered the cell. The commandos, he announced without warning, must leave. It was a

new day—December 1—and the next shift of police officers would
soon be reporting for duty.

The news jarred the men. They'd been on the run since they
parachuted into the country. Once again events had abruptly closed
in on them. They looked to their commander.

Holten-Pflug felt blindsided. How would he find a new hideout?
Where could they go? Yet he also knew with a suddenly desperate
urgency that he had to get his team more time in Tehran. A single
day—and then they would make history.

FOR MIKE, THE UNEXPECTED PROSPECT of having to spend more
time in Tehran landed like a spiteful curse. He'd been eagerly anticipating the departure from the insecure Russian embassy, with its
parade of thugs daintily waving their feather dusters in a transparent
charade, with its lush gardens accessible by subterranean tunnels.
He'd been looking forward to putting thousands of miles and a
range of steep mountains between the Boss and the six Nazi commandos. Only the escape had been postponed. The Boss would
not be leaving for Cairo until Friday. The knowledge that both the
president and the six Nazis would be in Tehran for two more days
reignited all his doubts and suspicions.

Yet just as quickly, once again his fortunes changed. At ten thirty
that morning the weather west of the city took a turn. A cold front
was passing through Cairo. And like the proverbial ill wind, it also
blew some good. The army meteorologist predicted that this volatile
weather would soon move east, storming through the Iranian mountain passes. When the president's plane flew on Friday, it would need
to climb way above six thousand feet to rise above dense clouds and
heaving turbulence—and Admiral McIntire, FDR's cautious physician, would have none of that. It was decided the president should
leave Tehran the next day, early on Thursday morning.

Mike rejoiced, and at the same time like a gambler on a winning streak he doubled down. He made an impassioned case to the

president's staff that once the day's meeting was concluded, there was no reason to spend another minute at the Russian embassy. And a lot of reasons not to.

You need to realize, he'd nearly pleaded, that as long as the six Nazi commandos are at large, they remain a threat. And his concern resonated. It was decided that at the end of the day the president would be driven to the US Army camp at Amirabad. It was at the foot of the Elburz Mountains, a twenty-minute drive from the airport, and best of all to Mike's wary way of looking at things, it was home to three thousand or so American GIs. That should be a sufficient bodyguard to intimidate six Nazis, Mike reasoned.

All he needed to do was shepherd the Boss through this last day of meetings, and then the president would be safe.

The Iranian police lieutenant, in the meantime, had solved Holten-Pflug's immediate problem, even if it was once again for a price. He drove the commandos to his own house, where, for 2,000 pounds a day, they were welcome to stay.

In the seclusion of the policeman's home, Holten-Pflug shared his new plan with his men. It was a strategy, he conceded, that was shaped by their diminished capabilities. They could not storm the embassies. Or poison the food. Or smuggle themselves inside. Those sort of shrewd schemes would be too ambitious, would require too much plotting, for what by necessity must be something more makeshift. As a result, the German major explained, he'd been forced to return to an assault that had once been considered in Berlin, and then swiftly abandoned.

They would ambush the Big Three as the official motorcades drove to the airport.

Originally, Schellenberg had rejected this manner of attack because it greatly reduced the likelihood that all three men would be assassinated. But now, after acknowledging the reversals that had been suffered as well as the precariousness of their present predicament,

Holten-Pflug had come around to seeing things with a measure of resignation. At this besieged juncture a single death would be a tremendous victory for the Reich. Yet at the same headstrong time, he still had not completely abandoned the gallant hope that all three men could possibly be assassinated, and he had plotted accordingly. His sense of his own destiny remained strong.

There were six of them, and three Allied leaders. The math was simple: they would divide into two-man units—a separate target for each. Holten-Pflug reserved the biggest prize for himself. With Gorechi at his side, he would kill the American president.

There had been the important question of intelligence: How would they know when the leaders would leave for the airport and what routes the motorcades would travel? But Holten-Pflug informed his men he had already discussed that problem with the police lieutenant. As had been the case when the Big Three arrived in Tehran, the Iranian authorities would be in charge of crowd control during the departures. The police would learn in advance when the world leaders would head to the airport and the streets that would need to be cordoned. This was information the policeman was only too eager to sell.

As for the actual attacks, each would be a test of the soldiers' courage, the standards they wished to live by, the values for which they were willing to die. They possessed a crate of Gammon bombs, an arsenal capable of ferocious destruction. A single well-thrown bomb would obliterate a vehicle and everyone inside. But to ensure the kill, it might be necessary for the commandos to become suicide bombers. They must be prepared to hurl themselves at the car conveying the head of state, pulling the pin on the bomb in their hands at the same instant. They would need to find the sense of high purpose that cherished the opportunity to die for the country and the cause in which they believed.

To a man, they accepted the challenge.

As the final day at the Russian embassy dragged on, Mike's mood was subdued and turning increasingly gloomy. Would the Boss ever finish? Would they ever leave? First, the conferences had lingered on interminably all through the day. Then the president had spontaneously insisted on hosting a farewell dinner for Churchill and Stalin. It was hastily arranged and, in comparison to the previous night's festive shindig, mercifully brief. But the discussions, to his agonized frustration, had resumed, and Mike had started to wonder if they would be leaving the embassy that night after all. He tried not to make any predictions, determined to focus on nothing but the demands of the moment. Yet his thoughts kept traveling back to the missing six commandos, and each time he made this journey, his fears were aroused anew.

The commandos, too, had suffered a setback. Once the concern had been raised, Holten-Pflug immediately realized its wisdom—as well as its significance. It was something he should have considered. It simply, he conceded with a fraternal candor to his men, had never crossed his mind.

One of his men had pointed out a large gap in the intelligence they'd receive from the police lieutenant. Movaqqar would be able to provide only the neighborhoods that would be blocked by the police barricades. Nothing more. The specific streets the motorcade would travel was not shared by the Allies. It would more than likely become apparent once his men concealed themselves in the crowds on the perimeter. But a troubling element of uncertainty remained. Would his men have sufficient warning to be at the right place at the right time? To get close enough to hurl a bomb—or themselves, if it came to that—at the appropriate vehicle? It would be, he knew, a matter of luck as much as anything else. If he had had more personnel, it would have been a relatively simple-enough operation. Position, say, two men to act as spotters, and they'd signal the street into which the motorcade would be turning. That'd give his men time to find a spot, to be prepared, to set the fuse on the bombs. Guided by this intelligence, the ambush would proceed without a hitch. Without it, there was no telling how things would play out.

The men sorted through this problem, only to arrive at the resigned conclusion that since there was no alternative they would be forced to rely on chance. They'd just have to hope that they'd be able to determine the routes and hurry into position. That they'd have time to set the fuses. But Holten-Pflug was realistic enough to grasp that wishful thinking was not an optimal battle plan. He had been this close, he had sensed, to achieving a great victory, and now fissures of doubt cracked his certitude.

Then Gorechi spoke up. If spotters were a tactical necessity, he knew where they could be recruited. The wrestler Ebtehaj had an entire network of men, and in the past they had done all sorts of dirty work for the SD and for Franz Mayr. For the right price, they'd slit throats. Pointing out the direction a car was turning would be seen as easy money.

The major exploded. He had put his trust in the wrestler only to wind up knocked senseless, bound, ready to be handed over to the Russians. How could you suggest working with him again?

Gorechi, with great tact, it must be presumed, pointed out to his commander that Ebtehaj had not been part of the group that had assaulted the team. Ebtehaj had not betrayed the confidence that had been placed in him. He had remained loyal to the Reich, and was a man of honor as well.

Holten-Pflug was not convinced of any of this. He considered it the height of recklessness to renew any association with Ebtehaj. Yet he also understood that without spotters to guide his men, the attack would likely be doomed. A determination needed to be made between two unsatisfactory alternatives: either he put his trust in a man he suspected didn't deserve it, or he condemned his mission to failure.

When he shared his decision, his words were not inspired by operational practicalities or the soundness of the translator's argument.

It came down to one overriding notion: he had been granted an opportunity to ensure his legacy—if he could summon up a soldier's faith, even when reason argued against it. Had he come this far only to cower in the final act?

Bring Ebtehaj here, he ordered.

42

T HE REUNION OF HOLTEN-PFLUG AND Ebtehaj was a perfect marriage of ambition and greed. The Nazi major shared
a carefully edited version of his plan and the role he expected
the spotters to play. He made sure not to suggest that it could turn
into a suicide mission or that the spotters could be swept up in
the blasts. The wrestler listened, and then the requisite bargaining
commenced. It ended with terms Ebtehaj thought were quite favor-
able. He'd provide six men for a total of 4,000 British pounds. Half
would be paid later that night when Ebtehaj returned with the men,
the remainder after the job.

The wrestler was nearly out the door when Holten-Pflug, no
longer able to restrain his seething anger, shared what else was on
his mind. The last time he'd trusted Ebtehaj he'd been betrayed.
He had put his confidence in men who claimed to be supporters of
the Reich, but who abandoned their allegiance in order to pocket
the hefty reward the Allies had offered. If that were to happen again,
he warned, he'd make sure the traitors paid with their lives.

Are you accusing me? Ebtehaj shot back. I was not part of the
group. Sure, I knew about the price on your head. Everyone in the
city did. A fortune. But when I make a deal, I don't go back on it.

Just so you know that I'm serious, said Holten-Pflug. Tell your
men: It'd be the last thing they'd ever do. They'd never live to
spend the reward money.

OUT ON THE STREET, HEADING to the café where he'd find his crew to tell them about the new job, Ebtehaj brooded about what the Nazi major had said. Betray him? It was more the case that he was betraying me. He'd never revealed the danger the spotters would be in. They could be blown to kingdom come in the blasts. And what about me? How long before the Allies would track me down? All the false promises about making me police chief. The Nazis were never going to win this war. That was clear. They were using me, treating me like a fool. Besides, who would pay the rest of the money if the major and his men get caught? Or killed? Either of which was very likely. A deal cuts both ways; they should know that. You lie to me, that invalidates any contract.

And he thought about the price the Allies had put on the six Nazis' heads. It was, indeed, a fortune. Five times as much as the German major had offered. It wouldn't have to be divided with his men. Even better, it'd be paid in full.

Ebtehaj decided not to go to the café. He headed to the house on Syroos Street instead.

IT WAS FREEZING AT CAMP AMIRABAD. An icy nighttime wind swept down from the mountains and slashed across Mike's face like a whip. But Mike wasn't complaining. It was nearly eleven p.m. and he'd just left the Boss in D barracks, the colonel's quarters, where he'd spend his last night in Iran. They had finally escaped from the Russian embassy only a half hour earlier. But at last they were on friendly territory, with a few thousand armed American troops for company to keep out any uninvited visitors. At nine the next morning they'd drive to the airport. A twenty-minute ride, and he'd be glued to the Boss's side the entire way. He was almost home free, Mike felt with a comforting glow of confidence.

Then he went to his room and the phone rang. General Arkadiev needed to talk to him.

CROUCHED BEHIND THE RUSSIAN'S JEEP, the general nearby with a pair of binoculars raised to his eyes, Mike had a good view of the one-story sandstone house down the long block. He had gotten there as fast as he could, commandeering a driver from the army camp as soon as Arkadiev had told him they knew where the six Nazis had gone to ground. It must be, he guessed, nearly one in the morning. The city was as quiet as a graveyard. But not for long, he suspected.

He had listened when a Russian officer—NKVD Mike decided—had given the husky Iranian wrestler his orders. The Nazi major is expecting you, correct? the officer had asked. The wrestler reiterated that it had been agreed he'd come by with six of his men that night. Good, said the Russian. When he asks where are the men, tell him to look out the window.

Mike saw what the Nazi major would see: Russian soldiers had taken positions up and down the block, and on the rooftops. Their weapons were pointed directly at the house. They had the building surrounded. If they opened fire, no one would get out alive. Is it really possible the men inside had heard nothing? he wondered anxiously. But he saw no signs of movement from inside the house.

The Russian had continued, looking directly into the wrestler's dark eyes. Tell the Nazi commander he has a choice. Either his men put down their weapons and come out with their hands above their heads, or we'll open fire. Understand?

Ebtehaj had ignored the question. What about my money? he asked.

You'll get your money, the Russian promised. Soon as we have the six Nazis.

Now the wrestler was walking across the street. Mike had his .38 in his hand, but he wasn't sure why. If it came down to a firefight, the Russians would handle things. They had the numbers, for sure.

It was not as cold in the city as it had been in the mountains, he would remember thinking for no particular reason. His eyes followed the wrestler. He could hear the tread of his feet on the gravel. A slow, unhurried walk. He heard the wrestler knock on the door, and he instinctively released the safety latch on his gun.

The door opened and a strip of light momentarily brightened the street. Would the Nazis see the troops? But the door quickly closed shut with a bang so loud that for an instant he thought it was a gunshot. Then there was only the tense quiet, thick in the dark night. This was the moment he'd been anticipating since he'd arrived in Tehran. He was poised to capture the men who had come to kill Roosevelt, Churchill, and Stalin. He had hoped he'd get this opportunity, and now it was almost there.

In his mind's eye he imagined the scene that was playing out inside the house. The wrestler would say that his men would not be coming, not tonight, not ever. Then it was as if he could hear the Nazi major's anger erupting. Would he make a threat? Point his gun at the wrestler? Mike had taken measure of Ebtehaj, and he suspected he was a cool customer, not easily ruffled. He would have told the major to look out the window. The house was surrounded.

Mike saw the window curtain flutter, but he also suspected that at this moment, with so much racing through his mind, it might have been his imagination.

Still, Mike knew the wrestler would relay the Russian officer's ultimatum: Either the six Nazis come out with their hands up, or they will be slaughtered.

Mike tried to put himself inside the mind of the Nazi major. He tried to imagine the long months of planning, of training, the constancy of purpose that, despite all the obstacles, had brought him and his men to this squalid little house in Tehran. He tried to understand the fires of ambition that had burned within the major as he pursued such a deadly mission. He wondered what drove him. Was it hate, or simply duty? Or something even deeper? And he tried to guess what the major would do when he realized all his

warrior's dreams had dwindled down to either meek surrender or
the massacre of his men.

At that moment there was an ear-shattering boom, followed by
a harsh white glow that must have lit up the night sky for miles. All
at once the building collapsed to the ground in a heap of smoking
rubble.

AT NINE THIRTY THE NEXT morning after a busy, sleepless night,
Mike watched as the president was strapped into his seat on the
C-54. In the aftermath of the explosion, Mike and Arkadiev had
tried to determine what had happened. As best they could understand things, rather than surrender the Nazis had decided to take
control of their own destinies. The remains of Gammon bombs had
been found in the debris, and, judging by the thunder of the blast, at
least a half-dozen must have been simultaneously detonated. There
were no survivors.

Mike went back to his seat in the rear of the C-54 and stretched
out as best he could. It was one of his rules that he rarely slept on
airplane trips; he liked to stay alert in case the Boss needed him.
But as the big plane rose above Gale Morghe Airport, heading west
toward Cairo, Mike closed his eyes. He was quickly fast asleep, at
last convinced the long night of the assassins was over.

Epilogue:
Secrets

REPORTERS WERE CRAMMED INTO A tight semicircle in the Oval Office facing President Franklin D. Roosevelt. The president sat in his wheelchair behind the massive walnut-veneered desk that had once been Herbert Hoover's. Mike stood, as he always did during the presidential press conferences, to the Boss's right, near a casement window, but never too far away. Outside, the weather was foul. It was December 17, 1943, and the press had come to hear about the conferences in Cairo and Tehran.

In time, the president began to talk about security problems during his trip. "In a place like Tehran there are hundreds of German spies, probably, all around the place," he said. "I suppose it would make a pretty good haul if they could get all three of us going through the streets."

"There was no use going into details," he added. Then the president laughed his hearty, booming laugh, and the press joined in, too.

Mike's face, though, remained set, as if cast in stone.

There were no follow-up questions from the reporters, and anyway the president had quickly moved on, talking about China.

IN THE DAYS, THEN MONTHS that followed, as the war raged and the events in Tehran receded from official memories, the actors who had knowledge of the secrets continued to guard them, too. And at the same turbulent time, their own lives moved on eventfully.

Berthold Schulze-Holthus, the Abwehr man in Iran, had finally overstayed his welcome with Nasr Khan. The Qashqai tribe handed him over to the British. In January 1945, he was swapped in an Allied exchange of prisoners with the Germans, and he made his way back to Berlin. When US soldiers took control of Tyrol, they found him enjoying the crisp mountain air in a chalet perched high above a precipice. They arrested him as a "decided security risk."

Franz Mayr, the SD stay-behind spy and Lili Sanjari's part-time lover, escaped British custody in 1946 and went to ground in Egypt. A forged British passport eventually led him to a new life in Switzerland.

Roman Gamotha, the Soviet double agent, remained wrapped in cloaks of mystery. According to one reliable report he was sentenced to "death by shooting" by a Soviet military tribunal on January 28, 1952. Another no less authoritative source had him alive in Egypt and training Fatah terrorists.

Cicero, to use Elyesa Bazna's code name, moved to Istanbul, where he'd hoped to retire on the treasure (about $1.8 million in 2020 dollars) he had received from the SD in exchange for his stolen documents. He discovered, however, that the British banknotes were counterfeit. With a thief's self-righteous anger he attempted to sue the postwar West German government. The case was laughed out of court.

Gevork Vartanian, the boy who had charged through the streets of Tehran with his Light Cavalry, fulfilled his youthful ambition of becoming a Moscow Center operative. He was awarded the Red Banner and the Red Star for his years of clandestine service, and at his funeral in January 2010, Russian president Dmitry Medvedev offered a eulogy for "a legendary intelligence agent."

Otto Skorzeny, "the Most Dangerous Man in Europe" who at the last minute walked away from Long Jump, also managed to escape a conviction in an Allied court for war crimes. He had been charged with disguising his commandos in US Army uniforms so that they could sneak behind the lines during the Battle of the Bulge. After the war Simon Wiesenthal, the famed Nazi hunter, included Skorzeny on his well-researched list of war criminals. At the same time it was also stated in reputable Israeli press reports that Skorzeny had been hired by the Mossad, the Jewish state's intelligence service, to hunt down former Nazis.

Walter Schellenberg, the operational mastermind of Long Jump, succeeded in outmaneuvering his rival (and friend) Admiral Wilhelm Canaris. He presided over Canaris's arrest, concentration camp internment, and subsequent execution. He also took over control of the Abwehr. At the end of the war, as he'd feared, he was sentenced by an Allied tribunal to six years in prison. As for the evidence that would reveal the full extent of his covert wartime schemes, he would write: "I had all the most important files of my department photographed on microfilm. The films were placed in two steel strong-boxes, small enough to fit into a briefcase. As a further precaution, a mechanism setting off an explosive was built into the box, so that the contents would be destroyed if anyone who did not know the combination attempted to force the box. Eventually both boxes were destroyed."

Mike Reilly went with FDR to Yalta, and he was at his side when the president died after a catastrophic stroke in Warm Springs, Georgia, on April 12, 1945. He said a prayer for his friend, and then, just to be certain, he gathered up the remnants of the Boss's breakfast to deliver to a chemist to be analyzed. Nothing unusual was discovered, but Mike had wanted to make sure for the last time that an assassin had not targeted the president on his watch.

Then there was the note that Stalin, after returning to Moscow, had sent FDR in the aftermath of the meetings in Iran. "I am glad," he'd written, "that fate has given me an opportunity to render you a service in Tehran."

What did Marshal Stalin mean? perplexed historians would

wonder over the course of subsequent decades. What service could
he possibly have performed for the president?

The answer would remain stored away, hidden deep in the secret
repositories where nations consign the failed dramas that had once
excited sinister hearts. Until now.

A Note on Sources

With a drum roll rarely sounded in any spy headquarters, let alone in the clandestine halls of Moscow Center, on November 18, 2003, the SVR, the Russian foreign intelligence service, held a press conference to announce the publication of a new book. *Tehran 43: Operation Long Jump*, written by Yuri Kuznets (Moscow: OKCMO, 2003; privately translated), was a detailed account of the Nazi plot to assassinate Roosevelt, Churchill, and Stalin at the Tehran Conference. It was based on the gold standard of espionage sources: previously classified Russian intelligence reports, NKVD analytical documents, and decoded message traffic. To herald the book's veracity, Vladimir Kirpichenko, a former deputy chief of the KGB First Main Directorate (foreign intelligence), who had access to the Moscow Center's archival materials in the Long Jump files, was trotted out. He praised Kuznets's account as "strictly documentary" and went on to confirm the startling story it told about the planning, execution, and ultimate operational collapse of the Nazi plot. And for further support, Gevork Vartanian, the boy hero of the Light Cavalry who was now a much-honored retired secret agent, appeared to bestow his eyewitness's imprimatur on the book. "We provided the security of the conference," he stated, feisty and indignant, "and we knew what was going on."

Spurred on by this event, I went looking for additional Russian source materials on Operation Long Jump and found other writings inspired by newly released files: Alexander Lukin, "Operation Long Jump," *Ogonek*, no. 33 (1990), August 15, 1965, 25, and no. 34

(1991), August 22, 1965, 25–27; Victor Yegorov, *The Plot Against "Eureka": The Lost Portfolio* (Moscow: Sovetskaya Rossiya, 1968); Nikolai Dolgopolov, "How the Lion and the Bear Were Saved," *Rossiiskaya Gazetta*, November 29, 2007; and "Triple Jeopardy: The Nazi Plan to Kill WWII Leaders in Tehran," *RIA Nowosti* vol. 4 (January 2007); "Tehran-43: Wrecking the Plan to Kill Stalin, Roosevelt, and Churchill," *Russian News and Information Agency Novosti*, October 16, 2007; Pavel Sudoplatov and Anatoli Sudoplatov, *Special Tasks: The Memoirs of an Unwanted Witness—a Soviet Spymaster*, with Jerrold L. and Leona P. Schecter (Boston: Little, Brown, 1984); and Christopher Andrew and Vasili Mitrokhin, *The Mitrokhin Archive and the Secret History of the KGB* (New York: Basic Books, 2001).

For someone like myself, a writer who had previously dug into the crevices of long-forgotten espionage operations to root out compelling tales, the declassification of the Russian documents signaled a new opportunity: I could at last tell the definitive story of the plot to assassinate the Big Three.

Equally promising, after I'd poked around a bit, I discovered an impressive collection of books and monographs published in the West that gave accounts of Long Jump that, to varying degrees, confirmed the Russian version of events. These included works by noted historians: Richard Deacon, *A History of the Russian Secret Service* (London: Frederick Muller, 1972); Nigel West, *Historical Dictionary of World War II Intelligence* (Lanham, MD: Scarecrow Press, 2008); John Erickson, *The Road to Berlin: Stalin's War with Germany* (London: Weidenfeld and Nicolson, 1983); Miron Rezun, *The Iranian Crisis of 1941* (Cologne: Bohlau, 1982); and Warren Kimball, *Churchill and Roosevelt: The Complete Correspondence* (Princeton, NJ: Princeton University Press, 1987). In addition, there were less rigorous (that is, flawed by pseudonyms, inaccuracies, and speculation) books and press accounts such as Laslo Havas, *Hitler's Plot to Kill the Big Three* (New York: Bantam Books, 1971); Bill Yenne, *Operation Long Jump* (Washington, DC: Regnery Publishing, 2015); and

Kyril Tidmarsh, "How Russians Foiled Nazi Plot to Kill Tehran Big Three," in the *Times* of London, December 20, 1968. Then there were hybrid accounts—that is, published as nonfiction, yet the categorization nevertheless struck me as dubious—documenting German black ops during the Cairo and Tehran summits that were of interest because the authors arguably knew a good deal more than they wrote: Stanley Lovell, the former head of Research and Development of the OSS, *Of Spies and Stratagems* (New York: Pocket Books, 1964); Walter H. Thompson, the police detective at Churchill's side in Tehran, *Assignment: Churchill* (Toronto: McLeod, 1955) and *Beside the Bulldog* (London: Apollo, 2003). And the Long Jump story was also told, albeit with some flights of cinematic fancy, in the feature film *Tegeran-43*, a Soviet-French-Swiss coproduction starring Alain Delon, as well as an episode in the thirteen-part British documentary series *Churchill's Bodyguard* that was based on Tom Hickman's book *Churchill's Bodyguard* (London: Headline, 2005).

Yet at the same time as I was encouraged by this mountain of credible evidence and research, I also had to pay attention to the naysayers. The concerns of Adrian O'Sullivan, *Nazi Secret Warfare in Occupied Persia (Iran)* (London: Palgrave Macmillan, 2014), who had done invaluable firsthand research in the Wehrmacht's archives, demanded to be heard. He completely dismissed Long Jump, charging it was Soviet "disinformation," a tale "generally associated with the literature of neofascist or antifascist historical revisionism" told by "purveyors of Stalinist mythology." Although, he did take a (small) step back from his politicized histrionics to wonder, "What is less clear is why the Putin-era intelligence services should find it expedient to resurrect and promulgate a baseless and obscure Stalinist myth set in wartime Persia." Having offered that concession, O'Sullivan returns briskly to his tirade and in the process ducks suggesting an answer to his question (including the most obvious one: because it's true). And Gary Kern in his "How 'Uncle Joe' Bugged FDR," an essay published by the CIA's unclassified journal, *Studies in Intelligence* 47, no. 1 (2003), plants one foot firmly in O'Sullivan's camp while also carefully keeping another outside the tent. "It is not altogether impossible that the Nazis did plan an attack on the Allied leaders, perhaps even at the Tehran conference," he concedes. But he also argues strenuously that the specific threat passed on to FDR by the Russians was nothing more than a scheme to get the president to settle into their bugged embassy. (It's a point of view that's challenged in a subsequent CIA Center for the Study of Intelligence essay by Warren Kimball, "A Different Take on FDR at Tehran," *Studies in Intelligence* 49, no. 3 [2007], who doubts the president would've been sufficiently naive to "have walked 'willingly' and knowingly into a surveillance trap" without a good reason.)

Clearly, the historical battle lines had been drawn. And clearer still, in attempting to tell the story of Long Jump, I'd be forced to weigh several wildly conflicting versions of events. This was familiar territory. I had traipsed into a similarly politicized minefield, for example, when I'd researched my account of how Russian codes had been broken leading to the arrest of a KGB spy ring, *In the Enemy's House* (New York: HarperCollins, 2018). I had to deal with histrionic arguments claiming Julius Rosenberg was set up, the charges a hoax, and the Venona decrypts an FBI fabrication. In fact, I'd come to believe that this sort of narrative obstacle was inherent to writing any spy story. In a world defined by secrets, where little is verifiable in public archives and even less is stated on the record, it's always a challenge to get at the truth—or, for that matter, to recognize it even when it's staring you in the face. In these real-life whodunits, there's all too often no butler revealed in the final act to take the blame. As James Angleton, the CIA's legendary counterintelligence chief, famously said (borrowing from T. S. Eliot), it's "a wilderness of mirrors," a world in which there are multiple interpretations, multiple solutions, multiple truths.

Consider, for example, a character who has a small walk-on role in this book, the spy code-named Cicero. It seems a certainty he was a German agent who delivered solid-gold Allied intelligence to his masters. Yet Malcolm Gladwell in a wonderfully astute essay ("Pandora's Briefcase," *The New Yorker*, May 10, 2010) recounts how just before his death Stewart Menzies, the British spymaster whose national secrets Cicero had plundered, told an interviewer another version. "Of course, Cicero was under our control," he revealed. To which Gladwell ruminates, "If you had been the wartime head of M.I.6, giving an interview shortly before your death, you probably would say that Cicero was one of yours. Or perhaps, in interviews given shortly before death, people are finally free to tell the truth. Who knows?"

Who knows, indeed? The question of truth in any spy story becomes even more daunting because intelligence assessments are fundamentally political dramas. Biases are proudly blatant. One man's tale of Russian derring-do is another's of Stalinist revisionism. There's always, as Angleton put it to the author Edward Jay Epstein, "a necessary duality" (*James Jesus Angleton: Was He Right?* [New York: CreateSpace, 2014]). There are two sides (for starters) to every story, and more often than not the side you see is straight out of Pirandello's playbook: it is so because you think it's so.

So, how did I approach the research and writing of this book? From my initial idea to tell the tale of Operation Long Jump, I had several narrative ambitions. I wanted to write a suspenseful, character-driven story of men, heroes and villains, caught up in a tense, desperate time who needed to find the courage and cunning to do their duty for their countries and to fulfill their own sense of honor. I was also determined to make it a factual account, a history as well as an adventure. However, at the same time it was purposefully not an academic study. I did not want to interrupt the flow of my book with a litany of caveats, with a constant chorus of "while-one-source-said-this, another-said-thats." And, most fundamentally, I wanted to write a true story.

Was this another impossible mission? I worried. Were the obstacles I'd be facing as steep as those that confronted (and ultimately doomed) the Long Jump commandos?

Nevertheless, I delved into all the research on Long Jump (see the chapter-by-chapter notes for more details). This included the treasure trove of recently declassified Soviet intelligence documents cited in the Russian accounts, translated Wehrmacht records (Bundesarchiv, Berlin; Bundesarchiv-Militararchiv, Freiburg), OSS and CIA files (National Archives and Record Administration, College Park, MD), British intelligence reports (National Archives, Kew; Imperial War Museum, London; and supplemented by A. J. Farrington, ed., *British Intelligence and Policy on Persia, 1900–1949*, Leiden: IDC, 2004), State Department records collected in *Foreign Relations of the United States: The Conferences at Cairo and Tehran, 1943* (Washington, DC: US Government Printing Office, 1961), and Secret Service documents and diplomatic papers at the Franklin D. Roosevelt Presidential Library archives filed within the Map Room Papers and President's Secretary File, as well as in additional FDR Library collections. There were also several memoirs that helped give a much-needed immediacy to the characters who populated this tale. These included Michael Reilly's *Reilly of the White House* (New York: Simon & Schuster, 1947); Walter Schellenberg's *The Memoirs of Hitler's Spymaster* (London: Andre Deutsch, 1956), which was further expanded by the transcript of his interrogation by British authorities after his arrest, as originally cited by Adrian O'Sullivan, and in Reinhard R. Doerries, *Hitler's Last Chief of Intelligence: Allied Interrogations of Walter Schellenberg* (London: Frank Cass, 2003); Winston S. Churchill's *The Grand Alliance*, vol. 3 of *The Second World War* (Boston, MA: Houghton Mifflin, 1951), *The Hinge of Fate*, vol. 4 of *The Second World War* (Boston, MA: Houghton Mifflin, 1951), and *Closing the Ring*, vol. 5 of *The Second World War* (Boston, MA: Houghton Mifflin, 1951); Berthold Schulze-Holthus's wonderfully vivid *Daybreak in Iran: A Story of the German Intelligence Service* (London: Mervyn Savill, 1954); and the many fulsome accounts that Otto Skorzeny wrote of his life and exploits, including *Hitler's Commando* (New York: Skyhorse Publishing, 2016),

For Germany: The Otto Skorzeny Memoirs (San Jose: Bender, 2005), and *Skorzeny's Special Missions* (London: Hale, 1957).

I also collected a small library of histories detailing World War II, wartime activities in Iran, and the Tehran Conference. It seems to me that for this sort of popular account it's unnecessary to list them all. Nevertheless, interested readers might want to start with Ashley Jackson, *Persian Gulf Command* (New Haven: Yale University Press, 2018); Robert I. Baker, *Oil, Blood, and Sand* (New York: Appleton-Century, 1942); Faramarz Fatemi, *The U.S.S.R. in Iran* (New York: Barnes, 1980); David Kahn, *Hitler's Spies: German Military Intelligence in World War II* (Cambridge, MA: Da Capo Press, 2000); John To-land, *Adolf Hitler* (New York: Doubleday, 1967); Richard Stewart, *Sunrise at Abadan: The British and Soviet Invasion of Iran, 1941* (New York: Praeger, 1988); Keith Eubank, *Summit at Tehran* (New York: William Morrow, 1965); John R. Deane, *The Strange Alliance: The Story of Our Efforts at Wartime Cooperation with Russia* (New York: Viking Press, 1947); Paul D. Mayle, *Eureka Summit: Agreement in Principle and the Big Three at Tehran, 1943* (Newark: University of Delaware Press, 1987); George Crocker, *Roosevelt's Road to Russia* (Chicago: Henry Regnery, 1959); Suleyman Seydi, "Intelligence and Counter-Intelligence Activities in Iran During the Second World War," *Middle Eastern Studies* 46, no. 5 (2010); and Anita L. P. Burdett, ed., *Iran Political Developments 1941–1946: British Documentary Sources—Iran Under Allied Occupation*, 13 vols. (London: Archives Edition, 2008). I also met with retired intelligence officials who spoke on background, insisted that their names not be used, but also encouraged my growing belief that the Long Jump secrets had been purposefully buried and were waiting to be unearthed.

When I was done, I had to make some decisions. I had to determine what was accurate in each account. I had to make judgments about which versions of the past seemed the most reliable, made the most sense. I had to fit the disparate pieces together. For example, Laslo Havas, who conducted some extraordinary interviews with participants in the mission in the 1950s when the trail was still warm, offered what struck me as a fanciful account of a pseudonymous woman asset working for Franz Mayr. However, after I read recently declassified British and American intelligence reports, it became clear to me that he'd been writing (with some liberties) about Lili Sanjari. I now had a key that would unlock at least a part of the story. And as I continued, more of the isolated pieces from the dozens of accounts began to merge together—and the finished puzzle took shape on the page. I had my true story.

Here are the rules I played by:

When dialogue appears in quotes, the words can be directly attributed to an actor in this story. They are taken from either his own writings—books, letters, diaries—or contemporaneous newspaper accounts. For example, Walter Schellenberg's conversation with Ribbentrop about the kidnapping of the Duke of Windsor is taken from Schellenberg's memoir.

When I describe what someone in this story is thinking or feeling, the thoughts and emotions were either first shared directly by the individual, appear in official intelligence reports, or were culled from previously transcribed interviews with those who had knowledge of these sentiments. For example, Mike Reilly's surging apprehensions when he arrived in Tehran were revealed in his chatty and candid memoir, *Reilly of the White House.*

When a location or an incident is described, the details are grounded in my research. For example, when a member of Franz Team makes his way to Tehran, I was able to use Wehrmacht intelligence files and British interrogation reports (many originally cited and translated by the industrious investigative historian Adrian O'Sullivan) to tell the tale with verisimilitude. And I was helped in my attempt to re-create life in Tehran's cafés by S. H. I. Moeini et al., "The Beverage Drinking Rituals and the Semantics of Alternative Culture: Tehran Cafés" in *Urban Culture in Tehran* (New York: Springer International Publishing, 2017). My feel for life in the prewar and wartime city was further enriched by John Gunther,

Inside Asia (New York: Harper & Brothers, 1939). And Forrest Davis, "What Really Happened at Tehran," *Life*, May 13 and 20, 1944, provides an intimate eyewitness account of the conference (although it was still a carefully censored report; FDR edited and approved the articles before publication according to historians).

Therefore, this is, to reiterate, a true story. But at the same time let me, in candor, flash an amber light of caution. The search for truth in espionage stories is always, to paraphrase Karl Popper, the search for the best hypothesis. Spy dramas are by the nature of the genre always works in progress. Nations reveal their innermost secrets by drips, not floods. Do we, for example, even today know whether the British sacrificed the city of Coventry to the Luftwaffe's bombs to protect the existence of Ultra, the top-secret wartime program that had cracked the Nazis' codes? How many pages has the US government declassified on the Kennedy assassination, and yet does anyone think the whole story has been told?

I received an answer of sorts to those questions during a conversation I once had at CIA headquarters with a distinguished agency official. He laughed out loud when I told him I was writing a true story. No one, he shot back, ever knows the whole truth when it comes to secret intelligence work. There's always one more file hidden away.

Which brings me back to Long Jump. At the unprecedented SVR press conference in 2003 that announced the declassification of the Long Jump files, a reporter asked, "Are there any secrets left concerning the Tehran Conference? And if there are still such secrets in the archives, when will they be disclosed?" Vladimir Kirpichenko, the former First Directorate chief, let the question float in the room for a long, pregnant moment. Then he answered: "I don't think any intelligence service in the world opens up to the last document."

And until they do, this is the definitive account of Operation Long Jump.

Following are the principal sources for each chapter of this book.

Sources

Prologue: "Stalin Bared Plot against President," *New York Times*, December 18, 1943.

Chapter One: Ian Colvin, *Flight 777* (London: Evan Brothers, 1957) and *Admiral Canaris: Chief of Intelligence* (London: Colvin Press, 2008) [Chief]; Ronald Howard, *In Search of My Father* (London: Saint Martin's Press, 1984); Ben Rosevink and Lt. Col. Herbert Hinze, "Flight 777," *FlyPast* no. 120 (July 1991); William Stevenson, *A Man Called Intrepid* (Guilford, DE: Lyons Press, 1976); Ian Onions, "The Mystery of Flight 777," *Bristol Evening Post*, 31 May 2010; Joaquim da Costa Leite, "Neutrality by Agreement: Portugal and the British Alliance in World War II," *American University International Law Review* 14, no. 1 (1988); Hugh Kay, *Salazar and Modern Portugal* (New York: Hawthorn Books, 1970); Ben Macintyre, *Double Cross* (New York: Broadway Books, 2013); Neill Lochery, *Lisbon: War in the Shadows of the City of Light* (New York: Public Affairs Books, 2011); "Portugal, the Consuls, and the Jewish Refugees, 1938–1941," https://www.yadvashem.org/righteous/stories/portugal-historical-background.html; Larry Loftis, "Ian Fleming, Lisbon, and the WWII Espionage Game," https://literary007.com/2017/02/10/ian-fleming-and-the-wwii-espionage-game; Royal Air Force Historical Branch, *Rise and Fall of the German Air Force, 1933–1945* (RAF Northolt) "Luftwaffe Operational Chain of Command"; Winston Churchill, *The Hinge of Fate* [Hinge]; Robert Forczyk, *Fw 200 Condor vs. Atlantic Convoy* (London: Osprey, 2010); E. R. Hooton, *The Luftwaffe: A Study in Air Power* (London: Classic Publications, 2010); Heinz Hohne, *Canaris* (New York: Doubleday, 1979) [Canaris]; David Kahn, *Hitler's Spies* [HS]; Walter Schellenberg, *The Memoirs of Hitler's Spymaster* [Spymaster]; Laslo Havas, *Hitler's Plot to Kill the Big Three* [Plot]; Michael Dobbs, *Saboteurs: The Nazi Raid on America* (New York: Knopf, 2004); Perry Biscombe, "The Deployment of SS Saboteurs and Spies in the Soviet Union, 1942–1945," *Europe-Asia Studies* 6 (2000) [Deployment].

Chapter Two: Records of the US Secret Service, National Archives [SS Records]; Mike Reilly, *Reilly of the White House* [Reilly]; Donald Ritchie, *Electing FDR* (Lawrence: University Press of Kansas, 2007) [Electing]; Hugh E. Evans, *The Hidden Campaign: FDR's Health and the 1944 Election* (Abingdon, UK: Routledge, 2002) [Hidden]; FDR Day by Day, FDR Presidential Library, http://www.fdrlibrary.marist.edu/daybyday/ [Day].

Chapter Three: Reilly; Anaconda, Montana, official website, http://adlc.us/; Jerry Calvert, "The Rise and Fall of Socialism in a Company Town," *Montana* 36, no. 4 (December 1986); "Mike Reilly Is Dead at 63; Headed Secret Service Detail," *New York Times*, 19 June 1973; SS Records; Jane Reilly Harte Obituary, March 2, 2009, *The Independent*, https://helenair.com/news/local/obituaries/jane-reilly-harte/article_6019ce63-5db7-5b85-99aa-2901a99d28fb.html

Chapter Four: Reilly; Doris Kearns Goodwin, *No Ordinary Time* (New York: Simon & Schuster, 1994) [Ordinary]; SS Records; Roosevelt Library, Secret Service Files [SSF].

Chapter Five: Reilly; Ordinary; www.alcaponemuseum.com; "FDR Hitched a Ride in Al Capone's Car," https://www.history.com/shows/brad-meltzers-lost-history/season-1/episode-5/fdr-hitched-a-ride-in-al-capones-car; SSF.

Chapter Six: Reilly; SSF; Ordinary; Hinge; John L. Chase, "Unconditional Surrender Reconsidered," *Political Science Quarterly* 70, no. 2 (1955) [Surrender]; Michael Howard, *Grand Strategy*, vol. 4 (London: Her Majesty's Stationery Office, 1972) [Strategy]; Winston Churchill, *Closing the Ring* [Ring].

Chapter Seven: Spymaster; Reinhard R. Dorries, *Hitler's Last Chief of Foreign Intelligence: Allied Interrogations of Walter Schellenberg* [Last Chief]; HS; Michael Bloch, *Ribbentrop* (London: Bantam, 1992) [Ribbentrop]; F. H. Hinsley and C. A. G. Simkins, *British Intelligence in the Second World War* (New York: Cambridge University Press, 1984) [Hinsley and Simkins]; Bill Yenne, *Operation Long Jump* [Long Jump]; Plot; Surrender; Strategy.

Chapter Eight: Spymaster; Last Chief; Canaris; Chief; HS; Plot; Long Jump; Ashley Jackson, *Persian Gulf Command* [Command]; Suleyman Seydi, "Intelligence and Counter-Intelligence Activities in Iran during the Second World War" [Seydi]; Hinsley and Simkins.

Chapter Nine: Spymaster; Last Chief; Command; Seydi; Adrian O'Sullivan, *Nazi Secret Warfare in Occupied Persia* [Secret Warfare]; HS; Christer Jorgensen, *Hitler's Espionage Machine* (Guilford, CT: Lyons Press, 2004) [Machine]; Anthony Read, *The Devil's Disciples: Hitler's Inner Circle* (New York: W. W. Norton, 2004) [Disciples]; Berthold Schulze-Holthus, *Daybreak in Iran* [Daybreak].

Chapter Ten: Reader Bullard, "Persia in the Two World Wars," *Journal of the Royal Central Asian Society* 50, no. 1 (1963); Secret Warfare; Hinsley and Simkins; National Archives and Records Administration, College Park, MD [NARA]; Daybreak; Wolfgang Schwanitz, *Germany and the Middle East, 1871–1945* (Princeton: Markus Wiener, 2004); *Diary of Franz Mayr*, National Archives (Kew) [Diary]; Seydi; CICI Persia Counter-Intelligence Summaries on Mayr, Moritz, and Gamotha at the National Archives, Kew, first cited by O'Sullivan [TNA]; Richard A. Stewart, *Sunrise at Abadan: The British and Soviet Invasion of Iran, 1941*; Hinge.

Chapter Eleven: Reilly; SSF; SS Records; National Museum of the United States Air Force, "Factsheet: Douglas VC-54C SACRED COW"; Spymaster; Last Chief; TNA; NARA; Plot; Yuri Kuznets, *Tehran 43: Operation Long Jump* [43]; Florian Berger, *With Oak Leaves and Swords: The Highest Decorated Soldiers of the Second World War* (Vienna, Austria: Selbstverlag, 1999), privately translated.

Chapter Twelve: Spymaster; Last Chief; HS; 43; Terrence O'Reilly, *Hitler's Irishmen* (Cork, IR: Mercier Press, 2008); Franz Kurowski, *The Brandenburger Commandos* (Mechanicsburg, PA: Stackpole Books, 2005); Plot; Long Jump.

Chapter Thirteen: Spymaster; Last Chief; "Sachsenhausen-Oranienburg," http://jewishgen.org.forgottencamps/Camps/SachsenhausenEng.html; "History of Sachsenhausen," http://www.jewishvirtuallibrary.org; Otto Skorzeny, *Hitler's Commandos*; For Germany; *Special Missions* [Skorzeny]; Secret Warfare; Plot; Long Jump; NARA; TNA; HS.

Chapter Fourteen: Spymaster; Last Chief; Plot; Long Jump; 43; Canaris; Chief; "Eden Hotel," http://www.potsdamer-platz.org/eden.htm; Reilly; SSF.

Chapter Fifteen: 43; Plot; Alexander Lukin, "Operation Long Jump" [Lukin]; Victor Yegorov, *The Plot Against 'Eureka'* [Eureka]; John Erickson, *The Road to Berlin* [Berlin]; Nigel West, *Historical Dictionary of World War II Intelligence* [Dictionary]; Miron Rezun, *The Iranian Crisis of 1941* [Crisis]; Long Jump; Spymaster.

Chapter Sixteen: Skorzeny; Spymaster; Last Chief; Plot; Long Jump; Lukin; Eureka; Berlin; Dictionary; Crisis; Secret Warfare.

Chapter Seventeen: Reilly; Spymaster; US State Department, *Foreign Relations of the United States: The Conferences at Cairo and Tehran, 1943* [Conferences]; Roosevelt Library Map Room files [Map Room]; Hinge; Paul D. Mayle, *Eureka Summit: Agreement in Principle and the Big Three at Tehran, 1943* [Summit]; Plot; Long Jump.

Chapter Eighteen: Skorzeny; Spymaster; Secret Warfare; Daybreak; Pierre Oberling, "Qashqai Tribal Conference," EXLAN, January 7, 2004; Lois

Beck, *The Qashqa'i of Iran* (New Haven, CT: Yale University Press, 1986) [Beck]; HS; TNA.

Chapter Nineteen: Daybreak; Last Chief; TNA; NARA; Plot; Canaris; Chief; Long Jump; 43; Lukin; Dictionary; Eureka; Diary.

Chapter Twenty: Spymaster; Last Chief; Surrender; Plot; Long Jump; 43; Dictionary; Lukin; Summit; Nicolas Farsen, *Corridor of Honor* (Indianapolis, IN: Bobbs-Merrill, 1958); Richard Deacon, *A History of the Russian Secret Service* [Russian Secret Service].

Chapter Twenty-One: Reilly; SSF; Plot; Long Jump; 43; Dictionary; Lukin; Russian Secret Service; Crisis; Pagvel and Anatoli Sudoplatov, *Special Tasks* [Tasks]; Christopher Andrew and Vasili Mitrokhin, *The Mitrokhin Archives and the Secret History of the KGB* [Mitrokhin]; TNA.

Chapter Twenty-Two: Skorzeny; Canaris; Plot; Dictionary; 43; Long Jump; Russian Secret Service; Max Hastings, *Das Reich: The March of the 2nd SS Panzer Division Through France, June 1944* (Minneapolis, MN: Zenith Press, 2013).

Chapter Twenty-Three: Reilly; SSF; Gary J. Byrne, *Secrets of the Secret Service* (New York: Center Street, 2018); Plot; 43; Eureka; Long Jump; Chris Mc-Nab, *Soviet Submachine Guns of World War II* (Oxford, UK: Osprey Publishing, 2014); Skorzeny; Plot; Spymaster; Last Chief.

Chapter Twenty-Four: Spymaster; Last Chief; HS; Plot; 43; Long Jump; Dictionary; Conferences; NARA; Ribbentrop; Elyesa Bazna, *I Was Cicero* (London: A. Deutsch, 1962); Anthony Cave Brown, *Bodyguard of Lies* (New York: Harper, 1975) [Bodyguard].

Chapter Twenty-Five: Reilly; NARA; Conferences; John R. Deane, *The Strange Alliance: The Story of Our Wartime Cooperation with Russia* [Alliance]; Spymaster; Last Chief; Bodyguard.

Chapter Twenty-Six: Secret Warfare; TNA; Daybreak; 43; Eureka; Plot; Long Jump; Dictionary; Tasks; SSF; Map Room; Alliance; Charles Pick Jr., "A Dry-Run Torpedo Just Missed Roosevelt," *Sunday Star*, August 27, 1948; Reilly; Day; Mitrokhin.

Chapter Twenty-Seven: Plot; 43; Long Jump; Eureka; Secret Warfare; NARA; Daybreak; Command; Seydi; Diary; TNA.

Chapter Twenty-Eight: Reilly; SSF; Plot; 43; Eureka.

Chapter Twenty-Nine: Plot; Long Jump; O'Sullivan; Daybreak; Reilly; "The Quanats of Iran," *Scientific American*, vol. 218, No. 4 (April 1968), pp. 94–107; Medi Saberloon, *Traditional Water Tunnels in Iran* (London: Archeological Press, 2010); Amir Afkhami, "Disease and Water Supply: The Case of Cholera in 19th Century Iran," *Yale F&ES Bulletin*, 2010; Command; 43; Eureka.

Chapter Thirty: NARA; TNA; Diary; Plot; Long Jump; 43; Eureka; Dictionary; Russian Secret Service; Skorzeny.

Chapter Thirty-One: Reilly; SSF; Day; Ring; Martin J. Bollinger, *Warriors and Wizards: Development and Defeat of Radio-Controlled Glide Bombs of the Third Reich* (Annapolis, MD: Naval Institute Press, 2010); 43; Eureka; Dictionary; Lukin; Plot; Nikolai Dolgopolov, "How the Lion and the Bear Were Saved" [Saved].

Chapter Thirty-Two: Reilly; Day; SSF; Map Room; Conferences; Plot; 43; Eureka; Lukin; Saved; Long Jump; Tasks.

Chapter Thirty-Three: 43; Eureka; Plot; Skorzeny; Dictionary; Long Jump; Lukin; Saved; Reilly; Summit; Gary Kern, "How 'Uncle Joe' Bugged FDR" [Bugged]; Warren Kimball, "A Different Take on FDR at Tehran" [Different]; SSF; Map Room.

Chapter Thirty-Four: NARA; TNA; Plot; 43; Eureka; Lukin; Long Jump; Reilly; SSF; Ring; Tasks.

Chapter Thirty-Five: 43; Eureka; Plot; Long Jump; Saved; "Gevork Vartanian: Spy Who Helped Foil Hitler Death Plot," *The Independent*, December 1, 2012 [Foil]; "Gevork Vartanian," *The Telegraph*, January 11, 2012 [GV]; Dictionary; Lukin; Crisis.

Chapter Thirty-Six: Ring; SSF; Reilly; Bugged; Different.

Chapter Thirty-Seven: Reilly; SSF; Map Room; 43; Plot; Long Jump; Saved; Lukin; Spymaster; Last Chief; Conferences; Day.

Chapter Thirty-Eight: Conferences; Ring; SSF; Map Room; Day; Reilly; "Zurkana," http://www.iranicaonline.org/articles/zur-kana; Fazad Nekoogar, "Traditional Iranian Martial Arts," http.//www.pahlavani.com; 43; Lukin; Eureka; Saved; Plot; Long Jump; Bugged.

Chapter Thirty-Nine: Foil; GV; 43; Eureka; Lukin; Saved; Dictionary; Plot; Long Jump; Spymaster; Conferences; Summit; Map Room; Ring; Day.

Chapter Forty: Conferences; Map Room; Day; 43; Eureka; Lukin; Saved; Plot; Long Jump; SSF; Foil; GV; Reilly; Bugged.

Chapter Forty-One: 43; Plot; Eureka; Lukin; Saved; Long Jump; Foil; GV; Reilly; SSF; Conferences.

Chapter Forty-Two: 43; Plot; Long Jump; Eureka; Saved; Dictionary; Reilly; Foil; GV; Day; SSF; Map Room; Files.

Epilogue: Reilly, "Stalin Bared Plot Against President," *New York Times*, December 18, 1943; Daybreak; Secret Warfare; TNA; Bodyguard; GV; Foil; "Medvedev Grieves Over Death of Legendary Intelligence Officer," *Tass*, January 11, 2012; HS; Skorzeny; Spymaster; Last Chief; Reilly; SSF; Conferences; Map Room.

Acknowledgments

Dr. James Joyce's prescription for the writerly life is "silence, exile, and cunning." Retreating to my hilltop hideaway, surrounded by dense woods, colonial-era fields and orchards, as well as a murky pond, I pretty much have the "silence" and the "exile" covered. It's the "cunning" that's the tricky part. And so as I attempt to fulfill this challenge, I count on the assistance of many wise and generous friends. Among them are:

Lynn Nesbit has been my agent for nearly as long as I've been writing, and after thirteen books together I rely on her wisdom and her friendship. Mina Hamedi in Lynn Nesbit's office is a newcomer, arriving just in time for this book, but I am nevertheless grateful to her for many kindnesses.

At HarperCollins, my publisher for my last four books, I work with people whom I respect and like; not always the case in publishing (or any business). Jonathan Burnham has been a gracious friend, and a publisher who actually reads—and insightfully, to boot!—the books he publishes. Jonathan Jao is the sort of editor I always wanted; my Maxwell Perkins, but no doubt more droll. And Sarah Haugen keeps things moving forward with intelligence and care.

Bob Bookman has been representing my work in Hollywood since the days before the talkies, or so it seems; he's an erudite presence in my life, and a source of wisdom and friendship. Jason Richman just came on board during the writing of this book, but he's plenty smart, wise beyond his years, and I count on his advice.

352 · *Acknowledgments*

Graydon Carter has given me opportunities to write for *Vanity Fair*, and now for his new internet publication *Air Mail*. I'm grateful.

And there are friends I turn to when things get rough. My sister Marcy, although directing a demanding and impressively successful business, is always there; she's the best. And I can also count on Susan and David Rich; Irene and Phil Werber; John Leventhal; Bruce Taub; Betsy and Len Rappoport; Sarah and Bill Rauch; Pat, Bob, and Marc Lusthaus; Ken Lipper; Claudie and Andrew Skonka; Nick Jarecki; Scott Silver; Destin Coleman; Daisy Miller; Beth DeWoody; Lacey Bernier; Arline Mann and Bob Katz; and Sara Colleton.

My three children—Tony, Anna, and Dani—have gone off into the world and are making their marks in ways that fill their old father with pride. Their accomplishments are a constant source of great joy.

And, not least, I have to thank Ivana.

Index

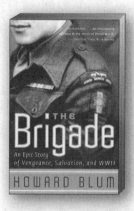
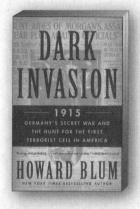
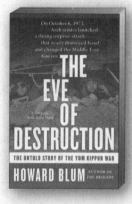
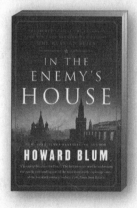
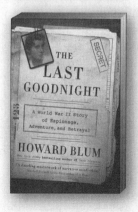